John Illsley is an English musician w̶ <del></del> KU-749-477
guitarist of the critically acclaimed band Dire Straits. With
Dire Straits, John has been the recipient of multiple BRIT and
Grammy Awards, and a Heritage Award. As one of the found-
ing members (with Mark Knopfler, his brother David and
drummer Pick Withers), John played a major role in the development of the Dire Straits sound. When Dire Straits finished
touring in 1993, John became involved in the art world. Having
carved out a reputation for himself as a painter, John had solo
exhibitions in London, New York, Sydney and across Europe.
He also co-founded the children's charity Life Education in
1987 which was recently integrated into Coram, one of the
oldest UK charities. John also owns a pub, the East End Arms,
in the New Forest.

MY LIFE IN
DIRE
STRAITS

JOHN ILLSLEY

WITH A FOREWORD BY
MARK KNOPFLER

PENGUIN BOOKS

TRANSWORLD PUBLISHERS
Penguin Random House, One Embassy Gardens,
8 Viaduct Gardens, London SW11 7BW
www.penguin.co.uk

Transworld is part of the Penguin Random House group of companies
whose addresses can be found at global.penguinrandomhouse.com

Penguin
Random House
UK

First published in Great Britain in 2021 by Bantam Press
an imprint of Transworld Publishers
Penguin paperback edition published 2022

A CIP catalogue record for this book
is available from the British Library.

ISBN
9780552177894

Typeset by Jouve (UK), Milton Keynes.
Printed and bound in Great Britain by Clays Ltd, Elcograf S.p.A.

The authorized representative in the EEA is Penguin Random House Ireland,
Morrison Chambers, 32 Nassau Street, Dublin D02 YH68.

Penguin Random House is committed to a sustainable
future for our business, our readers and our planet. This book
is made from Forest Stewardship Council® certified paper.

For Steph, James, Jess, Harry and Dee Dee, with love

Contents

Foreword

We were lucky we weren't teenagers — that would certainly have been fatal. Nearly everything we were to experience in the professional music game was for the first time, so we had to learn as we went, at ever-increasing speed through an ever-changing landscape.

John had wanted it all as badly as I did. He was a great companion for the trip the band took, and he continues to be a great mate today. John felt like an old friend from the beginning. Whenever we see one another now, which is often, it feels exactly as it did when we first met. He was a constant support, full of the positive energy and will-power required in a touring and recording outfit.

Although Dire Straits received a lot of international attention relatively early, I'm not sure that could happen now. John and I both feel extremely fortunate and always have: it was the era before down-loading and piracy, a time which could support careers in music. Nowadays, recording contracts often don't last for more than an album or two. The music business has become more impatient, less inclined to nurture talent and more likely to demand instant success.

So there's music, and there's the music business: two different things. But mainly, for us, it was a huge adventure and a hell of a ride, with all its comedy, absurdity, exhaustion, madness and sadness. Like everyone, we had to learn to cope with some of the more negative aspects of the game, but John and I always valued and appreciated the success. I'm writing this in my own recording studio, for example: all the hard work paid off. I know John feels the same.

The ride is not for everyone, not for those who can't take the pressures and the pace, for whatever reasons. It was a different world. And John has remembered a pretty big chunk of it.

MK
May 2021

Elbows on the balcony railing, I'm looking down on the Sunset Marquis pool, watching a guy spinning in his inflatable, nursing his Daiquiri, an uneasiness gnawing a little at my guts. My cocktail is different, a heady mix of nerves and exhilaration. I have been living off it for five weeks, night after night, coast to coast in the States. But tonight, the whirl-wind tour almost done, there is a double shot of nerves in the shaker, two parts nerves to one part exhilaration, with a dash of fatigue and a twist of disbelief. We're playing the Roxy.

Neil Young, Frank Zappa, The Temptations, Bob Marley, Van Mor-rison, Bruce Springsteen, Chuck Berry, Lou Reed, Jimmy Cliff, The Ramones, Patti Smith, Etta James, Jerry Lewis, B.B. King . . . and 'Tonight, ladies and gentlemen, all the way from London, England, yes, please give it up for . . . Dire Straits!'

Or, in my head at least, please give it up for four lads from the bor-ough of Lewisham.

That's how it feels anyhow — not quite believing it's real — and I am trying to get my head around the absurdity of it, pretend it's just another gig, like the ones we were doing a few months back. It's not a big gig, the Roxy, just a couple of hundred guests, but it's the Roxy. The Roxy! Tiny, but in its way, in kudos terms, as big as Madison Square Garden, the Hollywood Bowl, Wembley . . .

Right below me, Southern rock band the Ozark Mountain Daredevils, all bushy beards and long hair, are poolside, slumped on loungers, swilling long-neck beers, bantering with the beautiful Californian babes milling around in their bikinis. A couple of cool-dude waiters are floating between the tables handing out cocktails and clearing the empties. The music is low but amplified in the intimacy of the pool area, a small courtyard overlooked by two storeys of rooms on all sides. The sky over to the west is a deep burnt orange fading to grey and the outdoor lights come on, silhouetting the miniature palm trees.

There's a hand on my shoulder. It's Mark.

'You all right?'

'Yeah, great, it's just, you know . . .'

'Weird.'

'Yeah, weird. A long way from Deptford, that's for sure.'

'Embrace it. We could be in the Dog and Duck begging for a mid-week slot after the darts match.'

I picture us around our little wooden table, four pints of brown ale, rolling our fags, moaning about the band on the little stage in the corner labouring through their set of Beatles and Stones tracks, a few old guys on their bar stools reading the Racing Post.

Below me, a guy with an afro is walking into the shallow end with a beer in one hand and a smoke in the other.

Mark says, 'Come on, we've got to go. Reception just called — the limo's here.'

'Limo!' This time it felt right. We were in Hollywood, for God's sake. You didn't take the bus.

We knock at Dave's and Pick's room and make our way down, past the pool, Pick playing the air with his imaginary drumsticks, the real ones sticking out of his back pocket. One of the reclining Ozarks, a hot beach-babe sitting on his lounger now caressing his chest hair, raises his beer bottle by the neck.

'Way to go, guys!' He smiles. 'The Roxy — you made it, man. Enjoy!'

In the air-chilled lobby, the doorman nods and stands aside, pulling open the door to the street, and we are back out in the soft, dry heat, making our way down the carpet under the long golden awning. Spring, like autumn, barely exists in LA. The temperature hovers between 60 and 70 degrees and I am overdressed in my charity-shop DJ jacket and heavy Levi's. A smiling chauffeur in his peaked cap has the rear door open for us and we disappear into the huge interior of the shiny black Lincoln, bigger than the kitchen back in Deptford.

We pull away, swing left into Sunset Boulevard, downtown Los Angeles behind us, Beverly Hills up ahead. We are all silent, staring out of the windows, taking in Hollywood's neon bar signs, the roller-bladers and the lightly stirring palms. Our second time in a limo in as many weeks. (We find out back in London the record company has put them on our bill, like breakfast at the Portobello, and the sirloins and salt beef in Nassau.)

A small crowd of a few dozen is hanging outside as the chauffeur eases the limo to the kerb. The Roxy looks like a detached family house, minus the stacked logs and plus double swing-doors. Right outside, there are two Hells Angels-style bouncers and a lamp post with a big orange neon 'R', like a giant lollipop, planted in the sidewalk between the towering palms. We climb out, a few heads turn our way and a guy with a boogie box on his shoulder shoots through us on his skateboard, trailing the smell of weed.

The owner, Lou Adler, record producer of The Mamas & the Papas and Sam Cooke, greets us in the lobby — Pick playing air drums probably the giveaway that we must be the band he'd booked. You can't mistake Lou, in his beret, beard and shades. He's very friendly, and none the worse, it seems, for his recent kidnapping and split from Britt Ekland.

We shake hands, thank him for the honour of playing his venue and, yes, we promise to come and find him in the bar after the show.

'Hey, man, no idea you guys were English. That's so cool. The music sounds so, you know, American. Rock 'n' roll with a touch of the blues.'

Mark says in Geordie, 'Yeah, we've had that a lot since we've been here.'

The dressing room backstage is no bigger than the ones in the village halls back in England and, if we were lucky to get one at all, in the pubs too. We can swing a kitten, but not much more, and we're bumping into each other, cursing and apologizing as we get ready, heading out into the open of the passageway to neck a few beers before the guy comes and tells us it's time. 'The Roxy is full, guys, and it's ready to rock.'

When we flew out to the States we were in great shape, tight as a drum skin, not a chord or beat out of place, song after song. You can't hit the road out there unless your performance is at peak fitness. If you're not stage-ready and you're lucky to be playing on the right side of the tracks, they'll groan and shuffle away to the bar. In less courteous places, especially the unis and the hick towns, you'd better have some slick dance moves to avoid the shower of projectiles from the floor.

You probably won't see that in the Roxy, but I'd sooner take a hurricane of Bud bottles in Pig's Knuckle, Arkansas, than a glum silence in Lou Adler's joint. Screw up in the Roxy and influential people in the music world will soon get to hear you weren't up to much. Get the place jumping – and you never knew who would be in the audience any night at the Roxy – and the good news travels fast. These little gigs at iconic venues have a unique atmosphere, and the pressure to perform well was hard to put out of our minds. In front of a small, exclusive audience with big names from the music industry seated below, you really don't want to mess up.

We are on top of our game, roused by the sheer thrill of the experience, and we go straight on stage and into our set, no conferring, and kick off with 'Down to the Waterline': 'Sweet surrender on the quay-side / You remember we used to run and hide . . .'

Chapter 1

The Heart of It

If you were to run a line north to south down the centre of England, then another midway across from east to west, the point of intersection would fall bang on a little town called Market Harborough, or as near as makes no odds. It might even score a direct hit and pinpoint 'Stonehenge', the very house in which I grew up. It was halfway down Shrewsbury Avenue – a small close off an unmade road on top of the hill, overlooking the town to the north and, in all other directions, the gentle, rolling, hedge-framed countryside of Leicestershire and Northamptonshire. This is as far from salt water as it's possible to be in the UK, as far from the wide-open seas and the world beyond as you can get. It is the heart of Middle England and, for better or for worse, this is the world that shaped who I became, a small world that brought great comfort and security but a world that made me yearn for the distant shores of somewhere way more exotic.

One morning I was walking with my mother down the High Street in Market Harborough, the pavements busy with shoppers filing in out of the butcher's, the greengrocer's and the ironmonger's.

I was nine or ten, so it must have been about 1959. We were going to pick up my father from the Westminster Bank and drive him home in our Vauxhall Wyvern for his lunch. My father had risen to the post of manager and, although we were comfortable, he didn't earn a pot of money. Very few households had more than one car back then, so my mother did this every day of the week, also dropping him off in the morning and picking him up in the evening. The only time she got a break from her role as *chauffeuse* was when the River Welland broke its banks in the great floods of 1958. For a week or so, my father rowed himself across the dirty, swollen waters, looking a little incongruous in his three-piece suit, pipe stuck in the corner of his mouth.

Anyhow, that morning we were crossing the street when the whole scene froze as if zapped by a giant stun gun from the skies. Everyone just stopped, including us, and the traffic, light as it was, slowed sharply. Only one pedestrian was moving — a young man from India or Pakistan. I was transfixed. I had never seen a brown face and neither, so it appeared, had anyone else. Had the man been wearing no trousers and a top hat, he couldn't have triggered greater fascination. After a few moments, somebody pressed the play button, the scene moved on, the world resumed spinning on its axis.

In that fleeting, weirdly thrilling moment, the curtain had been yanked back and I got my first glimpse of the world beyond our sleepy little market town. It wasn't so much the man himself that intrigued me, but the reaction of the locals, the farmers hopping out of their filthy Land Rovers in muddied boots and flat caps, the grannies in knitted bonnets and the well-to-do housewives in pencil skirts and matching tweed jackets all frozen to the spot. I can't say for sure that it was at that precise moment I set my course on a life more adventurous than the one on offer in Market Harborough, but it was certainly around that time that my imagination began to take flight.

Insularity was a state of being for Britons in the fifties; the sight of a

My mother and father, Wilfred and Bubbles. Their marriage took
place in late 1939 shortly before he headed off to war.
I have a great deal to thank them for.

'foreigner' rare as hen's teeth. Most of Market Harborough's population had never set foot in London, let alone journeyed overseas. Only the old soldiers like my father, now in their thirties and forties, had 'crossed the water'. A trip to Leicester, eighteen miles up the road, was a major excursion; to Birmingham, about sixty miles, it was a right old adventure; and to London, a hundred miles, it was an epic that people would dine out on for weeks — and, for some, a tale even to tell the grandchildren. London might just as well have been Tokyo for the farm workers, bank employees and shopkeepers of Market Harborough.

One evening around the same time, in a rare break with the no-nonsense traditions of her kitchen, my mother put her reputation for good sense on the line and served my father with a curry dish. I was the official veg gatherer from the garden, as well as her *sous-chef* (chopper-in-chief), and I could tell by the smells from her stove that something new and exciting was in the air that evening. My mother, it was obvious, was a little nervous when she laid down the plate of steaming spiced food before him. There was a short silence, then my father slowly picked up his fork, leaned back a little and prodded it, like she'd served him roadkill. 'What on earth is this?' he asked, politely bemused, politely horrified even.

Like almost every other household in Britain at the time, most evening meals comprised some undressed meat, some potatoes and one type of vegetable, maybe two, preferably boiled to rags. (My mother was a fine cook, but that was the *mode du jour.*) Home-made fish and chips on Friday was the great excitement of the week. The Sunday roast was an event too, but it came with a price — leftovers on Monday. Curry was what people ate during the Raj because they were unable to get hold of minted lamb chops and boiled spuds or sausages and mash. Curry was never seen in a British dining room and, outside the major cities, there was not a curry house to be found on any High Street.

Whether Mum's curry was proof that Britain was on the verge of a great cultural transformation (which it was) or a sign of just how small-minded and conservative we were back then (which we were), I was too young to judge. The fact that I remember these two trivial incidents as significant childhood events tells its own story about the settled, parochial domesticity of British family life in the late fifties. How could we have guessed that British culture was a year or two from being given a mighty shake-up and left standing on its head? Maybe Mum's exotic, daring curry was the sign, a harbinger of things to come.

I don't remember our first home, a small semi in Leicester, because I was four years old when Dad borrowed some money from his mother and some from his bank, both at favourable rates of interest, and we moved into 'Stonehenge', so called I suppose because it was built from this warm, golden Northamptonshire stone. It was not the flashiest house on the street by a long stretch, but it was honest and comfortable with solid oak window frames and even a downstairs loo, which was considered quite fancy in those days. Why we had an outside loo as well, I can't tell you.

The garden was just under an acre, large enough to accommodate a veg plot to serve our needs most of the year. There was even room left over for Dad to create a grass tennis court, but one that bore only the faintest resemblance to Wimbledon Centre Court. Take the net away and it was pretty well indistinguishable from the rest of the grass. It was my task to mow and roll it and, although I took my responsibilities very seriously, the ball never bounced true, forever mocking the players by shooting away at all angles.

My two elder siblings got their own bedrooms — Richard, who was eight years older than me, and my sister, Pat, five years older. I shared the fourth bedroom with William, who was just over a year older — near enough to my birthday for me to confront my mum after some kid's jibe in the primary-school playground that I had been a 'mistake'.

'Of course you're not, darling!' she exclaimed. 'We were so keen to have you, we couldn't wait any longer.'

As the fourth child, I wasn't mothered too hard and, under William's protection, I was pretty well left to do what I liked outside

Holding hands with my brother Will for the first and probably the last time, in 1951.

school, biking for miles and miles along the country lanes, building rafts on the Welland, fishing for chub in the canal and, in the winter, sledging all day long down our hill and skating on the pond at the bottom. Many memoirs recall terrible childhoods, but I'm afraid I'm unable to lay claim to one. Mine was a happy one and there's nothing I can do about that.

Sure, my parents were strict. I would never have dared defy them or talk back to them. But they were always fair. We weren't churchgoers, except at Christmas, and we took Communion from time to time, but they instilled in us a very keen sense of what was right and what was wrong. When I was a bit older, living in Deptford and very short of cash, I wrote to my dad, telling him I was struggling a little and asking if he might help. He sent me twenty quid by return of post with a letter explaining that, because he was giving me the money, he was also sending the same sum to my three siblings, even though they were all in employment. You always knew where you stood in Stonehenge.

They were loving parents, although, in true post-war fashion, the love was never exhibited in words, let alone in a public display. Perish the thought. That would have made everyone go red and feel ashamed of their weakness. Like most others of the time, we were not a family given to hugging. Many years later, towards the end of my father's life, I thought, *To hell with it, I'm going to give him a hug before he dies.* I took a deep breath, but when I stepped forward Dad's face creased in alarm and he recoiled as though I had come at him with a six-inch blade. But I hugged him anyway.

Still, in that repressed non-verbal, non-tactile English way, we all knew we loved each other. We just never dared say it or show it, no matter how desperate we might have been to give or receive a warm embrace. You didn't build empires by sobbing and hugging one another, after all. I guess that generation, with a Lee-Enfield at its head, would say, 'Of course we love our children! They know that. It's obvious, but you don't need to harp on about it, for heaven's sake!'

My father had certainly done his bit for Queen, country and empire — not that he ever talked to anyone about it, except his old pals from the Royal Signals Corps, one of the first into action, to set up battlefield communications. Like any schoolboy, fascinated by tales from the war — a mighty war that had ended just four years before I was born — I was desperate to know about his experiences fighting across North Africa and up through Sicily and other parts of Italy. *Did he ever meet Monty? How close did he get to capturing Rommel? Were the Hun really awful cheats?* But he would rarely be drawn. He would just clamp his pipe in his teeth, ruffle my hair and say something like, 'Come along now, let's go and finish building your go-kart.'

It must have been strange for those soldiers, away for so many years, fighting those hideous battles, suffering heaven knows what degree of what we'd now call PTSD. The term wasn't even invented then. They still called it 'shell shock' but, to be diagnosed with it, you virtually had to be naked on all fours drinking from puddles before being led away by the men in white coats. My father would have seen some dreadful fighting, given his campaigns, but he never let on about the horrors. I often wonder how he might have suffered.

Posted to North Africa early in the conflict, he popped back on leave for a couple of weeks, not to return for four years. When he did finally come home, he met his son, my brother Richard, for the first time — a walking, talking son about to go to nursery school! I was about to say that I can't get my head around that — but I can. I ended up doing half a dozen tours of the world, each one lasting a year or so, roughly the length in total of the Second World War. There were no guns (except in Italy), no deaths, but the absence from home can't have felt any less acute than it had for my father. I never considered my father's anguish, never pictured him sitting in some tedious camp in the rear waiting for orders to go into action. It was only when I went on the road myself, leaving my wife and children at home, that I gave it some thought. You're playing music in front of large audiences, not gunning down Germans and Italians, but it's still a weird and dislocating experience being on the road, detached from that security and homeliness. But more of that later.

My father never really escaped the long shadow of the war, his six years of combat in distant lands. On demobilizing, he immediately signed up to the Territorial Army, and every summer he'd host a reunion with his old chums in our back garden. Half a dozen men, dressed in their fatigues and berets, would sweep into the drive in their jeeps, set up their field tents and unload all the impedimenta of war. There were no guns or artillery pieces, which was disappointing, but otherwise it was a perfect re-creation of a proper camp, complete with billy cans and jerry cans, ammo boxes and portable cooking stoves. It was the highlight of the holidays for me, and William and I would sleep out in one of the tents, the comforting stench of damp, musty canvas filling our nostrils.

The Second World War may have been one of the most momentous events in history, claiming the lives of millions, hastening the end of the British empire and re-shaping the world order, but as soon as hostilities ended, for most combatants, ordinary life restarted with barely a moment's reflection. My father was back in post at his bank within two weeks of his return, heading off in his three-piece suit after six years continuously in his khaki uniform.

He was a good man, my father, hard not to respect. Even now, heading into my seventies, when faced with a difficulty, I still ask, 'What would Dad have done?' Mum's character was the mirror image of his: thoroughly decent, unflappable, kind, loving, dutiful. Like him, she was Leicestershire born and bred, the daughter of a schoolmaster. Hers was a life of domestic toil, bringing up four kids, all the household chores falling within her brief. She went about it happily enough as far as I could tell, but I was observant enough to see it was hard graft. She shopped for and cooked all the meals, baked the bread every few days, drove my father to and from the bank four times a day, constantly cleaned the house from top to bottom, scrubbed and wrung all our clothes (until our first washing machine arrived at the end of the fifties) and, with me as a part-time helper, she tended to all the tasks in the garden too. She neither smoked nor drank — unlike her cigar-smoking, gin-loving mother — and her one escape from the rigours of housework was an occasional round of golf down at the club at the foot of the hill. She must have been quite keen because, like Dad, she was the captain there for a few years.

The only time my mother got a break from the kitchen was when we travelled up to Ashby-de-la-Zouch to take Granny out for lunch at the Crown Hotel. That was every bit as exciting as it sounds — so miserably formal, the atmosphere so stultified that it was no more fun than going to church. And they were excited to make me eat something called 'smoked salmon', which made me feel sick. Raw orange fish! Otherwise, we never ate out, partly because, apart from the bigger hotels, there were very few restaurants to eat out in, and partly because it would have been considered an abominable waste of money. Why shell out a tenner when Mum can cook it just as well at home?

There was little 'culture' in our lives. My parents weren't great readers or music-lovers and I don't remember any conversations around the dining table about the arts. That, too, I think was fairly typical of the time. My parents belonged to a practical generation, mending and making do, and getting on with the main business of creating an ordered household in which the children might grow up safe and happy, just as they had done. It came as a surprise then, after their deaths, to learn that my mother, who I knew had a gorgeous singing voice, had joined a choral society and that — this all after we had flown the nest — my father had turned to painting. Just as I was to do later in life, too. Clearing out their belongings, we found quite a number of Dad's drawings, and they were really impressive for someone with no formal training. I can't but wonder quite what they — especially my mother — would have done with their lives had they not been so fanatically dutiful in raising the family, putting all their effort, money and time into that, leaving themselves so little to nurture their own gifts and interests. There was nothing glamorous about their lives, but there was something a little heroic in their self-sacrifice and unmovable sense of duty to us.

Life probably wasn't a great deal different in Market Harborough to what it had been before the First World War. In 1954, the UK became the last country to end rationing, and within a few years the economy was surging. The boom in consumerism found its greatest expression in technology and gadgetry, whetting the appetite for all things new and, in youngsters like me at least, creating a yearning for modernity, for something different. In 1950, the year after my birth, half of British homes had no bathroom and millions of people shared an outside loo with their neighbours. Homes in remote rural areas had no electricity, food was kept cool in the larder, clothes were washed by hand, most people had a weekly bath in a tin tub and virtually no one had a car. By the end of the decade, televisions, washing machines, refrigerators, gramophones and vacuum cleaners were filling homes and most families outside of the cities had a car in the driveway, buffed and polished with pride every weekend.

My very first memory, a little before this boom, is watching the Queen's Coronation on a television set bought, like so many others, especially for the occasion. It's a cliché to say it, but this was an impossibly exciting moment for a four-year-old boy. I sat cross-legged on the floor in my shorts, transfixed, the room rammed with neighbours and friends, the little square screen in the corner flickering and fuzzing in shades of grey as Her Majesty made her way down the aisle of Westminster Abbey.

It seems laughable now, this lust for a modernity that now seems so quaint. Mum made the most delicious bread, but all I wanted was the sliced and processed stuff all the kids were boasting about at primary school, down in the heart of Little Bowden at the bottom of the hill. When finally I got to try some, with baked beans on top no less, I returned from my mate Mike's across the road feeling really 'with it', like I had now truly arrived in the modern world. So, too, for my mother when the Co-op opened, the first self-service shop in Market Harborough. Until then, Mum would tramp from one specialist store to the next, clutching her list, and the shopkeeper would hurry around the shelves picking out the items desired. The Co-op was no less than a revolution. Maybe Market Harborough wasn't such a backwater after all – that was the feeling in town. Who needs London when you've got a Co-op?

So, you get the picture of my childhood. Middle England, middle class, safe, happy and comfortable, but a tad grey, unadventurous and unimaginative. My only exposure to culture was the occasional trip to the pantomime and, most exciting of all, twice to London for the International Motor Show at Earls Court with Dad and once to see *My Fair Lady*. The great highlight of the year was the annual holiday in Cornwall. Weighed down by six passengers and our luggage, it took twelve hours for the Wyvern to crawl the 280 miles to our rented cottage overlooking Trevone Bay. (Today, that journey takes five hours.) The car was so heavy that when we reached the Somerset market town of Frome three of us had to get out and walk so that the Wyvern could make it up the steep hill.

My mother and father were expecting me to follow in their path and stick around in lovely, sleepy Leicestershire. Why wouldn't they? What other kind of good life was there? Why leave Market Harborough when it offered everything a young man might want? Pubs, shops (including a Co-op!), a cinema, beautiful countryside, walks, fishing, a golf club, a rugby club and, if you must, a railway station to take you into Leicester. And there were dozens of pretty and hearty farmers' daughters to settle down with. What on earth does

London have to rival such a contented life? All that squalor and pollution and fast women and con men.

Then William built himself a crystal radio from a kit — and any hope of me leading a quiet life in rural Leicestershire vanished overnight.

Chapter 2

Night Flight to Luxembourg

The crystal radio was a very basic bit of equipment that required no batteries, just a long antenna to pick up signals from nearby transmitters. In our case that was the big plug-in radio set downstairs. Unlike me, William was born with a gift for fixing and building things, undaunted by any challenge to his resourcefulness. If you gave him all the tools and laid out all the parts, he could probably work out how to build a car. I am exaggerating only a little. He was so good with his hands, no one was surprised that he ended up becoming a fine sculptor, potter and painter.

He finished assembling the radio kit in no time, and then we waited, all sleepy innocence, for Mum and Dad to put their heads around the door to say goodnight. Once the lights were out and they were safely back downstairs, he pulled his secret contraption from under the bed and plugged in the headphones. This was pretty well the height of mischief for ten- and eleven-year-old boys in the late fifties. To listen to American rhythm and blues music when we should have been getting our sleep in for school was to break an unwritten commandment. This degenerate music from across the Atlantic was regarded as seriously damaging to the development of the nation's moral health. In the court of parental opinion, this was William's crime, but I was a willing accessory to it, the lookout.

A little nervous, I kept my eyes on the door handle, ready to throw a slipper at William, but hearing the tinny buzz from my bed, I was soon filled with curiosity and envy. I think William must have picked up on my restlessness and excitement because after a while he said, 'Hey, come and listen to this. It's Radio Luxembourg. We'll take it in turns, one song each.' He's a good bloke, my big brother.

I lay down next to him, both of us staring at the ceiling — and my adventure in music began. Luxembourg was an independent station they were all talking about at his school, playing music you could hear nowhere else at the time. From the moment the sound erupted into my eardrum, it was obvious the songs being played were a very far cry from *Family Favourites* — and strictly not for grown-ups, especially ones who smoked pipes and polished their cars in the driveway on Sundays.

By the time I crept back to my own bed an hour or two later, I was unable to sleep, my head buzzing with the rasping rebel voices of Little Richard and Elvis Presley and heaven knows who else. I have tried to explain the utter, heart-thumping thrill of that moment to my children, who are plugged into their music of choice all day long. It's very hard for anyone born after 1960 to understand there was ever a world of virtually no media, least of all for the younger generation, no connection to a world beyond the playground, the street and the fields in which you played.

Until I was about ten, the *Eagle* comic, *Children's Hour* on the radio at five o'clock, featuring *Dick Barton Special Agent*, and *Family Favourites* — these were the frontiers of fun for a British child inside the home. On *Family Favourites*, mums, dads and the kids sat around the house radio and rang in their song requests. Most of the tunes played were crooning love ballads and big-band jazz, the kind of music that has young boys and girls staring at the clock, wondering when they might be released to go and do something fun, like build an Airfix model aeroplane. Tommy Steele and Max Bygraves were about as funky as it got.

In the mid- to late fifties, Lonnie Donegan, the 'King of Skiffle', was probably the coolest and most original act in Britain, with great appeal among the younger audience, but even he would have been considered far too racy for *Family Favourites*. That was until Cliff Richard and his backing band, The Shadows, turned up on the scene with 'Move It', probably the best rock 'n' roll song ever to come out of Britain. I'm serious. It was so good, so raw, that the older generation were seriously worried by its shameless lustfulness — all that sexual lip-curling and hip-swaying. It's a cracking piece of music, and it's a great shame that, very soon after its release and the minor scandal it triggered, Cliff retreated from the edge and took the safer path so readily. The Shadows were a highly talented band and guitarist Hank Marvin one of the greats.

The BBC was very much part of the traditional establishment, the voice of the older generation and by far the most powerful cultural 'influencer' of the day. The Corporation's efforts to thwart the young by controlling their tastes, feeding them homely and harmless fare and shielding them from dangerous American trends, was soon to prove futile. If anything, their effort to control and brainwash kids into liking the same music as Mummy and Daddy fuelled a powerful counterculture, as represented by Radio Luxembourg. What was emerging in the late fifties and early sixties — with the kids plugged into their little radio sets after the curfew — a few years down the line was going to lead to the unchaining of youth culture and a wild reinvention of popular music. Everything that the powers at the BBC and the wider establishment feared most.

The television wasn't much more exciting than BBC radio, once the space-age thrill of it had worn off. For a start, it only had two channels, BBC and ITV, and most of the programming was aimed at an adult audience, the schedule full of cookery programmes, *Hancock's Half Hour* and Westerns. The fate of the music programme *Six-Five Special* was proof that the BBC was hostile to catering for the tastes of the young. When it was launched in early 1957, it enjoyed instant success and was watched by millions, but the men in suits found all that swaying and strumming less appealing and soon began to interfere, putting pressure on producer Jack Good to include educational and information elements to the show. Good resigned in protest after a year and when ITV produced their own music show, *Oh Boy!*, playing non-stop music, as Good had wanted, the ratings for *Six-Five Special* plunged and the BBC pulled the plug on the programme at the end of 1958, making the disingenuous claim that its fall in popularity vindicated their decision.

With the BBC seen as the moral authority over culture, television was still regarded in many middle-class households as mildly corrupting, especially ITV, with its vulgar gameshows. I was never allowed to watch ITV — 'the other channel' — and I was strictly banned from watching *Coronation Street* because the characters didn't speak properly. Like most kids, I lived in a bubble, a perfectly happy bubble, but a very small one, in which most of the fun stopped as soon as I was called in from outside to get washed up for supper.

But Will's tinny little radio, the cheapest of gadgets, changed all that, wiping out the boundaries of my imagination and allowing me to dream. Until that night, I used to save up my pocket money for a bag of sweets, a comic like *Eagle* or *Victor* or maybe a new Matchbox car. Now all I wanted was a radio and some headphones of my own. I took on as many chores in the garden and around the house as my mother could find for me, and in a few weeks I was the proud owner of my own. My parents were fine about Will and me listening to the radio during the evenings, possibly because it freed up the television for them, but they trusted us to switch them off at night. I'm afraid we failed there, and we'd head off to school puffy-eyed and foggy-headed. That crystal radio might well explain why I was no scholar. The signal was not the most reliable and I spent a fair amount of time walking around the bedroom or dozing off in the corner in an effort get it back.

The radio became my portal into another dimension, a secret door to open every night that would allow me to float away into a fantasy world, whisking me from my bedroom in the English shires across the Atlantic and into the more vibrant and colourful world of the United States. It was a world constructed in my mind in sound and voices, not in visuals, because there were very few images of the place in circulation, no media to convey them. Watching *Gunsmoke* hardly gave you an insight into the life of ordinary Americans. My impressions of the country were built on the songs I heard coming out of that little radio set. I was never going to stay and settle down in Leicestershire. Radio Luxembourg had put an emphatic end to that possibility.

Rock music, rhythm music, rhythm 'n' blues, the new popular music, beat music . . . no one really knew what to call the new sounds emerging; they only knew that they were not jazz, not folk, not ballads, not big band, not even rock 'n' roll because, by 1958, the Teddy Boys had cleared off and that revolutionary movement had already passed. These were new sounds in search of an identity and an audience — and they found a very willing one in me and Will, and in virtually everyone under the age of about twenty. There was nothing unique about my experience. Far from it. We were part of a huge nationwide movement. We just didn't know it yet. We were biding our time in our bedrooms.

This is possibly going to sound far-fetched, but I have always believed it to be true: pop music, rock music — whatever you want to call it — filled the great emotional void in young people's lives at a time when it was frowned upon to express emotion. This natural urgency to connect, to express yourself, may even have been the main driving force behind everything that was unleashed in the sixties. In the fifties, housewives might dab an eye listening to Dean Martin or Frank Sinatra, but no one talked openly about love or the longing for it. That was considered unseemly or wet and weak, shameful even. And God forbid any talk of sex. Not a chance. Yet our generation was no different emotionally to any that had come before it or after.

The parents tapped their feet and hummed along to Perry Como, Doris Day and Pat Boone, concerned not to let their feelings carry them away too far. But for me, certainly, listening to American music on the sly, and then openly — and loudly! — in my bedroom, I felt as if I was giving licence to my feelings, setting them free, being true to myself. It felt right, allowing the music and the emotions expressed to talk directly to me. Music was emotional rescue.

Today, when I hear a track like 'That's All Right' from Elvis's Sun Sessions, it carries me straight back to my bedroom in Market Harborough. The music went deep, and it stayed deep, lodged in there for good. My reaction to the music, lying in my bed, was intensely physical. I was quite literally shaken and shivered by it. The next day, bouncing down the hill to school with my satchel swinging, it was still resonating and buzzing. The feeling I get when I play live today is almost exactly the same. It was as if someone had put a syringe in my arm and injected me with a very powerful stimulant. I believe recent scientific research has shown that roughly half of us respond to music in this extreme physical way. It is probably the reason why The Who, The Rolling Stones and Elton John announce a new 'farewell' tour every few years; why once successful but now forgotten bands will still play the pub and small-club circuit for peanuts and a pint of beer. They need the hit.

After a couple of years of furtive radio listening under the covers, the invention of cheap gramophones allowed Will and me to up-grade our musical experience. We no longer had to wait all night for Pete Murray or Fluff Freeman to play our favourite music on Luxembourg. We could go and buy it! And listen to it over and over. Until The Beatles took off in 1963, it was very hard to get hold of vinyl, most records being imported from the States and there being so few record shops in those days, so it was very exciting to get your hands on one. People treasured their vinyl and took great pride in their collections. The bigger the collection, the higher your status.

We bought a Dansette Popular with four speeds, the most common record player of the time and retailing at an eye-watering eleven guineas. That's roughly two hundred quid in today's money. At first it was only the singles we were interested in, the seven-inch 45 rpms, and as soon as Will had saved up enough, after Cinema Club on Saturday mornings we'd head down to Greens, the only music shop in Market Harborough. Aged twelve, I didn't have the earning power to splash out just over six shillings on a single (about a fiver in today's money), so the first records were all Will's. But that didn't stop me haring out of the school gates and up the hill to listen to his latest purchases before he got home. I'd stack them on top of each other and lie on my bed, waiting for the satisfying clunk of the vinyl and click of the needle as they dropped down on to the turntable one after another. The first single of my own was The Beatles' second release, 'Please Please Me'. It took time and a great many household chores, but our collection soon began to grow, and I still have many of them today, my name or Will's written in the corner of the plain sleeve.

Fairly quickly, it became clear that listening to the music was not enough. I wanted to play it. The guitar was the instrument that was changing music so rapidly and radically and I wanted one badly. Trouble was, they were mighty expensive. Word in the playground was that the only affordable one was the Rosetti Lucky Seven, but even that was about ten pounds, a vast amount of money, the equivalent of a skilled worker's weekly wage. It took me months and months to save up my weekly two shillings and sixpence pocket money while working like a demon in the garden, cutting grass, digging potatoes and helping Dad clean the Wyvern. I bought no comics, no sweets, no fizzy pop, and finally I was able to walk into Greens one Saturday morning, hand over the wodge of cash and place my order. Most guitars back then were American, expensive to import, but Rosetti was a UK distributor, selling instruments manufactured in the Netherlands. The Lucky Seven was the budget option.

It was a beast of a guitar, but I wasn't to discover that fact until a few years later, when I got my fingers on a half-decent one. Will had an acoustic of his own and soon we were picking away at the strings, trying to replicate the sounds of Elvis, The Beatles and a young folk singer called Bob Dylan.

Our parents probably thought the guitar was the instrument of the devil, but they feigned indifference, happy, I guess, that at least we were learning to play an instrument and not smoking cigarettes down by the railway tracks (although we did that as well!). We had a basic chord book and some sheet music and, once I had mastered where to put my fingers, Will showed me some simple chords on his acoustic, starting with the three basic blues ones, E, A and B. I found it very hard, but I persevered for hour after hour, barely emerging from my room all day in the holidays and at weekends, at first going from E to A, and from A to E, then expanding the repertoire until my fingers hurt and my brain was fried. You have to really want to learn to play the guitar, or any instrument. It's why there are so many barely used guitars lying around in the world's bedrooms, attics and basements. It takes endless practice to break through and get to the stage when it becomes automatic and you're not thinking about it, just feeling it.

So it was some time, a couple of months probably, before I felt ready to attempt a song. I laid out the sheet music, put on the simplest record in our collection and, inflicting a terrible assault on the song's integrity, tried to join in. It was thrilling to nail a few chords, but frustrating when I stumbled and the song got away from me. But I kept at it, and I kept working on new chord structures too, combinations of C, G, F, A minor. It was a full year before I had most of them in the bag. It was a revelation and a relief to discover that if you know about twelve chords, you can play a lot of songs. How well you play them is another matter but, once you start messing around with chords, you never stop. Even today, almost sixty years on, if I see my guitar leaning against the wall and I have five minutes to kill, I pick it up and start strumming, just as I did in my bedroom all those years ago.

The basic chords cracked, playing became an obsession, to the exclusion of all else. I abandoned the sheet music and played along to the records. That's not an especially impressive achievement because most early rock songs are very simple arrangements and Dylan songs — take 'Blowin' in the Wind', for example — are so beautifully uncomplicated they're almost like children's nursery rhymes. The sheet music was more hindrance than help because it always seemed to lag behind the record, particularly with the Beatles tracks. Years later I was to learn this was because when the tracks were recorded the engineers had speeded them up a touch to give them a little more verve.

The Rosetti Lucky Seven was a very crude instrument, but it was probably a good thing that I had to learn the craft the hard way. (Both Keith Richards and George Harrison also learned to play on a Rosetti and, for that reason alone, it deserves an honourable mention in the Rock 'n' Roll Hall of Fame.) Will and I would pore over the latest guitar magazines, gazing longingly at the Gibsons, Rickenbackers, Martins and Fenders. All we might be able to afford was a Watkins Rapier but, without an amp, that was never under consideration either. When I upgraded to a half-decent Hofner, I was delighted to discover that not all guitars are born or built equal. It was like getting behind the wheel of a Merc after passing my test in a Robin Reliant.

For two years, the Lucky Seven and I were joined at the hip, and I will always have a soft spot for my first guitar. When I wasn't sleeping or in the classroom, I was sitting on my bed, staring out over the rolling hills of the Leicestershire countryside, battling through the chords, trying to keep up with my new heroes and idols, indulging in the fantasy of being up there alongside them on that stage or in the studio. Some kids dreamed of scoring the winning goal at Wembley in the FA Cup final. I dreamed of being in a band. But not for a moment did I ever think it could become a reality. My immediate reality, that I was going away to boarding school, a very old-fashioned English boarding school at that, was more in tune with the age of Queen Victoria and the world of Gilbert and Sullivan than the new Elizabethan age and the world of Elvis and The Beatles.

Chapter 3

Banjos, Beatings and Bass

Will came back for the Christmas holidays after his first term at boarding school full of stories of bullying, flogging and 'fagging' — the time-honoured tradition of a new boy acting as a slave to a senior. The school prefects at Bromsgrove were known as 'jowts', he said, which immediately made me think of the orcs in *The Lord of the Rings*, the Tolkien trilogy everyone was reading at the time. The jowts sounded equally as fearsome as the orcs, apparently finding any excuse to reprimand, punish and even beat a junior for the most minor infraction of 'the rules'. Just stepping off the path on to a corner of the immaculately manicured lawn led to a heavy cuff over the head and an hour in detention or a summary boot in the pants, even a full thrashing from the most belligerent prefects. It sounded terrifying — and I was going to be joining him there the following year.

I had been looking forward to Will coming home so much. It felt as if he had been away for years, but it was only three months. I had found it hard being the only child left behind in our once full and happily noisy household. Richard and Pat were now working full time, Richard for the Royal Insurance Company and Pat as PA to the boss at Walkers Crisps, down the road in Market Harborough. Will had been my constant companion, room mate, fellow explorer of the Leicestershire wilds and, above all maybe, my musical mentor. Now I'd only get to see him in the holidays, and I felt an aching sadness looking over at his empty bed, his blankets and eiderdown neatly folded into squares at its foot.

Yearning for company, I spent a lot of time on Dad's ancient sit-up-and-beg bike, cycling to villages as far as ten miles away, over the hills and along the twisting narrow lanes, just to spend an hour or two with a mate from school. One of them lived in the little hamlet of Tur Langton, and I was happy to make the long round trip, whatever the weather. We'd sit in the nearby haybarn, smoking the Woodbines he'd nicked from his father's pub, the Crown Inn. I didn't like smoking one bit and I was sick the first few times, but it was something to do, a naughty thrill to break the tedium of my weekends. It wouldn't be long before I overcame my disgust for cigarettes and became a proper smoker, like most teenagers of the time, but at first I did it just for hell of it, not to be moping around in an empty house.

After primary school in Little Bowden, I had moved to Brooke House, a little prep school in Market Harborough, the idea behind it, as with all 'preparatory' schools, being to prepare the child for the rigours of boarding school. But unlike the impression Will had painted of Bromsgrove, Brooke House was a happy place and I enjoyed it, though my memories of it are hazy. Two of the teachers made a big impression — a sexy young French teacher (all the way from France itself) who we all fancied rotten, and a very elderly English master who had a yellow face from being gassed in the Great War. He was a very good teacher who inspired me to read a great deal more, and we were always delighted as well astonished when he made it to the end of a class without dying. He read us our Wordsworth and Tennyson as if every wheezing breath might be his last.

My best friend was Willy Gilbertson, the most rebellious boy in the school. He only lived a few miles away, but he became a boarder when his parents could no longer tolerate his anarchy at home. He wasn't a lot more law-abiding at school, in spite of the strict discipline, causing a great scandal when, after a row with the headmaster, he dismantled his metal bed and hurled it from the first-storey window, badly damaging the French teacher's Austin Metropolitan.

Despite a general sense of wellbeing, my principal memory of Brooke House is an unhappy one. During break one day, the headmaster's crazy sheepdog managed to escape and came bounding and slobbering across the playground in search of prey. He had plenty of appetizing options, all those bare legs in shorts like raw legs of lamb, but he decided that my flesh looked the juiciest and sunk his gnashers into my calf. It was such a deep bite I had to go to hospital and have a dozen stitches and a tetanus jab. The dog was immediately taken away and put down. No winners there, then – and I felt a little guilty, sad that the dog had paid the ultimate penalty for what was probably no more than the same high jinks in which we had been indulging in the playground.

This wasn't my first trip to hospital. I was quite an accident-prone kid. Playing in the garden one afternoon, aged four, I had dropped a paving slab on my foot and spent two nights in an empty ward at the Leicester Royal Infirmary down in town. It was the first time I had been away from home and the misery of it was so great it played on my mind for years after and made me dread the day I'd have to leave the comforts of Stonehenge and go away to school like my elder siblings. On another occasion, in a really dumb attempt to get my parents to buy me a proper bike, I worked up as much speed as I could and crashed Dad's rusting hulk into a heavy gate post. I suffered heavy bruising and cuts and was lucky not to break a bone. My cunning ploy didn't work either. Dad just bought a new front wheel. Christ, I must have been bored.

I was aimless and lonely at home, so music came to play an even bigger role in my life and I spent every evening and much of the weekends up in my room, stacking up the singles on the Dansette and playing along on my crappy Rosetti Lucky Seven, kidding myself I was Little Richard. When the day finally arrived and my heavy trunk was lifted into the back of the Wyvern, I was a boiling pot of conflicting emotions as we drove the ninety minutes through an ice-age landscape to Bromsgrove, halfway between Worcester and Birmingham. Part of me was eager for an adventure, to grow up and get on with life, and I was also looking forward to the company of other kids; the other part of me was chilled to the bone with fears of what lay in store, a shivering fear not helped by the sub-zero temperatures getting the better of the car's heating system in the savage winter of 1963.

To a thirteen-year-old, eighteen-year-olds might just as well be thirty or forty, and I wasn't relishing the prospect of falling foul of their officially sanctioned discipline and unchecked bullying. We were to be the last generation to experience an English boarding school as our great-grandfathers had. Change was in the air and very soon these schools would start to become more liberal and humane, little by little. It was January 1963 when I started at Bromsgrove, but the experiences that awaited me were little different to those of a young boy there in 1883. I was also sad to be leaving Stonehenge, where I had felt so happy and secure for ten years. It was a very anxious and timid boy my parents left standing in the snow on the steps of Broom House watching the Wyvern slip and slide its way down the drive to the school gates, back to the carpeted comfort and centrally heated warmth of home.

The winter of 1962–3 remains one of the coldest ever recorded. From just after Christmas through to Easter, the whole country lay under a deep blanket of snow, many of the more remote lanes remaining impassable for the entire period. Four feet of the stuff lay across the Bromsgrove grounds, and piles twice as deep towered like prison walls where it had been cleared along the drives and squares. To walk up to the main school was to pass through a long, icy corridor and even I, very tall for my age, was unable to see over the top.

Except for a small coal fire in the housemaster's study, there was no heating in Broom House and, the housemaster being something of a sadist, there was no chance of us boys being allowed in to share the warmth. Far from it. At lights out in the 'bedder' — our dormitory — he'd stroll in and open every window as wide as it would go, arctic air being good for building the character of callow young boys, of course. On my first night, and for many to follow, I went to sleep, eventually, to the sound of boys whimpering with cold under their thin woollen blanket. It was the coldest winter since the Middle Ages, so the papers were saying, but still the housemaster did not relent in his fanatical character-building enterprises. Dressed in every item of clothing we possessed, we effectively slept those three months outside. The only warmth we felt that entire term was out in the shed, where all twelve of us would huddle like sheep after returning from classes in the main school. There was a rusty wood-burning stove, but we soon exhausted the meagre supply of twigs and discarded timber, so we just hunched up in a small pack, shivering, teeth chattering.

There was no communication with our parents other than twice a term, when they were allowed to come and take us out for Sunday lunch. We'd be released after Matins but have to be back in time for Evensong. I was a little homesick that first term, but crying was considered shameful and it was something you did only under your sheets or behind the locked door of a toilet. It was a great relief knowing that William was somewhere nearby. His nickname, for reasons unknown, was Louie, and I soon became known as Little Lou, even though I was taller than him, soon to be six foot five. Will's protection, and me being tall, helped keep most of the bullies at a distance and I soon worked out that the ones among us who played by the rules and kept their heads down could get by with only a modicum of bruising, though it was both physical and emotional.

As the tallest boy in the year, keeping my head down and staying inconspicuous was not that easy — and it soon turned out that I was not that compliant either. I was no tearaway, but I soon developed a reputation as a bit of a rebel. The rules were laid down by the school but enforced by the jowts. Whenever you stepped out of line, you were tried in the kangaroo court of a dark corridor or a senior's room and sentenced to what was known as 'Jowts' PT', a cute name for what amounted effectively to some creative form of torture, flogging on the backside with a shoe being the standard punishment. These punishments were meted out as much for fun as for justice, and if a jowt was in the mood he'd happily give you a few whacks for not tucking in a shirt, for undoing a top button or for talking after lights out. If an offence was considered sufficiently grave, the jowt would solemnly (or laughingly, depending who it was) take you to your housemaster or, worse still, to the headmaster himself, the highest court of judicial authority, and that inevitably brought a more severe sentence.

I took the first of many beatings after I was caught during prep reading the James Bond book *Dr No*, considered by the school authorities to constitute pornography. This was only a couple of years after the famous *Lady Chatterley's Lover* obscenity trial, in which lawyers argued that D. H. Lawrence's novel — later to become a school text — should be banned from sale. Even two years on, we were told that expulsion was the fate awaiting anyone who dared to debase himself with a copy of this outrageous exercise in indecency. When I did finally get my hands on the book, I was deeply disappointed to discover that it was no more titillating or exciting than *The Rainbow* or Chaucer's tale of *The Wife of Bath*.

You couldn't help but wonder who was getting the greater sexual thrill: the wayward boy found reading the 'filth' of authors like Ian Fleming or the red-faced bachelors administering the caning of naked bottoms to punish the offender. The offence of reading *Dr No* was deemed grievous enough for me to be marched into the Supreme Court of the headmaster's study. I cannot tell you whether Dr Lionel Carey derived any erotic satisfaction from whipping my bare behind with his 'wagger' — a very thin cane — but, no stranger to the tankard and the carafe, he was always in fiery mood after lunch, which is when he liked to execute his penal duties. Looking down his bright red nose, he gave me chapter and verse on my degeneracy and then, obliging me to bend over, thwacked my little arse until my buttock cheeks burned and my eyes watered. Well, that'll teach me!

Quite a number of our teachers had served in the war, which might explain the insistence on severe discipline, regimented protocols and the occasional eruption of violence, and there was no more military character at Bromsgrove than my housemaster from my second term onwards. Broom was a sort of holding house for new boys, and as soon as a space was freed up I was transferred to Gordon, in the heart of the school, run by — or rather, commanded by — the fearsome John Hedley, quite possibly the hardest man I have ever met. Hedley was a former Chindit, a proto-Special Forces unit that had specialized in deep jungle warfare against the Japanese in Burma. You didn't make it into the Chindits unless you had a character forged in fire and iron. He was also recruited into the Special Operations Executive (SOE), working as an agent and saboteur behind enemy lines, and wrote a book about his wartime exploits. Terrifying, yes, but John Hedley was a decent man, hard but always fair.

He was, however, no fan of the guitar, The Rolling Stones or The Who, and it was over my obsession with music that we often clashed. When The Stones released their rousing version of Chuck Berry's 'Come On', I played it over and over. When I was senior enough to have a room of my own, I was allowed to practise my guitar for an hour in the evening, but I didn't always stick to the exact letter of that rule and frequently found myself standing in his study, forced to hand over the instrument. I had two guitars at this stage – an acoustic and a bass – and both spent much of their time at Bromsgrove gathering dust in John Hedley's broom cupboard.

'You and your infernal banjos, Illsley!' he'd fume. 'You really need to knuckle down and apply yourself to something useful. Where's strumming a banjo going to get you in life, eh?'

Many years later, after my father passed away, I found letters that Hedley had written to him, expressing his concerns that my love of music was seriously undermining my performance at school. The phrase 'infernal banjos' is used several times.

It was true that I was unlikely to secure a place at Oxford or Cambridge, but I wasn't a complete failure. I had two years in the First XV rugby team (being tall, I was a great asset in the lineout) and I also broke the school record for the discus! And, through Hedley, I was appointed head of the CCF (Combined Cadet Force) band. He saw it as an opportunity for me to be drilled in some 'proper music'.

To be fair, he was right to be worried about me: I was a bit of a failure in my academic studies. I was something of a dreamer, always staring out of the window thinking about girls and music, sneaking away to the attic for a crafty smoke or, when I was a bit older, at weekends down to the pub, where we'd buy bottles of pale cream sherry out of the back door, then sit in a field and make ourselves sick drinking it.

In spite of the harsh Victorian-style regime, the school did manage to produce a number of successful creative characters, the most well-known being the poet A. E. Housman. The actor Trevor Eve and the writer Nicholas Evans were there at the same time as me, proving that the school cannot have completely neglected its development of the 'softer' subjects and pursuits. Further evidence that the culture of the school was changing was underlined by its appointment of a new art teacher, Don Faulkner, a man who was to have a huge influence on me, and one I admire like few others. We have remained great friends ever since. He made an instant impression on me when he walked into our first class that morning, hair trailing over his collar and holding an acoustic guitar. We all looked at each other in amazement. A teacher with long hair was not a common sight in English schools then.

'What are you gawping at?' he asked.

'Well, sir, you're holding a guitar.'

'Very observant. And I'm going to sit down and play it while you get on with some painting.'

'But what shall we paint, sir?'

'For a start, you can move all those desks to the walls and turn this into a proper art room, and then get yourselves some paper, some paint and some brushes and get on with it.'

'But what shall we paint, sir?' I repeated.

'Whatever you damn well like! Use your imagination, your powers of observation. That's what artists do, you know.'

Well, this was different from sitting in serried ranks of desks sketching an empty wine bottle for a still life. It was one of those moments in your life when the perspective shifts. My view of the world was never quite the same after that first encounter with Don. We all picked up our brushes and, as we let our imaginations do the work, he sat in the corner looking cool and strumming Bob Dylan tunes. I was sixteen then, in my third year, and from that day on the art room became my sanctuary, a refuge from the harsher world beyond. It was the day I realized there was always a way out of whatever hell you might find yourself in. There was always sanctuary somewhere, be it in art, music or the company of a good man. Or woman.

'I'll be here all the time,' Don said. 'Come in whenever you like, even if you just want to hang out and chat.'

The older I have become, the more I have come to respect John Hedley, but at the time it was very hard to imagine him making the same offer, and I needed no second invitation from Don to indulge in his company and enjoy his outlook on life and art. The world needs all sorts of different characters to function but, at that moment, in mine, I was way more receptive to the Don Faulkners than to the John Hedleys. After that, I didn't feel so bad that music and art were pretty well my only interests at school. I no longer felt like a failure. I could search, without guilt or shame, for who I really was and wanted to be. Over the coming weeks, then months and years, Don made me realize there were other ways to be happy, to be successful, to be who you are. I'm sure we have all had these angels who dropped into our younger lives and pointed the way. Don Faulkner was mine.

And it was just as well, because I flopped in all my mainstream academic subjects. I have the excuse of being a June baby, one of the youngest in my year, but there were others born around the same time who did perfectly well and way better than me in their exams. Maybe it was because I came from such a secure and loving family and didn't ever feel I needed to prove myself. Maybe it was my love of music because, truly, that was my only great passion then; it had a way stronger pull than the visual arts, and I lay awake every night with my radio and was always borderline imbecilic with sleeplessness in the morning.

The easy answer was that I was thick. But I wasn't. I was no scholar, but I was no dunce either. Whatever. Who the hell knows? But the fact is that I screwed up my O levels so badly I had to retake a year. I sailed through them the second time, but then took only two A levels. I got as close to a Z in physics as you can, but got an A in art, thanks to Don, an incredible teacher who drew superb grades from his pupils, not by sticking to the curriculum but by rebelling against it. He taught us more about life than the rest of my teachers put together, and I can still hear him today: 'There is no single, absolute, prescribed way of doing anything, only your way. It's all down to you, who you feel you are, who you want to be. You are in charge.'

Don's philosophy was invaluable, and so it would prove, but the fact that I had only one good A level meant I had no chance of getting into university or even into art college, while William got into Loughborough. You needed two strong A levels, which seems mad now. Surely a proficiency in art should be sufficient to get into art college? What use would a C in physics be? With hindsight, though, I'm quite pleased about the way things went. Had I scraped into art college, it's highly unlikely I'd have experienced the rich life I have. I could have ended up painting watercolours in the Market Harborough area and playing Slade covers in the Nag's Head at Christmas time. Nothing wrong with either of those pursuits, but they weren't for me.

Music and art. Music and art. I was eighteen and, frustrating though it was for my parents, they were my only true interests. I am seventy now, but nothing has changed. Music and art, music and art. Looking back, there were three big moments in my time at Bromsgrove, moments that nudged my life on a different course to what might have been expected. Meeting Don Faulkner was a huge life-changing moment, but the manner in which I joined my first band was another. Will had started one, with himself and Hughie Mason on guitar, Charlie Sowden on piano and Paul Turner on drums. I was desperate to join, but with two guitarists already (a year older and that much cooler), there was no way in. Once again, Will gave me the leg-up in life. Why didn't I become a bass player?

'But I don't have a bass!' I protested.

'It's okay, I'll make you one!'

God, I love my brother, because that's exactly what he did. He built me a guitar, and ten years later I was playing bass in Dire Straits. It's amazing, isn't it, how life turns on these small moments? Had my brother's band needed a regular guitarist, as I had hoped, I'd have jumped at it. I'm not bad, but I'm not a brilliant guitarist like, say, Mark Knopfler or Keith Richards, and it's highly unlikely I would ever have enjoyed a career in music if I had stuck at the acoustic or electric guitar. I couldn't have known it at the time, but although the fact that Will and his mate Hughie Mason had first dibs on the regular guitar slots in the band was a major frustration, it turned out to be the most important turning point in my life. If it hadn't been for that, God knows how my life would have panned out.

At first, I took off the two top strings of my acoustic — B and E — put on a 'pick-up' and bashed around on it, working out notes as best I could, and it was a good education, learning the bass so crudely. Then William, a great craftsman with any materials, built me a bass guitar, a very presentable one, with all the correct frets and strings. It was a fine piece of work but, as he admitted, it did look a little like a garden tool — so it became known as 'the Spade'. I wish I had kept it, rather than chucking it when I moved on. I couldn't have known what an important artefact of my personal history it was to become. But I do have a picture of me playing it on stage at school in our band, The Knott. Yeah, The Knott! A small moment in the history of popular music, but a massive story for us at the time. How cool were we? We had amps and everything — albeit ones that created less noise than the average home speaker today. And we played in front of the whole school on Saturday evenings before the screening of the weekly film, me doing all the singing because none of the others knew the words — and they were all too shy. We played only covers — The Animals' 'House of the Rising Sun', Cream's 'Spoonful', The Who's 'Can't Explain' and, my favourite, 'That's All Right' by Elvis.

It was all a bit of harmless fun — certainly not the first, deliberate step of a career move. It was 'cool' to be in a band and, as I wasn't brilliant at much else at school, it was a little chance to grab some self-worth, lap up some kudos. The most important thing to come out of it was the launch of my love affair with the bass guitar. I quickly understood its importance in relation to the harmonic structure;

First band — 'The Knott' — with my brother Will and Hughie Mason, homemade speakers and a borrowed Hofner bass.

that a song falls apart without the bass and drum holding the rhythm together. Most kids want to take the starring role of the lead guitar, but the bass was perfectly suited to my temperament. At this time, I didn't want to be the guy at the front of the stage. I was happy to hang back and be the guy trying to hold it all together, bringing a touch of order to the chaos.

I can't say for sure that music and art gave me more confidence, made me stand a bit taller, but I strongly suspect they did. We all need to feel good about something, and I do know that in my last year I felt strong enough to take a moral stand, something I would have never dreamed myself capable of just a year earlier: I stood up to John Hedley. Major J. D. H. Hedley, a man who made you feel sorry for the Japanese fanatics he battled in the jungles of Burma. I went along to his study with a couple of other house prefects and told him we were no longer prepared to administer beatings to the junior boys. He went completely nuts, raving about how we were tearing apart the moral fabric of the school that had existed for centuries.

'I'm sorry, sir, but we no longer want to do this. It just doesn't feel right.'

I'm as proud of that as I am of anything I did in my school years.

Chapter 4

Girls and Gigs

The sixties seemed to bypass Market Harborough. They took one look at the place – the flat caps, Clydella shirts and tweed skirts – and, seeing that their work would be cut out, swerved off in search of more pliable locations to convert to a fresh outlook on the world. The decade was also to leave the lightest of footprints on Kettering, one of Britain's less remarkable towns. It was to the technical college there, twelve miles down the A6, that I ended up being sent, either to further my education or to finish it, my parents pursuing the logic that any qualifications from any institution had to be better than none.

Kettering Tech was not exactly Balliol, Oxford, but as it turned out I quite liked it for that. It was certainly a relief to be out of grey flannels and starched collars and studs. It was with great pleasure that we, the leavers of 1968, tossed away our straw boaters on Saturday, 29 June, the school's end-of-year Commemoration Day, and streamed out of the school gates. We were happy as skylarks and horny as rams, like convicts after a long stretch, breathing the fresh air of freedom and thrilled by the adventure of a life on the outside.

Three months later, I was pulling on a new pair of jeans and a charity-shop suit jacket, getting into my Ford Popular (cost: ten pounds) and heading in the other direction to the leafy squares of Bromsgrove and into a slightly depressed industrial town famous for its production of shoes and boots and not much else. For a year, in a rather half-hearted sort of fashion again, I set about trying to get A levels in English and physics. But to get me where?

My father wanted me to follow him into banking, but I knew in my guts that wasn't going to happen and that some sort of show-down was looming. So, what was I going to do? I knew I'd have to work that out at some point, but for a year I was happy enough to drift about the tech and head out at lunchtime to eat burgers and drink shakes down at the Wimpy (*the* place to hang out in Ketter-ing). After classes, I'd sometimes head to the snooker club with some mates (the second-coolest place to hang out), but more often hit the pub or the Wimpy with the girls.

Girls! Wow. I had barely met any. Straight out of an all-boys school, I was mesmerized by these exotic creatures, having been denied access to their company for so long but now sharing the same class-room. After eight years in the exclusive company of boys, I now spent most of my free time rubbing along with the female of the spe-cies. I had never had a female friend, but now I had a whole bunch and, frankly, they were probably the only reason I kept up my studies at the tech and didn't pack up to find some sort of apprenticeship or employment. You grab what fun you can when you can, and girls, burgers and snooker — they were all way more fun than reading Mil-ton and trying to master the mysteries of electrical circuits and the structure of the atom. Today, I'd probably find those subjects quite interesting (quite), but back in the day, my sweet Lord, it was dull. It all seemed so irrelevant. Girls, on the other hand, seemed very rele-vant indeed.

It's so hard for school-leavers to know what to do with their lives.

How can they? They have had no experience of life. For all I knew, I may have had it in me to become an outstanding boatbuilder, bookbinder or bicycle designer. But how was I ever going to know where my talents and interests lay when I knew little else but the insides of a classroom and a textbook? I just knew I had to hang in there, without upsetting my slightly concerned parents too much, try not to stare out of the window as much as I did at Bromsgrove and, well, just see what turned up. That was pretty much my life plan and vision of the future at this stage. No point looking beyond the burgers, the birds and bashing the black over the baize into the top-right corner.

Change and progress might not yet have come to Market Harborough and Kettering, but they certainly came to my bedroom and my burgeoning record collection. This new wave of music, the charge led by The Beatles, The Yardbirds and The Stones, was so different to what had gone before in 'popular' music. For a start, you never really used to get 'bands', apart from big jazz bands. You just got a singer with a rhythm section tucked somewhere behind in the shadows. The singer wore a suit, grinned into the camera and crooned into the mic, wooing housewives everywhere with songs written by someone else. But these new songs were being penned by the people actually singing them.

The songs felt so fresh, coming from the heart, from true, everyday experiences, that I could relate to them directly in a way I had never managed until then, or even felt was possible. Listening to American rhythm 'n' blues on Radio Luxembourg as a kid was massively thrilling, but I had no idea what the performers were singing about, and I didn't really care. It was the sounds. Even Elvis, who I loved, never 'spoke' to me. He was an exotic, a rebel, a medium to convey me into another universe. But from about 1963 onwards, I lay there on my bed in Stonehenge staring at the ceiling, thinking and feeling, *Finally, someone is singing to me, for me, about me.*

No kidding – the first time I heard The Kinks' 'You Really Got Me', it was as close to a religious epiphany as I have ever had, at least up till then. I had never heard anything like it, for the simple reason that nothing like it had ever been written before. It was a similar experience with The Who's 'My Generation'. The music of the sixties is spoken of as a revolution, but it was as much an emotional revolution for the people listening to it as it was a shift in cultural tastes and musical form. These new bands gave voice and validation to young men like me.

I am not a dewy-eyed retro-idealist about the sixties. It was all about the music for me. Nothing else. I didn't give a toss about the fashion. Sure, it was fun to watch the one brave girl in Market Harborough who dared walk down the High Street in a mini-skirt and, as with the Asian lad ten years earlier, witness the whole scene around her freeze in horror. But decking myself in some sort of tribal uniform never crossed my mind. I had had enough of uniforms. Today, when they put up some footage about the sixties, all you get is guys in Afghans, everyone on the spliff and the acid and flocking to Carnaby Street. My only experience of that was the odd snatch of sassily dressed London youths in a news report on telly.

I plugged into the sixties by going to gigs as often as I could. My first was to see Joe Cocker and the Grease Band before I started at the tech. Incredibly, he was playing in a field right outside Market Harborough. Woodstock it was not. Honestly, there can't have been more than thirty or forty people there, but he sang as if he were playing to twenty thousand. It was just after the release of his cover of The Beatles' 'With a Little Help from My Friends' and I was blown away, watching him shaking with passion as he belted it out.

In 1967, I saw the Jeff Beck Group at Hinkley Town Hall, with Jeff on lead, Ronnie Wood on bass, Aynsley Dunbar on drums, and, on vocals, Rod Stewart, who came on stage swigging from a half-full bottle of whisky. Rod and Jeff had a big row halfway through the set because Jeff kept changing chords and messing up the key for Rod, who became enraged and started screaming at him. But it didn't stop the show, although it looked like it might at one point, with the two of them squaring up. It was by far the loudest music I'd ever heard, booming through huge Marshall speakers, my insides shuddering from the vibrations. Most amps and speakers then were paltry compared with what was to come. A home music system with good speakers today can generate roughly the same volume as many gigs back then. Very loud music was rare, and to hear it that night, shaking every atom in my body and rattling the fittings and fixtures, was quite an experience.

Even louder were The Who, playing the Granby Halls in Leicester in 1968, and coming on at the end to cause utter mayhem after great little sets from Joe Cocker and a brilliant but little-known Leicester outfit called Family. The Who only played four songs and then devoted the rest of the night to smashing the stage to pieces, the crowd joining in with the destruction down in the auditorium. I stood there dumbstruck, watching guitars being broken in half and stabbed into speakers, cymbals flying, and all the while, John Entwistle on bass, calmly playing on amid the chaos.

These were heady experiences and, in hindsight, I guess they were changing me in an imperceptible way, nudging my life in a direction without me being aware of it. The gig that probably made the greatest impression was Jimi Hendrix at the Gaumont in Worcester in April 1967. Outside of a small circle of music fans, Hendrix was largely unknown at the time and he was the third or fourth support act to The Walker Brothers. Also on the bill, completing the weirdest of line-ups, were Cat Stevens, The Tremeloes and Englebert Humperdink!

Hendrix played 'Hey Joe', 'Purple Haze', 'Like a Rolling Stone' and 'Wild Thing', and you knew you were in the presence of a very original and special talent, like nothing else out there. I had never seen or heard anyone play a guitar like that, and I'd certainly never seen someone set fire to one, but that's exactly what he did during 'Hey Joe'. As with The Who, it was one of those electrifying, slightly terrifying, awesome experiences that was to stay with me for ever.

Hendrix's reputation grew after his performance at the Monterey Festival a couple of months later, but it was about a year and a half later, in January 1969, that he burst to national prominence. Jimi and his band, The Jimi Hendrix Experience, were performing on Lulu's prime live show, *Happening for Lulu*, and I was at home on the sofa, tuning in, as I did every week. After a brilliant version of 'Voodoo Chile', the band were working their way pretty lamely through 'Hey Joe', when Jimi pulls up and says, 'We'd like to stop playing this rubbish and dedicate a song to Cream.'

Lulu's face was a picture — all this going out live on the BBC, with half the country watching! The supergroup Cream, with Eric Clapton, Ginger Baker and Jack Bruce, had split up in late November 1968, bringing the curtain down on one of the most influential bands of the era. That was sensational news and it had been slow to filter through. Jimi and his band then played a brilliant version of Cream's 'Sunshine of Your Love', and I can feel the tingle and shiver now as I recall my astonishment at the news and at Hendrix's bravado and brilliant tribute. As soon as it was over, we were all on the phone, frantically pulling at the slow-moving rotary dials. 'Did you see that?' 'Did you see that?!' This was the year of the first moon landing, but Hendrix on *Lulu* was my moon landing. He got banned by the BBC for this outrage, but he wouldn't have cared less. The following year, he was dead.

The plan had been to keep The Knott going after the other four members had left school, Will heading to Loughborough Art College to study furniture design and the other three going straight into jobs. We managed to play a few gigs the following year, the only memorable one taking place at Market Harborough rugby club.

It was staged in the home changing room shortly after the players had finished scrubbing up after a match. The dirty brown water was still in the big communal bath when they chucked a few boards of plywood over it and we took to the stage to set up. Necking yards of ale and aftershave, the rugby boys couldn't have cared less if we'd played covers of 'Bill and Ben, the Flowerpot Men' and 'Puff the Magic Dragon', but we did okay and, I have to add, the acoustics were as good as any I've played in a small venue.

That was pretty well the end of the line for The Knott. It wasn't exactly the same as Cream or The Beatles calling it a day, but it was still a sad realization. It was my first band, I had learned to play bass, albeit fairly crudely, but above all, for me, it was the thrill of playing live and the satisfaction of making a steady improvement. I had come to realize that music was always going to have to play some role in my life. In what capacity or at what level, I had no idea, and the thought of being in a proper band never crossed my mind. But, having played the bass and mastered the basics and a bit more, it was right there in my bones and soul now, and would stay there for good. I was always going to play music, and I was always going to be a bass player.

At Kettering, I searched for bands to join, but there weren't a great many to be found. In fact, there wasn't a great deal of anything that might be considered fun or creative to be found in Kettering at the time. I played in a three-piece blues band for a bit, with a half-decent drummer and a good guitarist who played nice and bluesy, trying to imitate his hero, Eric Clapton. But we were fairly crap as a three-piece, playing to a few half-empty pubs, changing our name after every gig in case word got around about how poor we were and the next landlord declined to book us. I moved on to what might be loosely termed a 'soul' band with a sax and trumpet player and, quite possibly, the only Chinese guitarist playing in a British band back then. He was one of the first Chinese to study in the UK and probably the most memorable feature of that microscopically small footnote in British musical history.

I'd like to tell you that at least my studies were a roaring success. But they weren't. Far from it. I failed both A levels. No surprise for physics, as I didn't even bother turning up for the exam. They say that if you're going to fail, make sure you fail big. I certainly didn't disappoint on that count. My parents may not have seen my latest academic catastrophe as a smart move, but maybe, just maybe, my intuition, my gut instinct knew what it was doing. Deep within, I think I had an unarticulated feeling of horror about the conventional, provincial life that my parents, like all parents, praying for their child's security, wished for me.

So, what the hell now? First up was to face my parents. They didn't give me a rollicking. It was worse; they gave me disappointment, powerfully expressed in glum and anxious faces, Dad in his arm-chair knocking out his pipe, as if trying to knock some sense into me. Every parent will know what they must have been thinking: *What are we going to do with this child?*

I knew I was going to have to pay some sort of penance for my flop in the classroom; I wasn't so inconsiderate as to fail to appreciate the sacrifice they had made in spending all their hard-earned money on educating their children. I had hardly given them a great return on their investment. My father rubbed his chin thoughtfully and said, 'Well, John, I suppose it's the workplace for you now. I've taken the liberty of making a few calls . . .'

My heart was freezing and sinking.

'. . . and there's a place on the Marks and Spencer management-training scheme. It's a great opportunity. What do you think?'

What was I to say? *You can stick that one, Dad?* So, I said, 'Er, okay.'

Off I trooped in my suit for a series of interviews and, incredibly, having got through the first three, I was in there for the fourth and final and it was going just fine. There were three men with grey hair ranged behind a long table and I was answering one of their questions when the bad cop among them interrupted and — I guess, trying to throw me off balance — asked, 'How do you go upstairs?'

'Sorry, I'm just answering your colleague's question, sir.'

'I don't care. What's your answer?'

'I'd walk up the stairs, I suppose. Maybe take the lift, if there was one.'

'Wrong answer. You'd run up them.'

So, I failed that too, and it was back for another chat with Mum and Dad in the sitting room at Stonehenge.

'John,' Dad said gravely, 'I've spoken to some friends in banking and there's an opening at Lloyds Bank in Rugby.'

Nightmare scenario — but my mother's face was creased and pleading. Again, what else to say?

'Er, okay. I'll give it a go.'

It only lasted a month, but it was without doubt the most miserable month of my life. Thank God for The Beatles' *White Album*. I played that over and over every night until the needle almost bored its way through the vinyl. Truly, it saved my sanity. The *White Album* and my guitar, which almost grew a voice to beg me to give it a rest. I'd handed in my notice at Lloyds after a week but had to serve out another three. A word of advice: don't go back to the sixties and become a trainee bank clerk in a provincial town. I've never read Dante's *Inferno*, but I'm guessing that experience would be one of his outer circles of hell.

So, more disappointment, more uncertainty, more frustration at living at home, no money. For beer and cigarette money, I took a job working in Symington's, a soup factory, down in town. I was the dogsbody tasked with cleaning out the mixing machines. Being an accident-prone dreamer, one evening I forgot to turn off one of the machines I was cleaning and put my hand into it. There was a terrible grinding noise and a bolt of quite unbelievable pain. When I pulled my hand out, my right thumb was hanging off just below the nail, and I was rushed to the hospital in Kettering — a very good one, thank heavens. The surgeon said he wasn't sure whether to take it off or sew it back on.

'I'm a guitar player. Put it back on, please.'

So he obliged, mercifully. Half an inch deeper into that mixing machine and I would never have played a guitar again and my whole life would have turned out entirely differently.

It was clear that Market Harborough wasn't really working out for me. I had to get out before it was too late. But where could I go? My thumb mended, I went to play a twenty-first-birthday gig for my mate Paul Turner, the drummer in The Knott. I got talking to his dad, who owned a timber business in Wolverhampton, telling him I was at a loss as to what to do for work and was keen to move on somewhere, anywhere. He said he had contacts at a huge timber importer and distributor in London that he bought all his wood from and he'd give them a call.

A week later, I was packing up the Ford Popular in the drive at Stonehenge: a bag of clothes, my guitars, my records and the Dansette. I'm not sure if it was relief or anxiety that was etched on my mother's face this time as they waved me off. Probably a bit of both. I loved my parents, and it was not them I was running away from with such joy. I just wanted a life, I wanted adventure, so where better to start looking for it than London? I had heard a few times that when you're bored of London, you're bored of life. The move sounded good. But would I find what I was looking for in a timber company in Erith in Kent? At least it wasn't that far from London.

Chapter 5

Timber and Tenements

It was the summer of '69, I had just turned twenty and my train was rattling through the bleak dockland landscape of south-east London: Bermondsey, Millwall, Rotherhithe, Deptford . . . It wasn't until many years later that I was to discover that I was missing out on a giant hippy party. While I was staring out the window, slightly aghast – so this was Swinging London? – the rest of the country was apparently walking around naked, smoking weed, making love and wearing daisy chains. I'm afraid the summer of '69 would pass me by.

It was only about fifteen miles from Charing Cross, but my journey from London took over an hour and you had the impression the driver was slowing up every now and then to wind down the window and have a chat with a mate. We pulled into Erith, a place so ugly it made Kettering look like Vienna. It struck me as a sensible act of self-preservation to take off my tie as I made my way through a scene of post-industrial desolation to the timberyard of Burt, Boulton & Hayward (BBH). Safely inside the gates, I put it back on and got lost among giant stacks of poles, planks and shaved tree trunks until, finally, I found the prefab office building.

'So, why are you here?' said Dennis Holland, a friendly old chap with a massive RAF moustache and a florid complexion.

'You're the second person to ask me that today. The chairman in your HQ up on the Strand just said the same. He sent me down to see you. He had no idea either. I'm here for a job.'

'Did he now? What do you know about timber?'

'Nothing, except that it's made of wood.'

'Hmm . . . well, that's a start. Tell you what, why don't you become our first trainee manager? Fifteen quid a week sound all right?'

'Perfect.'

BBH was a major business, providing all the telegraph poles for the south of England and most of its railway sleepers. The yard was there in Erith to be close to the Thames, where the logging ships from Finland and Russia delivered their cargo, all of it unloaded by hand by crews of stevedores whose pints you most certainly never wanted to spill. These, I was to discover, were tough, tough men that even John Hedley might struggle to command.

I had done my six weeks' training in each of the six departments, including the mill and the docks, before I settled into sales, and it wasn't long before Dennis called me in.

'I don't know why we've never done business with the GLC,' he said. 'It's the biggest employer in Europe, the biggest builder in Europe, and it's currently putting up thousands upon thousands of new houses and scything down the world's forests to do it. For some reason, no one here has ever managed to find out who buys in their timber.'

I got on the phone and, by the end of the morning, having been passed around the labyrinth of offices of the Greater London Council, I found myself talking to a bloke called Dave.

'It's about fucking time someone from your fucking company phoned me. And yeah, I do buy the wood, every last splinter of it.'

'How about lunch or supper?'

'Great, I love food.'

I knew nothing about food or London restaurants, so Dennis told me to take the guy to Inigo Jones; one of the best in London, he said. Dave brought his cartoon cockney girlfriend, we had a rare old knees-up and I got the GLC account. The deal was simple: the GLC were to buy all their timber from BBH, and I was to take Dave and his 'bird' out for a slap-up meal once a fortnight. Who said business was tough?

It wasn't long before the GLC started putting in absolutely massive orders, and Dennis was grinning so hard his moustache would have stretched from ear to ear, had it not already been doing so. After six months, my account was worth £1 million a year, about £15 million in today's money. I'd like to claim that was down to some sort of Rockefeller business genius lying latent but undiscovered in me. But no, I just took the guy out for steak and as much wine as he could drink.

I lived in a nondescript semi-detached boarding house in a nondescript suburban street in the nondescript borough of Bexleyheath, run by Doris, the seventy-five-year-old landlady. I gave her five pounds a week and she gave me a cooked breakfast to floor a lumberjack and an evening meal, usually chops and mash, sausage and mash or shepherd's pie and peas. I spent the tenner left over from my pay packet on fuel to run the car and beer to run me. There was literally nothing to do in Bexleyheath in the evenings unless you had a powerful telescope to look at the stars. Dennis was kind enough to inform me there was an excellent strippers' pub that did an excellent Sunday roast — a suggestion I never followed up, tempting as it was. Any change of scene would have been welcome after a few months.

So, for six months, I did my work, had a few pints with my colleagues, went back to Doris for my grub, then up to my room to play my guitar and stick records on the Dansette. There was very little good new music coming through. It had all just dried up, so I went back to my favourites: Dylan, Van Morrison, Cream, The Kinks, The Stones, The Beatles, The Yardbirds, Muddy Waters, and so on. I missed playing in a band, but there was nothing I could do about that for the time being. I had become quite anglocentric in my tastes, but always with a leaning towards the blues. Britain had become the crucible of modern music over the last decade, absorbing the influences of different strands of American music, black and white, and mixing them into its own potent and unique sound. Once again, it was music that saved my sanity.

I made the occasional trip into central London, but I knew only a handful of people in the city and there was not much point in going up to the West End to wander about by myself. A highlight should have been going to see The Stones play in Hyde Park on 5 July 1969. It was a free concert, and police estimates put the crowd numbers as peaking at close to half a million. In spite of that, there was a weird and slightly depressing atmosphere, possibly because founder and guitarist Brian Jones had died two days earlier, and possibly because the PA was so weak that you couldn't hear much unless you were crammed in at the front. It might also have had something to do with the unsettling sight of seeing Jagger perform in a sort of white dress. It was the first time the band had played for two years, and they admitted afterwards they had played badly. There was a ton of weed and booze being passed around but, far from being on a high, I slipped back on the train to Doris's for my chops and mash, feeling slightly deflated by the experience. I loved The Stones, but I was unlucky to catch them on a bad day.

I met some brilliant people at BBH, and I stayed in touch and went back for drinks with them long after I'd moved on, but the dreariness of life in Bexleyheath could go on for only so long and I was on the alert for good companionship, preferably female. Around Christmas time, I found it in a girl called Diane, who I got talking to in a pub after work. My life picked up the day I met Diane, a social worker from Salford and the only girl from her school to go on to higher education. In fact, my life changed radically the day I met her, and I soon said goodbye to lovely old Doris and her chewy chops and moved into Diane's little flat in Woolwich.

We made a strange couple at first, her being a very short working-class lass with a strong commitment to socialism and me being a very tall, middle-class, privately educated lad in middle management with no commitment to any political cause whatsoever. Diane changed that, opening my eyes to worlds — and world views — that were as far from the cosy environment of Market Harborough and Bromsgrove as you could imagine. She was an activist and a campaigner, a full-on card-carrying leftie, and she inspired me to start reading and taking an interest in the wider world. I was soon reading Engels and Marx and going on Ban the Bomb marches. It's a thrill to have your mind opened, I discovered; to have your conscience shaken, your horizons broadened. You can always change your mind, but just keep thinking and questioning.

Two episodes in particular blasted me out of my complacency, out of my lazy indifference to the lives and plights of others. The day she took me back to Salford to meet her family was one. It was like stepping back into the late nineteenth century — and I loved it, for showing me the real world. Not much could have changed, that's for sure. There was row upon and row of red-brick terraces in an area forgotten by industry and the modern world, blighted by high unemployment and suffering extreme deprivation. I had never been further north than Leicester, and this was a soul-shakingly different world to anything I had come across. We had an outdoor loo at Stonehenge, but we also had two in the house. We also had more than one fireplace, but it was not the only means of heating our home. Hers was an old-fashioned working-class home where the front room was left unused except at Christmas. Life was lived in the little kitchen. Everyone smoked hard, drank hard and ate chips. Fish was a treat.

What struck me most was the powerful sense of community, everyone so friendly and looking out for each other; the pub on the corner was rammed during opening hours. There were no drugs on the street but, my God, a lot of beer was drunk there. They didn't need social workers in their street, Diane said. Nor any police. If a kid went wayward, he was sent round to Diane's mum, who gave him a dressing-down and threatened to put her son, Fred, on to him if he stepped out of line. You really didn't want Fred put on to you.

The week up there made a powerful impression on me and, driving back south, I felt a little ashamed by the good fortune I had enjoyed and my failure not to have made the most of the opportunities I had been given. I was an altered man when I arrived back in London, and I knew that significant changes lay ahead.

If I was shocked by what I saw in the back streets of Salford, I was genuinely distressed by what I witnessed in London's East End when, not long after, Diane and I volunteered to take part in the 1971 Census, going from house to house, flat to flat, gathering details of people's lives to provide a snapshot of the nation's population. 'Dickensian' is a word used so often to describe poverty and urban decay that it has become almost meaningless, but the term perfectly described the world we encountered.

Our beat was Poplar and the Isle of Dogs, in what is now the business and finance district of Canary Wharf, just a few hundred yards across the Thames from the pleasant and affluent borough of Greenwich, where we sometimes went for a drink. I've been to the modern incarnation of the Isle of Dogs, with its skyscrapers and malls, and two worlds further removed from each other is tough to picture. The conditions in which people were living were shocking: squalid flats for two or three inhabited by ten or more, many of them immigrant Asian families. On most floors, there was just one toilet to be shared by every flat in the corridor.

In the space of a few months, my world view — if it deserved the dignity of that term — had been knocked for six. (Remember, with so little media then, you had to make an effort to be informed. No excuses, but there was a lot more ignorance, or lack of awareness, then.) At school, I had no interest in what I was obliged to study, other than art, but now I was motivated. I was going to go to university and educate myself, come what may. After a year at BBH, I started evening classes at Woolwich Tech, studying sociology, to get the diploma I needed to study the same course at a more advanced level at Goldsmiths, part of the University of London, its campus up the road in New Cross, on the limits of Deptford.

Even on my little salary I could afford a mortgage, and so Diane and I bought a little terraced house together in Bexleyheath and began a life of quiet domesticity, serious study, even more serious politics and, in my case, manic DIY and loads of loud music. It was strange, becoming more comfortable materially yet more troubled in my conscience.

After I got my diploma from Woolwich Tech, securing my place at Goldsmiths, I went to inform Dennis that I was leaving the firm. He almost fell off his chair.

'Sociology? University? Why on earth would anyone want to do that? We're just about to make you the youngest board member in the history of the firm! And what about your account? It's doing so well. You're set up for life, boy! Don't be a clot and throw it all away.'

I had a lot of time for Dennis, a funny and kind man, and I tried to explain that, at twenty-three, I was too young to settle down to such a comfortable middle-aged lifestyle. I wanted challenges, adventures, to push myself, to see what else was out there, maybe do some good for others. He was genuinely upset at the prospect of losing the contract with the GLC, so I agreed to his compromise: I wasn't to tell

Dave I was leaving, I'd still take him out for his fortnightly piss-up in a posh restaurant and BBH would pay me a half-salary and let me keep my company Hillman Hunter. That worked out at about three or four grand a year and, to be honest, my new socialist principles were not quite so incorruptible as to turn down funds that would see me through my studies. But, in the event, I gave the job up after six months. I had so much more money than the other students, it didn't sit at all comfortably with me, not least because I had a grant from the college as well. I wanted the full grimy student experience, cold beans out of a tin and all that.

It was probably inevitable that Diane and I would split up, me being in my new world, with so many new friends and diversions. I was a student; she was a full-time social worker. She had changed me as a person, and I will always be grateful for her shifting my perspective of the world, influencing me to take a different direction. She represented another of those turning points in the journey of life, another example of the serendipity that guides our destinies. Just as Will's band having two guitarists forced me to take up the bass, just as flunking my exams and failing to get into art college left me in limbo and forced me to go to London, so too had Diane pushed me down a path I could not have foreseen. She had been the most significant agent of change in my life up to that point.

I did something for her too, I hope; a mellowing effect, perhaps, on her radicalism. Without letting up on her socialist principles and activism, she certainly enjoyed the petit-bourgeois comforts of our home! We had balanced each other out, correcting our extremes, making us see the world from other sides, I suppose. When I moved out, I gave her full ownership of the home, which was worth about £12,000, in return for a couple of grand. Within a month, a friend of a friend moved in with her and I believe they stayed with each other.

I moved into a council flat on the Crossfields estate in Deptford, vacated by a student friend who had gone travelling the world for a year. The Crossfields was an early post-war social-housing estate comprising twelve red-brick blocks and split in two by the arched brick viaduct of the North Kent Line. Each 'house' had five storeys, the washing slung like forgotten bunting along the communal walkways. Most of the houses had been deemed 'unfit for family habitation', so a great number of the residents were students from Goldsmiths, plus artists, musicians and general layabouts wanting to do not very much other than smoke weed and drink beer. I was to get to know the community very well, and it was great. There were 'normal' working people living there too, making the community an interesting mix, and on the whole everyone got on.

So, I packed away my jacket and tie, threw on my T-shirt and jeans and started growing my hair — hair I would barely cut for a good couple of decades. It was a ten-minute walk to college in the morning, up Deptford High Street, past the Sally Army hostel, all the tramps emerging for the day, and over the railway line into New Cross. If you were to come back late at night from the Union bar when all the shops were boarded up, it was advisable to do so in a group. Drunk, stoned, dreamy students were easy prey.

Mum phoned up a lot at first, worried to death about me having chucked in a solid job to go broke and live in a run-down council flat. Having proved myself at BBH, I think they understood that I knew what I was doing and let me be, to work out life for myself. I was as happy as I had ever been. Finally, aged twenty-three, my life was beginning. For the first time, I was living it on my terms. I was fully de-institutionalized, free from family pressure. I was smiling and laughing a lot more and, incredibly for a student, I was out of bed on time every morning, excited to head into college. I was making friends fast, and not just because in the first few months I still had some BBH cash to splash at the bar.

There was one unsettling incident in those early days that shook me up and left a dark cloud hanging for a while. One evening I came back to the flat, up on the fourth floor, to find that my door had been kicked down. Entering hesitantly, it was as if Charles Manson and Jackson Pollock had dropped in after an acid and scrumpy bender. The whole place had been smashed to pieces, including a bunch of my favourite records. There was blood on the floor, ceilings and walls. On the wall was painted, 'John, you're a fucking bastard.' I was completely freaked out and went and stayed at a mate's. It turned out that the girl I had slept with not long before had a boyfriend. And a very angry one, judging by his interior-decorating skills. It was a one-night stand, and I had no idea she was attached. So, once she told me, I sought him out on the campus, apologized and explained. He was really cut up. The good news was that they stayed together, and he and I became mates. Sort of. It was the only trouble we ever had on the estate, despite it housing a mixed bag of characters who had been thrown together from all walks of life — and it had come from the Goldsmiths crowd, rather than the locals.

Knowing my friend was coming back from her travels, I needed to find a new place to live and was delighted to see a notice on the Goldsmiths board offering accommodation in another flat on the Crossfields. I was loving it there. It had become my home, every other night spent in the Oxford Arms, with the more alternative residents of the community. I moved into number one, Farrer House, which had a mattress on the concrete floor but, as yet, no furniture, as promised by the council. Even though it had four bed-rooms, it was one of the flats deemed unfit for family habitation. There was a small gas fire in the sitting room, a fifties gas stove in the kitchen, a payphone and a pay-as-you-go electricity meter.

My BBH money long since gone, I was soon as skint as the rest of them and, the rent being £9.48 a week, I started to hunt for a flat-mate to share the burden. A mate at college said he knew of a local social worker — half the population of south-east London at the time seemed to be a social worker — and he said he'd get him to give me a call, if he was interested. A couple of evenings later, the phone rang and, incredibly, I was in the flat and not in the Oxford Arms.

'Hi, is that John? I'm Simon's mate. He said you might have a room going free on the Crossfields.'

'Not free, mate, it'll cost you £4.78 a week. But yes. You want to come and check it out?'

'It's fine. I know those flats. I've done work in them. Okay to move in Sunday?'

'Well, sure, yes. Whenever you like. What's your name, by the way?'

'Dave. Dave Knopfler.'

'Dave what?'

'Knopfler.'

Dave turned up as arranged, and I was delighted to see he was carrying a guitar case.

Chapter 6

Mr Knopfler, I Presume?

The mid-seventies are often regarded as the lowest point in modern British history, but for me they were as happy as any years of my life. The Heath Conservative government had declared five states of emergency in four years, there were crippling strikes, spiralling inflation, collapsing stock markets, militant union barons with more power than the political parties, dirty and unreliable trains and erratic malfunctioning telephones, power cuts were an accepted part of life, the IRA was exploding bombs all over the place, football hooligans were running riot, the skinheads of the National Front were menacing immigrants, there was graffiti and litter everywhere, and street upon street of terraced houses were being bulldozed to make way for brutalist tower blocks, which people thought were the answer to every community's problems. London was more of an eyesore than it was in the Blitz. Everywhere you looked, it was shabby and decrepit, nothing really worked, and every day the headlines in the newspaper spoke of a once great country in severe decline and on the point of total collapse.

But down in Deptford, we were having a ball.

Maybe it was because Deptford was so far ahead in the race to the bottom. There can have been few districts in Britain so unglamorous, so deprived, but on the Crossfields estate and the Goldsmiths campus, we didn't care so long as we had enough money to buy beer, fags and the odd bag of weed. I loved Deptford, its greasy-spoon cafés, its ancient pubs, its friendly tramps, its haunting history with all those derelict warehouses and rusting dock machinery up the Creek towards the Thames. There was a bleak but beautiful poetry to the place, and it had a strong, beating heart to it, the attitude being, 'So we live in a shithole, but it's our shithole.'

After the heyday of the sixties, the general music scene in Britain had become fairly uninspiring in the early to middle years of the following decade. There was lots of 'experimental' rock in the album chart, and the singles chart was dominated by lightweight, insipid, easy-listening pop songs, very few of which were to stand the test of time. The Bay City Rollers were being hailed as the new Beatles and Terry Jacks's saccharine 'Seasons in the Sun' topped the charts for a month in early 1974. Enough said. This was also the golden era of the novelty song — The Wombles, The Wurzels and comedy actor Windsor Davies with 'Whispering Grass'. If you loved your music as I did, there wasn't a great deal of new talent out there to drop on to the turntable. Bowie, Cockney Rebel and Eric Clapton were the only contemporary acts speaking to me. I took refuge in my favourites: J. J. Cale, Muddy Waters, Bob Dylan, Van Morrison, B.B. King, Leonard Cohen, Cream, The Stones, The Kinks and The Beatles.

Part of the problem was that most of Britain's best rock stars had fled overseas to avoid eye-wateringly punitive tax rates, which were a real problem back then. The Stones had scarpered to France, Bowie to New York, Rod Stewart to California. It was a full-blown exodus, and it was no surprise they were in headlong retreat. Thin Lizzy's single 'The Boys Are Back in Town' and the album *Jailbreak* earned them £200,000 (about £2 million today) but after tax they ended up with just over thirty grand for the whole band, before deductions for their management team and agents. They had worked hard to finesse their craft, sacrificed a stable life, brought great joy to many people for posterity, but they were being paid like apprentice dust-men. Elton John, whose early albums with lyricist Bernie Taupin I really enjoyed, was the bestselling artist of the day, shifting about 30 million albums in 1975 alone. Everyone presumed he was drowning in money, but he was receiving only about three pence in every pound. It was barely worth him getting out of his four-poster and clearing his throat. Great that he's done okay since, but he certainly wasn't coining it in back then.

These were highly charged, highly politicized times — perfect for studying sociology at Goldsmiths, in the golden era of stereotypical bearded leftie lecturers and, it must be said, virtually no female lec-turers. It was a very left-leaning university, my department especially so, but the ideological fervour I had embraced with Diane waned a little. I soon realized I didn't want to be a card-carrying ideologue of any stripe, and I never have been since. Maybe it was the sight of one of my militant socialist lecturers pulling on his corduroy jacket and getting into his BMW at the end of his short day, off to bang one of his female students. Maybe it was meeting up for drinks with my old mates from BBH and suburban Bexleyheath, all good people, capi-talists all, I'm sure, but hard-working and decent, just trying to get on and earn a crust.

I wanted to learn as much as I could, I wanted to open my mind as much as I could, and I worked pretty hard, but I never joined a party or a society at Goldsmiths, never got involved in a campaign — except once, I think, for cheaper beer at the Union bar. It was not until I got to Goldsmiths that I realized that the people I had encoun-tered at BBH — the teak-tough dockers and stevedores, as much as the office and yard employees — had opened my eyes to the world every bit as much as the academics, activists and ideologues of the university. They were real people doing real jobs and living real lives. I wasn't going to let politics define and restrict me. I may have been living in a small world, but the world of my mind had become a much bigger space, and I wanted to treat people as I found them, whatever their political affiliations.

David Knopfler turned out to be a perfect flatmate. We shared the same sense of humour as well as a love of music. He was off social-working by eight-thirty and, in our area of London, he wasn't ever short of work. I was off to uni for ten and, having our own sets of friends, it was a pleasure when our paths did manage to cross. He was a very open guy, willing to talk about anything. We had an easy relationship, had similar musical tastes and from time to time we strummed guitar together.

After the wilderness years of Bexleyheath, where guitarists were thin on the ground, playing music was making a strong comeback in my life. Uni gave me plenty of time to improve my technique, there was a bunch of bands on campus who I messed around with and, more than just an attraction to her character and looks, it was no surprise that my next girlfriend was heavily involved in the music scene. Jean was in the year above me at Goldsmiths but also ran an agency for folk singers up in Kentish Town.

She'd recently broken up with the singer Bob Davenport, from the north-east, like her, and a big name in the world of folk. He was a friend of Bob Dylan's and had played with him on a number of occasions. I didn't know much about folk, beyond Dylan, Joan Baez, Pete Seeger and Woodie Guthrie, and I knew next to nothing about the English scene. Jean introduced me to the leading players, including Martin Carthy and the Watersons, and the extraordinary guitarist Richard Thompson from Fairport Convention, who came to have a big influence on me. People can be sniffy about folk, as they can be about poetry, but even if you don't like it, you can't ignore its importance in our musical tradition and its influence on rock. If nothing else, for me, it helped open my mind and widen my musical tastes.

In a moment of madness in October 1974, Jean and I decided to open a record shop in the vacant outlet below her agency on Kentish Town Road. We called it Honky Tonk Records. The name was inspired by the DJ Charlie Gillett's show of the same name on Radio London. We wanted to sell the best of the new music that wasn't getting airplay anywhere, just as Gillett was trying to play it to his audience. Charlie was one of the few DJs on the radio playing anything new, alternative, or little known, and anyone with a true interest in music — that is, music outside of the charts — tuned in to him religiously every Sunday. He was interested in albums, not singles; artists, not trends; anything that he rated; and he played a lot of the music I loved, like Little Feat, Ry Cooder and J. J. Cale, and new UK bands like Ian Dury and the Blockheads and Graham Parker & the Rumour.

More in wild hope than in expectation, I wrote to him at Radio London, asking if he had any suggestions for our stock list. I was truly surprised when I received a reply, almost by return of post, with a really encouraging letter and a very long list of recommendations. Jean and I probably weren't the most driven of shopkeepers, not being there much of the time, and the shop closed its doors, to the sadness of nobody, in May 1975. I'd like to say we gave it a proper crack, but we didn't really. Lazy students. Little could I have known that just two years later Charlie Gillett was going to re-enter my life and have the most sensational impact upon it.

The music scene at Goldsmiths was pretty vibrant, and every Saturday night some decent acts came to play at the Students' Union, including the great British blues player John Martyn, a big name in the day. It's a gig I remember vividly, mainly because the brilliant Danny Thompson was on double bass. I was mesmerized. By then, I was playing in a blues band of my own, a three-piece – drums, guitar and me on bass – and we called ourselves Blind Alley.

We were very excited about all the gigs ahead of us and even more excited when, for our very first public performance, we managed to wangle ourselves as the support act for a cool, quite alternative band called Kilburn and the High Roads. So we went on, as planned, a packed, pissed floor at the Students' Union swaying before us, and we played okay – or so I thought. After about fifteen minutes this funny-looking bloke with a rectangular head marched on from the wings, grabbed the mic and barked, 'Right, that's enough of this shit. Go on, fuck off!' The audience cheered and we skulked away. The man was Ian Dury, and that was Blind Alley's last as well their first gig.

It was July 1976, at the height of the heatwave. I had just finished my finals and woken up in bed with the manageress of the pizza restaurant down the road in Greenwich. I was hungover like a dog, but it had been a fun night out and life felt pretty good, knowing I hadn't screwed up the biggest academic challenge ever asked of me.

Heading back the one stop to Farrer House, the train rattled on to the rusty old lifting bridge, my head ringing in rhythm with every jerk of the carriage. Low tide on Deptford Creek revealed its carpet of oily mud patterned with bottles, fuel drums and shopping trolleys. Beyond the bridge, all the way to the sharp bend before the Thames, were rotten wharves, crumbling warehouses and idle cranes. We slowed into the station and, high on the viaduct, through my reflection in the filthy train window, I could make out that the curtains in our flat were still drawn. David must have had a late one too.

I ground out my cig in the ashtray of the armrest, rubbed some blood back into my face, cursing those last few pointless drinks. I trotted down the steps and dashed on to the 53 bus. So, another day dawns in Deptford – what to do with this one? Practise some chords, I guess, hit the greasy spoon mid-afternoon, kill all three meals in one sitting, then back down the Oxford Arms with some mates for a few beers and – fat chance – to watch a half-decent band.

Thoughts of how I was going to spend my day, as ever, expanded into how I was going to spend my life, as I made my way through St Paul's Churchyard and into Crossfields. That old question kept coming back to haunt me: what now? What to do with a sociology degree in a global recession? I was almost twenty-six, for God's sake.

Whenever I was away from it, I always pictured Crossfields as black and white and grainy. But we hadn't seen a grey sky for weeks. It had been hot, hot, hot. I tramped over the browning grass, swung past the burnt-out Anglia, ducked down the alley, its walls strewn with anarchic imperatives and banalities: *Eat the Rich! ... Sorry About Your Wall ... I Fought the Law ... Bang Head Here ... All Property Is Theft ... Who Needs Skool? ...* And now a fresh one that had appeared overnight, in dripping white: *NF OUT!* It was a corridor of anarchic philosophy – 'punk' was going to be the big new thing, so everyone reckoned.

Ernie was stretched out on his bench in the little square, an open toilet for Crossfield dogs and passing vagrants, a litter bin for everyone else. His mouth was ajar, face to the heavens, arm swung over the bottle of VAT 69 on the ground. I pulled out a couple of fags and dropped them into his coat pocket. I liked Ernie. Everyone liked Ernie. One of the friendliest tramps from the Salvation Army hostel on the High Street, he enjoyed the occasional day or night out in our 'park'. The residents were good to him and, having nothing to nick, he had nothing to fear. None of the students or assorted artists on the estate resented the fact that, thanks to the social, he probably had more money than we did. But we had a roof over our heads, we had our youth, we had our dreams. Ernie had his VAT 69 and his fags.

On the forecourt, a kid weaved in among the cars on his Raleigh Chopper wheelie bike – nicked, no doubt. If you farted on the Crossfields estate, someone would nick it. All property was theft, just as the graffiti said. Your Chopper is my Chopper, your car is my car — that was the prevailing outlook in inner south-east London. As an aimless middle-class, lapsed-Marxist sociology student, dressed by Oxfam and victualled by the Oxford Arms, hanging out in our spit-and-sawdust sitting room, I didn't have much of a problem with that.

Number one Farrer House was on the ground floor of the five-storey council block, and I made my way through a tunnel of washing, bootsteps echoing beneath the walkway. I wiggled the key in the faulty lock, finally finding some purchase, and shouldered it open.

Parched, I turned straight into the galley kitchen, filled the kettle and fired up the gas ring. The sink was piled with dishes and mugs, the sideboard showcasing the remnants of a late-night feast: half a loaf of Mother's Pride, a jar of Sandwich Spread, a box of TUC crackers, a tin of Fine Fare baked beans with a fork stuck in the crusted mass.

I clicked on the radio, turning the volume right down so as not to wake up Dave. Brotherhood of Man's 'Save Your Kisses for Me' . . . Do me a favour. I nudged the dial . . . The Wurzels' 'Combine Harvester' . . . I twisted the tuning knob a tad further . . . The Stones' 'Fool to Cry' . . . That was better, and I left it.

I lobbed the teabag into the bin, stirred in some sugar and took one step across the hall into the living room — and recoiled sharply, sloshing my tea.

'What the . . . ?'

There was a man lying on the cement floor fast asleep — the promised carpet had never materialized — and his head, propped against the only chair, was at right angles to his body. The guy had an electric guitar across his chest. To one side of him, the giant square ashtray spilled over with a thousand butts; on the other sat a couple of empty bottles of Newcastle Brown. His face, sheet-white, revealed a hint of

David. This must have been the brother he had mentioned. He stirred and groaned, and an eyelid unstuck itself.

'Cup of tea?' I asked.

When I came back, he had cleared up the fags and the beer bottles and I heard him splashing his face in the bathroom. I picked up his guitar, a Gibson Les Paul Junior. Nice.

He came back in and I handed the tea to him. He held out his hand and, in a mellow Geordie accent, he said, 'Mark, by the way. Mark Knopfler, David's brother.'

'I guessed as much. Heard a lot about you. John — John Illsley. Nice one.'

He sat down on the only chair and I perched on the old sofa bed I had found in a builder's skip a few weeks earlier. We fell into an easy chat about this and that. I took to him at once. There was a natural air and softness about him, and you could see him thinking hard before he answered a question. The conversation drifted towards music and he picked up his Gibson and started playing.

He plucked a few strings and twisted the tuning pegs. Then he really started playing, messing around with riffs and snatches of tunes. He had a curious finger-picking style. I had never seen anyone play a guitar like that, but even just fooling around, it was a great sound — a bit country, a bit rock — but fresh and original. Dave was right — his brother could play.

After a while, I asked, 'Fancy a fry-up?'

'Sure.'

We went up to the greasy spoon on the High Street and had the Full English with a side of liver.

Chapter 7

Punks on the Lawn

I never asked my parents for financial assistance throughout my three years at Goldsmiths. That was a matter of personal pride and out of respect for them. If I was going to chuck in a really good job, as I did, what sort of son would I have been to go to them with a begging bowl, asking them to fund me through a sociology degree, a course in which they saw neither sense nor merit? I lived off my grant and picked up a few quid here and there for casual work and the odd gig with a band thrown together for an occasion. So long as I could drink, smoke and eat — roughly in that order — I really didn't mind being broke.

By the time it was all over and the grant had dried up, I was truly skint, and Dad was good enough to send me that cheque for twenty quid of propping-up money (worth about about a hundred and fifty quid today) until I found some employment. I was at the counter in the Lloyds Bank on Deptford High Street cashing it in when two gunshots brought plaster crashing down from the corniced Victorian ceiling. The robbers were shouting and everyone else was screaming and I rather wished I hadn't crumbled that weed into my coffee after all — a little trick I'd learned at uni to take the edge off the morning. I stayed dead still, stunned and terrified, shaking as hard as everyone else.

One of the three robbers went to the counter window next to mine, another played lookout, and the third prodded us with his sawn-off shotgun, herding us until we were all face-up against the far wall. Mine was pressed against a cheap reproduction of a Victorian landscape — all hideous dark greens and browns with some cows standing in a misty pond of dew and a spire in the far distance — and in the reflection of the glass I could see the other robber belting the manager, who, so far as I could understand it, was refusing to open the safe.

It took about three minutes for all the tills to be emptied and the swag to be handed over. The robbers ran out and we all stood frozen to the spot in complete silence. After about a minute, the cashier I'd been with appeared from beneath the counter and said, 'Sir, shall we just carry on? Let me cash that cheque for you.' Then, as I wandered over, she added, 'Oh, no, we don't have any money, do we?' I think we were all in shock. The police arrived, sirens screeching, we all gave our contact details and carried on with our days. One evening a few days later there was knock at the door in Farrer House. Dave and I were strumming away in the sitting room, quite stoned. Imagining it was a neighbour wanting to borrow some milk, I pulled open the door and, standing in a fug of smoke, I was met by the sight of a bobby, helmet and all.

'Is this a good time, sir?' he asked with a smile, nostrils flaring. 'I've come to take your statement about the robbery.'

'Good a time as any, I guess.'

I let him in and diverted him into the galley kitchen, Dave opening every window in the flat as fast as he could. I recounted my version of events, the policeman scribbled into his pad, we shook hands and he left, gracious enough not to make any reference to the aroma. This was Deptford. They never caught the robbers.

The heatwave of summer 1976 was soon over and I was back in Deptford after spending a few weeks with Jean in her native Newcastle. We'd had a wonderful time, lounging around in the sun, picnicking at Whitley Bay, Druridge Bay and further up along the Northumberland coast, but we both knew in our bones that it was the last hurrah after three very happy years together. We had reached a point when life tells you to move on, whether you like it or not. Circumstances dictated and overruled what remained of our love. Truth be told, love had mellowed into friendship.

Back in London, I was quickly establishing another friendship — with Mark. As with Dave, it was a very easy and natural relationship and, again as with Dave, our album collections had much in common: J. J. Cale, Ry Cooder, Little Feat, Bobby 'Blue' Bland, B.B. King and a lot of reggae. Although they were entirely different characters, each gave you the same feeling of warmth, humility and honesty. Like with Dave, I felt an immediate connection with Mark; he was one of those people you know you're going to be mates with for ever, unless one of you moves to Tahiti. The two of them were good mates as well as brothers and I loved hanging out with them, all of us united by music.

The brothers had a similar vibe, but their outward manner was different. Dave was an open book — what you saw was what you got; he never hid anything. Mark, no less warm and thoughtful, was a little more reserved and you had to turn the pages to read him. He didn't tell. You had to ask, and when you did, he'd sometimes sit for a disconcertingly long time, thinking hard before he gave you his answer. He was, it became clear quite quickly, a deep thinker, but with a bellyful of humour ready to erupt at any moment. They say that only about 20 per cent of communication is verbal and, whatever he did or didn't say, I knew that I had made a friend for life.

After a couple of years as a reporter on the *Yorkshire Post*, Mark was lecturing in English at Loughton College in Essex, but he started coming down to Deptford virtually every weekend. He was playing guitar in a group called the Café Racers, an upmarket pub band playing mostly blues and rockabilly. One night the bass player dropped out because his wife went into labour and Mark called to ask if I could step in. The gig was at the King's Head on Upper Street in Islington, a well-known venue for up-and-coming bands that doubled as an arthouse theatre. Though small, it was the most prestigious venue I had ever played, and it went well. It was great to be playing in a band with Mark. Back then, he was just playing, not singing.

At this stage, I knew him only as a truly gifted guitarist, a cut above anyone I had played with, and his unique style made him stand out all the more. He told me he had been having a go at writing songs. He was as interested in writing and literature as he was in music. Language was his thing, it's what he taught, but I thought little more of it.

So, the days idled by over the autumn and winter of 1976 and into the spring of 1977 and I was very happy in my little world in Deptford: full English breakfast in the Star Café on the High Street with Dave or Mark, messing around on the guitar during the day, the odd gig, the odd bit of temporary work to earn a few quid, and then down to the Oxford Arms for a few pints with our mates on Crossfields in the evenings. It's hard to recall exactly what you were thinking over forty years ago, but I was definitely mulling over the idea of some sort of future in the music industry. Put it another way: I have no recollection of giving serious thought to any other specific line of work, let alone making plans for one. Really, I was drifting, just hanging out, playing music, listening to music. I played with the Café Racers now and then, and over a pint after one gig, Mark said, 'Why don't we put a band together?'

Not long after, he played me a song he had been working on. He had called it 'Sultans of Swing', the name of an amateur jazz band he and Dave had seen playing in a half-empty Greenwich pub, just a bunch of ageing guys playing music for the sheer love of it. He played it on his newly acquired red Fender Stratocaster through a 1960s Fender Vibrolux amp that I had recently given him. This was the moment when I realized something special was going on. It was just him and his Strat but, not long into it, I became aware I was listening to lyrics and a melody of true craftsmanship and originality. He still has the Strat and the Vibrolux today. Bought for a hundred quid or so, the guitar is probably worth about £30,000 on the open market — and a great deal more on account of its owner.

When Mark moved into Farrer House that spring, he was working on a number of songs, and the inspiration for a couple of them came from the times we used to spend hanging out in the West End, mainly in Soho, the city's seedy soul, full of hookers and sex shops, drunks, misfits and eccentrics. It was vibrant and full of colour. One evening we were up there and dropped into an art exhibition after making our regular call to the Barocco Bar off the Charing Cross Road for a bowl of pasta, and then into Angelucci's on Frith Street for a coffee. It was modern art on display, abstruse and meaningless to me; comic, almost, in its imaginative randomness and lack of technical skill: a pile of bricks in one corner, a TV showing a Ford Popular being driven around some urban streets, a ball of string on the floor. When we drove back to Deptford, Mark was in the passenger seat scribbling into his notepad. A week later, we were in the flat and I was messing around with some reggae sounds on my bass. Mark said, 'Hey, that might just work on this song I've been toying with since that art exhibition. I've called it "In the Gallery".'

He had the bare bones of a few songs now, and the three of us spent many evenings in the flat playing our guitars, helping to bring a little more clarity and musical structure to them.

With the songs taking shape, the band was coming together, but we needed a drummer to complete the line-up. Mark knew a guy called Pick Withers, who he'd played with in a pub rock band called Brewer's Droop and had gone on to become the house drummer at Rockfield Studios in Monmouthshire, where some big names had recorded, including Dave Edmunds, Hawkwind and Queen. Pick was a professional musician who had done lots of session work and it was our good fortune that he had a bit of time on his hands. Knowing Mark could play, he agreed to make the trip down from north London to Deptford one evening for a session with us. We gave him a pouch of Old Holborn and some petrol money for his trouble.

We set up in the back bedroom, which Mark and I had lined with old carpet felt in a futile attempt at soundproofing and, us all being smokers then, the atmosphere was soon thick with smoke. There was barely room to move, and we had to be careful not to get overexcited and crash the headstocks of our guitars into one another, or into Pick's cymbals. It was obvious from the first few minutes that Pick was a very good drummer. He was quite a light player, sensitive, more jazz than rock in his feel and instincts. I had played with a number of drummers, but no one in this league.

Drums and bass are the engine room of the band, the foundations on which all else is constructed. It may not be the most glamorous element of a band, but the rhythm section is crucial to the whole operation. Pick and I fell into step at once — at least, that's how it felt to me. Straight away you felt him pulling us all together into something tighter and more solid. He had a beautiful touch and really listened to the songs, his play instantly bringing sharper definition to them. That first session was a genuinely exciting moment, a moment when the happy chaos of creativity was given some order, some clear form. It's vital for the bass player and drummer to sync, and playing with Pick that first time was one of those great moments of revelation you experience in music from time to time. Aha, now I get it!

Pick was an interesting character too, likable and with an

unpredictable sense of humour, but inscrutable, not giving too much away about himself, happy to play his drums, smoke his roll-ups and then disappear back up to north London once we were done. I think Pick saw that something a cut above the ordinary was possibly in the making, and our sessions in the flat became a regular thing — we'd entice Pick to come to rehearsals by buying him fish and chips. After a couple of sessions, our friends started joining us, standing in the narrow hallway or sitting in the living room, as there was no room for anyone else in that tiny rehearsal space. Amazingly, none of our lovely neighbours ever complained. I have to assume that they were listening to the music upstairs through the ceiling, or across the way through the walls, and that they were enjoying it! We were learning our craft, but having a laugh too.

There have been a number of stories about how the name Dire Straits came about, but we are in broad agreement that it probably came from a keyboard-playing pal of Pick's north London flatmate Simon Cowe, who was in the band Lindisfarne. We'd agreed to keep rehearsing together and to start hunting down some gigs, so we needed a name. Simon apparently said to Pick, 'You've never made any money, mate, and you're always in dire straits. How about that? Dire Straits!'

I don't remember the subsequent conversations, but we all warmed to it. The name of a band is not that important, if you ask me. If the music is good, the name just becomes your identity, the name you play under. No one buys an album for the name of the band. The Beatles and The Stones — you think of their music, not the name. That's the name we agreed to adopt, but only after our first-ever gig, on the 'lawn' outside Farrer House in July 1977, when we still played as the Café Racers.

That first gig was a punk festival with us as the odd ones out, the misfits. It was a very hot and windy day, and we let the other bands use our flat as the base. I can't quite bring myself to call it the 'dressing room', because that would be to bestow the gig, and number one Farrer House, with a dignity that neither deserved.

Punk was in full cry at the time, and I have to confess, apart from a few acts like The Clash and the Sex Pistols, I was no fan. It was great that a form of music had turned up to rage against the establishment, though, because the music business needed a shake-up. Punk was a shout of anguish at a low point for both music and society. It made perfect sense. It was angry music, almost anti-music. That was the point of it, wasn't it? To distort, to pervert, to mock, to do away with harmony and craft, and the anarchy of its outlook was reflected in the tuneless chaos of the 'songs'. But they weren't stupid, these guys, at least not the leading proponents of the movement. Some were putting on an act, and the best of them were consummate performers. Maybe that was because quite a few of them were middle-class lads who had been to art or drama school.

I'm not sure 'consummate' best describes the bunch of 'musicians' who settled into our flat that afternoon for the festival of music being performed out on the lawn to the bewildered enjoyment of about thirty or forty Crossfields residents, most of them pretty stoned. They filed out one after another, gobbing into the wind and shouting about overthrowing the established order and civilization as a whole. It was never quite clear what their new world order would be — the important thing was to smash up the old one. I'm sure they'd have worked the details out later.

Most of them were rudimentary players and we spent a great deal of time tuning their guitars for them before they hit the lawn, only for them to put them back out of tune as soon as they started playing. Harmony — aaaghh, no! All the power for the gig ran from a single cable that trailed back into the flat, scarcely bothering our electricity meter, which we had fixed with a copper bar and insulating tape so that the dial stopped and sometimes even went backwards when the fridge came on.

The PA system, which we borrowed from an up-and-coming local band called Squeeze, barely deserved the name. We struggled against the strong wind blowing into our faces and what sound there was was carried away behind us so that we were effectively miming silently to our small audience, who were lying and sunning themselves on the grass. There's a picture of us from that day, and our hair is going backwards, just like the sound we made. In spite of playing before so few people, I remember being quite nervous. But we were surprised how well it went and, kicking back afterwards, you'd think we'd just played Madison Square Garden, not the lawn, Farrer House, Crossfields estate, Deptford.

Looking back now, you can see it all more clearly. At the time, we never really thought about our identity. I don't think we gave much thought to the fashions of the day, so there was no 'look'. We didn't belong to a movement or aspire to be part of one. As a band, we were developing our own style and identity — an attitude that we maintained from there on. Disco and punk were the dominant, happening sounds of the day, and the drift was towards what would become known as 'new wave', with bands like Talking Heads, Elvis Costello and the Attractions, The Police, Squeeze, The Boomtown Rats and Blondie. We were just doing our own thing in a musical world of our own, and if people liked what we did and there was an appetite for it, then great, so much the better. That was a bonus.

With Pick on board, there was real momentum to the band now. We felt solid. We practised hard and we worked at trying to get gigs, dropping into venues and ringing around from our payphone in the flat. We started local, and the first significant slot we secured was at the Albany Empire on Deptford Church Street, close to the Star Café. The Albany was great for supporting the local music and arts scene and we often shared the bill with or played the night before or after Squeeze. They came from the Greenwich area and had a really distinctive sound, unlike anything that had preceded or was to

Taken at low tide on the Thames by the Wood Wharf studio.
We were definitely not used to being photographed in 1978.

follow. Good lads, too. It was a proper venue, and people from outside Deptford and Greenwich were drawn there by the quality of the shows. Squeeze were great fun and, with a number of truly original songs, they clearly had the talent to make the breakthrough.

We used to fit the amps, guitars, mic stands and cables into my old Rover – which meant everyone else had to get to the gig under their own steam. My bass bin went in the boot and I had to tie the boot lid to the bumper as it wouldn't shut. We played a number of gigs at the Albany in the summer and autumn of 1977 and I very nearly didn't make one of the earliest ones – our second or third – because I fell off a horse earlier in the day and damned nearly broke my back. Dave's girlfriend, Chris, who used to spend a lot of time in the flat, worked in a stables up in Essex and one morning she asked if I'd like to come up and ride out. I am no horseman but, with nothing else on, I said, 'Yeah, why not?' I'm always up for a new experience, but I had no idea what I had let myself in for.

You can't grow up in the Leicestershire countryside and not mount a horse at some point in your youth. It has the finest riding country in England, and there are horses every which way you turn. So, I had probably ridden about three or four times, without much enthusiasm but enough to master the basics, like sitting the right way around. Being very tall, the stable lads gave me the biggest bloody horse you have ever seen, more mastodon than pony, and off we trotted into a field, me feeling distinctly apprehensive.

We started with a walk, as you do, graduated into a trot, which was fine by me but quite as far as I wanted to go up the speed scale, thank you very much. Chris needed to give her mount a good gallop for the exercise, and when she broke into a canter, mine sniffed a party and erupted after her. We were really travelling now and I was already getting nervous, but then her horse started leaping over hay bales and, mine, disobeying all my pathetic efforts to restrain it, had no in-tention of missing out on the fun. We went over the first, and I was clinging on for dear life, absolutely terrified, then over another and another. It was on the fourth that the horse really took wing, and I lost my balance as we came back to earth. The strap under its belly hadn't been tightened properly, the saddle slipped and I slid sideways and went flying across the field and crashed on to my back.

I've had my fair share of accidents over the years, but rarely have I felt such extraordinary pain. I thought I must have broken my back. I couldn't move; I just lay there, whimpering in agony. The paramed-ics thought the worst too, taking an age to get me on to a stretcher and into the back of an ambulance. Fearing I had damaged my vital organs, the staff at Chelmsford Hospital chose not to give me any painkillers, and I lay writhing in pain throughout all the procedures and scans they carried out.

It turned out I hadn't broken my back but had suffered heavy bruising there, and to my ribs and, worst of all, my lungs. Mark came up in the afternoon to pick me up and we drove slowly back into London, me lying on the back seat, groaning. Mark said, 'We'd better pull over and find a payphone to call the Albany and cancel the gig.'

'No way. This is a big break.'

'Well, you can't play lying down, mate.'

'I'll be fine.'

Back at Farrer House, I swallowed enough painkillers to tranquil-lize the horse I had been riding and smoked some medicine of my own. I hobbled into the Albany, where they gave me a bar stool, and I played the gig like Val Doonican at his Christmas Special. I don't remember a great deal about it, but I'm told it went very well.

Mark was working on new songs, but we didn't yet have full com-plement for our sets at this point, so we played a few covers, usually some J. J. Cale, some Ry Cooder or, for a bit of a crowd-pleaser, some Chuck Berry or Brenda Lee's 'Sweet Nothings'. Some nights we played to a full house of a couple of hundred; others it would be half empty and we'd drink our free pint, divvy up the thirty quid between us and head back to the flat at midnight. The cost of the PA system alone pretty well took care of our performance fee. Per gig, we each ended up with enough for a packet of fags and a couple of pints. That's not a sob story or an exaggeration, it's just a plain fact and it's the experience of most bands starting out.

We loved playing the Albany, literally a stone's throw from the flat, but to be playing your local over and over, as we did that summer and autumn, eventually created and compounded the sense that we weren't going very far in our musical journey. (Being an arthouse the-atre, and a liberal establishment that encouraged minorities, the Albany was always regarded as a bit of a leftie hangout, and when it was burnt to the ground in an arson attack in July 1978, a few

Outside the entrance to Wood Wharf rehearsal studio.
Can't believe we agreed to pose for this one.

months after our last gig, the National Front were considered the main suspects, though it was never proven and no one was ever charged.)

Eager to break out of our home territory, we started seeking out gigs further afield, targeting the pubs known to welcome up-and-coming acts. Islington was fertile ground, with the King's Head and the Hope and Anchor a few hundred yards apart from each other on Upper Street. Mark was in a highly creative period and soon we dropped the cover versions and we could fill the show with our own songs. We were beginning to attract a small following, so if the poster went up in the window of the King's Head or the Hope and Anchor people came back to see us. That was very encouraging and fed into a sense of momentum.

Without a roadie or a van, we were our own crew and carried on using my old Rover to transport the equipment: amps and bass bin in the boot, guitars on the back seat. Mark and I would drive it to the venue, Pick would come in his own car with his drum kit and Dave would make his way by Tube or train. The Hope and Anchor was especially challenging because bands performed in the small cellar and the only way to get the kit in was to lower it down the chute the

Not the first time the band's name was spelled wrong.

brewers used to deliver the beer barrels. It was even harder getting the equipment out at the end of the gig, muscling it back up the chute to the street. The cellar was a tiny space, holding no more than 120 people, and one night it was so crammed that someone knocked over the PA system on one side of the stage and it made absolutely no difference to the sound.

We also got gigs at the Tramshed in Woolwich. There was a feeling that if we just kept playing these well-known little venues, we had a chance of making it to the next level. Mark had written half a dozen good songs now, so we had the material, we had the hunger, but what we didn't have was the money for a demo tape to punt around the radio stations and record companies. It cost a small fortune to hire a recording studio and put some tracks down on tape. Maybe that's why so many middle-class bands finally make the breakthrough. Somehow, they find the money to put themselves out there.

We barely had two Rizlas to rub together, let alone two pound notes. Then, one morning in late summer, I scooped up the post from the doormat and there was a handwritten letter — from Dad. Inside, there was a cheque for five hundred quid. Gran had died in January and left all the grandchildren the same sum. Thank you, Gran! Five hundred quid, a big sum — about £3,000 today. There was only one way I was going to spend that money.

*1957 in my
Sunday best to
meet Grandma
for lunch.*

*My dear father
puffing away next
to his children.
How things
have changed.*

The very first Dire Straits gig, at a punk festival playing under the name of the Café Racers. A strong wind blew most of the sound into the flats behind. Despite appearances, there were more than two kids in the audience.

Standing in the Thames mud again for an early Albany Empire gig poster.

Our iconography moved on over time.

Above: A mad weekend of relentless interviews on our first visit to Amsterdam in 1978. Why do photographers love brick walls as a backdrop?

Below: Amsterdam 1978 – doing one of the eccentric TV shows that made us feel a bit queasy but gave us great exposure.

Taken in Montserrat, where we recorded Brothers in Arms. *Not sure we would do a shot like this these days.*

Mark's guitar roadie wanted a photo of the National resonator against the beautiful Caribbean sky. Just one photo was taken by Deborah Feingold and it became the iconic cover for the album.

Photographer Bob Mazzer captured me and Mark in full
flow at Wembley Arena in 1985.

Chapter 8

Five Hundred Quid

Rent: £9.40 a week. Weeks in year: fifty-two. Cheque from out of the blue: £500. £9.40 x 52 = £488.80. Take £488.80 away from £500, and you've got a fortnight of breakfasts and beer money. But I wasn't doing the maths that way. The equation was far simpler than that. We wanted to record the five songs we felt were our strongest so far.

The principal factor was this: did we want to give ourselves a genuine chance of making it in the music world? To do that, we had to have a demo tape. As I held the cheque in my hand, I experienced a slight ballooning of hope. We had a meeting in the flat after a practice session that week and the boys promised to pay me back when, er, you know, as soon as . . . well, thanks, John. Genuinely, I didn't care if I never saw a penny of it back, and I said as much. All the others would have done the same. (For the record, I got it back when we received our first royalty cheque.)

Put a demo tape out there, and then we could never sigh over our pints in the years to come, bemoaning the fact that we never gave ourselves a shot at a record deal. Whatever happened from there on, things were going to play out as fate intended. Had poor old Gran not died when she did and I'd never got my hands on that five hundred quid, who knows how it would have all turned out? Most likely, we'd have stayed on the pub and club merry-go-round for a while longer, Pick would have moved on to another band or back to session work, one of us would have got a job, we'd play together every other weekend or so and the band would probably have disintegrated. The stress of penury, the slow demoralization of working around the pub circuit — same venues, same faces, all for a fiver a night — would eventually take its toll. There comes a point in every band's development when it has to stop the hoping and the practising, face up to reality and get on with another life. That's the fate of most aspiring bands.

With a demo tape, we had something that could be played on the radio or listened to by a record company. Us waiting to get spotted playing in the pub was like an aspiring model waiting to be spotted in a supermarket by someone who worked in an agency. It happens, but it's very rare. We rang and asked around, seeking out good studios within our budget. Five hundred quid didn't get you very far in the recording world — and we could forget about all the fancier set-ups. The name that kept cropping up was Pathway Studios in Newington Green, north-east London. It was a small set-up dealing mainly in demo tapes, not in putting records down, and it was establishing a bit of a name for itself. The Police, Elvis Costello, Nick Lowe, The Damned, Madness, Sham 69 — none of whom were big names then — all used Pathway around that time. We booked in for a weekend in late summer 1977.

By the time we made our way up the steps to 2a Grosvenor Avenue, we were in pretty good shape, musically. We didn't have the time, money or need to put all our songs down. We just needed the best possible versions of the ones we'd chosen: 'Sultans of Swing',

'Wild West End', 'Water of Love', 'Down to the Waterline' and one by Dave called 'Sacred Loving'.

We had rehearsed hard, the band was tight and I felt that I had come on as a player. Where once I had felt I needed to push myself forward and fill all the space in order to get more involved in the song, now I had learned that, for the bassist, less is sometimes more, that leaving something out was often better than putting something in. Along with Pick on drums, it was my role to lay the solid foundations on which the guitars and the vocals could sit. I had come to realize that good playing was essentially about feel. I stopped trying to play every note the same every time; I started playing them as they felt right in the moment and for the song. I kept it really simple, and I've been playing that way ever since.

The recording studio was tiny, bigger than the bedroom at Farrer House but still a pretty tight squeeze with all the equipment, and we felt quite at home there. There was a cupboard of a control room in the corner with space for about three people, at a push. There was no producer, just an engineer, a nice guy called Chas Herington, and his equipment was perfectly adequate for capturing the simplicity of our music. There was a Brenell reel-to-reel one-inch tape deck; the final version would be bounced down to a quarter of an inch tape. Three of the eight mics for the tracks were suspended over Pick's kit, there was one for each of the three guitars and a couple for vocals. I was on my newly acquired Fender 59 Precision — a wonderful gift from Mark, who knew I'd been hankering after one but simply didn't have the money. He was on his red Strat with his Fender Vibrolux amp, and Dave was on his Telecaster.

We had to work fairly quickly and were in there for ten hours on both days until we were happy we'd got it right. On the Sunday evening we waited in the flat upstairs as Chas worked on the final touches in the control room. He didn't have to do too much. The songs pretty well went straight down on tape and there was only a little mixing necessary. Besides, the equipment then was so unsophisticated there was very little that could be altered after the event. We'd laid down good versions, we knew that, but anticipation was in the air, and we were hanging around to hear how it had all come out. We had never heard a recorded version of ourselves. Nothing we had played live or in practice had ever been put down. The songs we were making existed in a state of suspension, only to come alive when we got together to play them. It was a buzz to know we were going to have a permanent record of our efforts for posterity, whatever happened to the band. Our music would be there for ever — well, the demo would be, at least. Even if it was to become the smallest footnote in the history of British rock music, it could now never be erased.

There was great excitement when Chas called us in to take a listen to what we'd put down. We crammed into the broom-cupboard control room, a couple of us having just our heads craning around the door. It was a strange experience to hear ourselves coming out of the speakers — it was as if it wasn't us, but another band. The sound quality was great and the version of 'Sultans', in particular, was excellent. It sounded very pure. There are many people who believe that this is the best recorded version of the song we ever made, and I'm inclined to agree. Who knows? I love it. It's a strange phenomenon, a song. You can play it a thousand times, but every single version is very slightly different. Again, it all goes back to feel, to the band clicking and syncing in a particular way, plugged into the same mood and vibe.

Not long ago, I found a copy of the demo tape in the bottom of a box and sent it off to have it 'baked' at Mark's British Grove Studios in London, to make sure it didn't disintegrate, which it might do after so long. When I heard it again, I was moved by nostalgia, thinking of the band all young and fresh-faced, squashed into that tiny control room, hearing that recording for the first time. That little tape was our passport to the future, authorizing our access into the world of professional music, giving us the opportunity to be heard.

It seemed inconsequential at the time, chatting to Chas on the steps of Pathway, thanking him for his efforts, about to head off, the tape and two copies stowed safely in Mark's coat pockets. We got on really well with Chas over the weekend, and he was hinting that he was thinking of moving on from Pathway, as he was getting a bit bored of being stuck in the unlit claustrophobia of a small studio. Lighting was his passion, and we agreed that if the demo tape led to anything and we went on the road, he'd come to do the lights. It just seemed like an exchange of pleasantries right then but, as events were to unfold, it was an important one. Chas was soon one of us, and he was going to stay with us right the way through. He was going to bring something really special to the party.

We had a tape with a few songs on — that was all. Now we had to get people of influence to listen to it. It was well known that sending a demo tape in to a major record company was as good as tossing it into a skip. They received demos by the dozen and, like unsolicited manuscripts with literary agents and publishers, there simply wasn't the will, or the resources, to listen to all of them. Most demos, like most manuscripts, fail to meet the standards required, so why would you bother making your way through the hundreds of submissions that came in every week?

Without an agent or a manager, we sat around in Deptford wondering what on earth to do next. We hadn't really thought through the next phase of the operation. It was a late Sunday morning and we were listening to Charlie Gillett's *Honky Tonk* show on Radio London when we saw our opening. 'Why not send a copy to Charlie?' Mark suggested. He was such a great supporter of new acts, every A&R man in town tuned in to his show. Few people knew more about the history of modern music, and few people cared more about its future. Charlie Gillett was a highly regarded music journalist and writer and, as I discovered when I wrote to him about my record shop, a very kind and conscientious man – there was already a connection there.

What harm could there be in writing to him and asking him to listen to the demo and give his full and frank opinion? At least then we'd know where we stood among the ranks of hopefuls out there. If he was positive, then great – he might be able to push us in the direction of a record company, his own Honky Tonk Records, maybe. But it came with a risk, because if he was politely ambivalent about our efforts, suggesting that we needed to go away and work on it, or that it wouldn't fly in the current market, then that would be pretty much game over. We'd be left with no other obvious course of action than to send copies in to a major label on a wing and a prayer.

We owe a great deal to Charlie Gillett, the first DJ to play the Straits on the radio. A lovely man in all respects.

I had no idea where he lived so I wrote to him at Radio London. I didn't want to call him, because that seemed way too intrusive and presumptuous. As with my previous letter to him, I wasn't really expecting a reply, but like last time, I got one virtually by return of post. He was polite enough to say he remembered me and, sure, he said, why not drop the tape into him at home on Wednesday afternoon?

Mark and I drove over to his house just off Clapham Common, our destiny buried in Mark's pocket, blew out our cheeks and pressed the doorbell. Charlie Gillett was a bit of a hero to us both, and we understood what was at stake here. Charlie could not have been kinder. He welcomed us in, made us tea — offered us a plate of biscuits, even — and we sat and talked music for over an hour. His curiosity about the band was flattering. He wanted to know everything about us — our influences and favourite bands, where we'd played, how many songs we had in the can — and he was intrigued by the idea of two brothers being in the line-up. He was brought up in the north-east too, so maybe he felt some connection with Mark and Dave.

He explained that he never listened to new music in front of the people who had produced it for fear of upsetting and embarrassing them if it wasn't for him. As we left, he invited us to the 100 Club on Oxford Street, where he put on his *Honky Tonk* show, and said he'd be in touch and that he'd be straight and honest in his opinion. There was no point in raising false hopes, he said, adding ominously that he'd give us back the tape when he was done with it.

So, the die was cast. We had crossed our Rubicon. We wanted a straight and fair judgement on our efforts, and there was no one better to pronounce it than Charlie Gillett. Encouraging words from him, and on we would push. That's what we were expecting — a letter, most probably, maybe a phone call. What we weren't expecting was for him to play any of the songs on our demo on his Sunday-morning radio show, a slot followed so closely by all the A&R guys.

Short of cash as ever, that Sunday, Mark and I had signed up to help a mate move some furniture. We spent the whole day lugging stuff around and into the back of a van. Ten pounds richer, we piled into the Oxford Arms for a few pints before closing time. Sunday night was a popular one for our little community of artists, musicians and ne'er-do-wells on the Crossfields estate and the place was full of smoke and banter as we pushed through the corner door. A bit of a cheer went up as we entered and, as we approached the bar, we got a slap on the back and some broad grins.

'Well done, well done. Amazing! Brilliant news.'

'What is? What are you on about?'

'The radio! Charlie Gillett played "Sultans of Swing" on the radio this morning.'

'You're bloody kidding!'

'No, and it gets better. He said "Sultans" was one of the best new songs he's heard in years and that he was going to play it every Sunday until someone signed you guys up.'

After that, as you can imagine, we drank a lot of pints.

Chapter 9

Panic in the Shower

Charlie called us at the flat the next day and told us that within minutes of him playing 'Sultans' his little studio at Radio London had fielded half a dozen calls from A&R men from the major labels. He said Johnny Stainze from one of the Polygram labels jumped out of the shower to hear it properly and stood dripping as he listened, then called Charlie at once. Another was driving along the A3, pulled over on to the hard shoulder, then found the nearest phone box to call from. They were all asking him, 'Who the hell are these guys? Never heard of them!' Charlie explained politely that was because this was the first time they had ever been played on the radio.

'Can I give these guys your number?' he asked. 'They won't stop ringing and they're very keen to know all about you and talk to you. It's a bit of a mob.'

It wasn't long before the phone in Farrer House was ringing like a telephone exchange. I exaggerate only a little. Our payphone was mounted on the wall by the door and, one after another, the calls came in: Phonogram, EMI, A&M, Virgin — every big player, plus a bunch of names I had never heard of. We very rarely took calls in the flat — except occasionally, when our mothers checked in to ask if we had found jobs and make sure we were eating properly — 'God, yes, Mum, the job hunt's going really well! — but that was about it. There was no answering machine and no table or chair, so every time we got a call we scrawled the details on the wall. It began to look like a graffiti mural in an urban ghetto. The name and number of the local weed dealer, the only other number up there previously, soon got lost in the tangle of scribbling.

Our quiet little world in Deptford was starting to spin at a dizzyingly fast rate. We had no manager or lawyer to advise us and we felt completely out of our depth. How would we know what a good deal looked like? How do you negotiate one? How many albums do you sign up to? What's a decent percentage for foreign rights? We were ripe for the taking but determined not to be ripped off, eager though we were to get signed, record an album and start touring.

We were keenly aware of the debt we owed to Charlie Gillett. A genuinely delightful man, he had catapulted us out of the Sunday-morning minors and into the major league. It didn't follow that just because we were going to get a deal we'd become an instant and roaring success, but we had a chance of building a fan base now. We would be heard by a nationwide audience, maybe even a continent-wide one, and who knew how the punters might respond?

Charlie loomed large in our lives in this period. In early September, he invited us to play at the late-summer party of his *Honky Tonk* radio show. It took place on Clapham Common and we performed from the bandstand to at least two thousand people, by far our biggest audience, and a nerve-jangling taste of the big time. He also invited us as guests to his *Honky Tonk* show at the 100 Club in Oxford Street. We saw some great blues acts, including Sonny Terry and Brownie McGhee, and a London duo called Chas & Dave were also on the bill. They were not well known at this time, but they were

*Our second-ever gig was at Clapham Common Bandstand,
in the summer of 1977, to over 2,000 people. Totally terrifying.*

great fun and brilliant instrumentalists. But that evening will always
be memorable for other reasons. Mark bumped into an old girlfriend
and we hung out with her and her friend, a beautiful and charming
Australian girl called Pauline. She and I clicked at once and soon became an item. Later, in 1981, we would become husband and wife.
Charlie Gillett was certainly having a major influence on my life! A
record deal in the making and a wife-to-be. Thank you, dear Charlie,
taken from us far too young.

Our main focus was on getting a deal and we had a bunch of
regular cassette tapes made up from the demo tape to send out to
record companies. Charlie had a small indie label and he made polite
overtures about us signing for him. It could have been awkward
turning him down, our sights set a bit higher, on the major labels
with greater reach, but he was extremely gracious when we declined.
He understood.

It was an exciting, crazy time for us, Mark and I crisscrossing London by Tube and black cab to visit the record labels who had expressed an interest. We were bombarded with questions: Who's in the band? Where do you play your gigs? How many songs have you got? Based on the sound of 'Sultans', some of the labels thought they were going to be meeting a pair of Americans and were taken aback that Mark was a Geordie and I was from rural Leicestershire. It was true that there was a hint of American influence on some of the songs, but to us our music had always felt very English. However, it was a perception that was to last.

Money offers were put on the table, some of them silly, some insulting, but we wouldn't be bounced into a deal. We had to get it right. This was our one and only chance.

Charlie continued to play 'Sultans' every Sunday over the coming weeks, fuelling the interest in us and leading to a bunch of gigs at more prestigious venues, including a string of nights at the Hope and Anchor and a week's residency at the Rock Garden in Covent Garden. It was owned by an American guy, who, like everyone else, it seemed, believed us to be an American band based in London.

We were innocents in the music industry, but we weren't completely wet behind the ears. It helped that we were a little older than most aspiring bands; we had the confidence to question the offers. Now in our late twenties, Mark and I had age on our side; we'd seen a bit of life. So, when one company offered us £1,500 for a couple of albums, we laughed and left. It's amazing, the tricks and the schmooze the record companies deploy to reel you in. A man called Richard Branson with a new company called Virgin was hot on our case from the outset. Virgin Records then operated out of a mews house off the Portobello Road in Notting Hill, west London. Launched by Branson and his cousin Simon Draper a couple of years earlier, they had had a huge success with Mike Oldfield's *Tubular Bells*, a brilliant album but one that was an unlikely hit, as it was

The Hope and Anchor, with the one free beer they gave us along with our £25 fee.

entirely instrumental and pop-classical hadn't ever troubled the charts and radio stations prior to its release. Oldfield was a sound engineer and Virgin gave him free time after hours to work on his project at their Manor Studios in Oxfordshire. I don't believe the finance of the deal was especially advantageous to Oldfield, but he got a studio, an album and worldwide fame out of it. Working all by himself, it was an extraordinarily creative achievement, and it gave Branson and Virgin the financial clout to build a global empire.

We had a meeting with Branson in the mews office and, though I can't remember the details, I do recall that Mark and I weren't overly impressed by the deal on offer, so, as with the others, we went away to mull it over, hoping all these companies would come back with a better deal. We knew enough about business to know that's how negotiation worked. About a week later, the whole band were invited for an evening at a Greek restaurant up in Paddington, not far from Virgin's offices. It was hilarious — like something out of a film. On arrival, we were ushered into a private room where there were quite a few extremely attractive women, all of whom worked for Virgin and none of whom were overly or formally dressed. A waiter came in with a tray of ready-rolled joints. At dinner, each of us sat next to one of the women and there was quite a lot of wandering-hand business under the table, and those hands were not ours.

Richard was a very charming host, like a Bedouin tribal chief in his desert tent, and over the course of the evening we felt the full power of that charm. After we'd eaten, there were more joints, and everybody was getting pretty high. It was all great fun, but Mark and I were quietly taking it all in, occasionally exchanging knowing glances. We weren't that naïve or impressionable, but neither were we going to pass up a cracking night out for free. Had we been twenty-one and not twenty-nine, we might well have been seduced by the glamour of it all. Many years later, when Dire Straits had long since ceased playing, Branson gave a TV interview in Ireland and ruefully admitted he had miscalculated that night. One of the newspaper articles that flowed from it was headlined 'The Night I Blew One Billion Dollars', and he was humble enough to realize there were probably better ways to have won us over. He thought we were going to show up and sign the next morning, but we were in bed in Deptford.

The one guy we really rated was the one who performed the fewest seduction tricks — Johnny Stainze from Phonogram. He was dead straight from the off, absolutely loved the sound of the band and was keen to get a serious, grown-up offer on the table. We liked him and trusted him and we were reassured by his knowledge of music and his devotion to us. Unlike many of the others, he never promised us overnight success and he was not interested in offering us a singles deal. He wanted us to make great albums over a period of time.

Stainze and Phonogram were the front runners, but still we needed to be sure we were getting the deal that would enable us to fulfil our ambitions. We didn't want to get bound into a contractual prison sentence that would leave us out of pocket and unhappy with our lot for years to come. Mark knew the eminent journalist Richard Williams, and Williams insisted that we got a lawyer and recommended a firm called Simons, Muirhead and Allan, which had offices just off the Strand. They were experts in music-industry contracts and had worked on behalf of a number of big names. It wasn't going to be cheap, but it was worth it to have the peace of mind that we weren't going to be sold down the river.

Robert Allan was our lawyer and he collated all the offers; there were loads, and they all had a legion of different clauses and stipulations that we could make neither head nor tail of. We'd spent a year or so being paid in pints, peanuts and fivers. Now we were talking sums running into five figures and deals that were going to run for several years. While all this was going on behind the scenes, we were playing a lot of gigs and, all of a sudden, the A&R guys were turning up in numbers and trying to work on us. It was a relief to let Robert get on with all that and filter out the best of the offers. Robert liked to take us to the famous old Covent Garden restaurant Rules, a short stagger from his offices, and we enjoyed the restrained glamour of it all. I had never eaten pheasant in a brandy, cream and peppercorn sauce before. It was all very grown-up.

We had about six or seven pretty decent offers on the table when, steered by Robert, we felt ready to decide. It was Johnny Stainze's no-bullshit level-headedness and transparent love of our music that won the day. He said Phonogram wanted to build us slowly, nurture our career, give us the time and space to work on new material. They wanted us for the long haul and were prepared to invest. 'We'll be more than happy if your first album sells five thousand copies,' they said.

We signed the deal for five albums in the run-up to Christmas that year. We got £47,000, about a quarter of a million in today's money, but it was an advance we'd have to pay back through royalties. It was not exactly a pot of gold, but it was solid and seemed fair . . . at the time. The important thing was that we had a huge record company behind us, they loved our music and they were keen to let us grow.

We were suddenly going to be getting some cash in our pockets. Thankfully, Robert Allan knew a firm of accountants who looked after a few bands, so we took his advice, and that was the start of a forty-two-year relationship with Harris and Trotter. Under the watchful eye of Ronnie Harris and his team, we have safely navigated the financial implications of being a successful rock band. Taking no risks and playing it 'Strait', Ronnie has become a friend and trusted adviser.

Not long after signing, we were invited to meet Phonogram's managing director at their new offices in Park Street between Park Lane and Oxford Street. We'd heard a few amusing stories about Ken Maliphant, a colourful Scot from Kilmarnock. We were a reasonably big signing and he wanted to meet us. It was late morning when we were shown into a big, plush office, and Ken was at the drinks tray pouring himself a large Scotch and, judging by his warm, jovial welcome, it may not have been his first. As we shook hands, there were some interesting vapours coming off him, and his bright red nose told its own story about his refreshments regime that morning.

Ken was extremely friendly and complimentary about our music, highly excited by our new partnership. Weaving over to the music centre, he fumbled with a cassette tape and, after a minute or so, Johnny Stainze, looking a little sheepish and embarrassed, went to help him work out how to put it in and pressed the play button. On came 'Down to the Waterline', and Ken did a little jiggle and exclaimed, ' "Sultans of Swing" is one of the best songs I've ever heard! It's wonderful, marvellous.' What you realized soon enough was that, in the music industry, you had the clever business and money guys like Ken, and then you had the foot soldiers like Johnny Stainze, the ones who knew their music and without whom the whole operation would collapse.

The deal in the bag, now all we needed was a manager. You can't go out on the road by yourselves. You need to have someone to book the venues, haggle with promoters and get the best deal. I suppose we could have done that ourselves, but our situation had changed. There would have been little time for playing and rehearsing if we took on all the admin as well. Gigs are often arranged at short notice, extra ones added as you go, according to demand. And there were no mobile phones, of course, so communication was haphazard and conducted from offices. When a band isn't playing, drinking it off and then sleeping off the drink, they tend to be wolfing down a breakfast and getting on the road to the next venue. You need someone pulling the strings and making the bookings for hotels and the equipment and just generally dealing with all the admin, leaving the band free to play and get drunk. That's always been the convention and it seemed like an eminently sensible arrangement to me, even if it meant parting with a percentage of our hard-earned cash.

Proof that we needed someone to manage the business side of our affairs was provided the night we had our fingers burned by Jake Riviera — Elvis Costello's and Nick Lowe's manager. We played a gig organized by him that autumn at the Troubador, off the Cromwell Road in west London, where we were the support act for Elvis Costello and the Attractions. Being in charge of the band's business at this stage, such as it was — all the accounts fitting on the back of a fag packet — after the gig I went to find Jake and get our tenner off him. A tenner!

Jake patted his pockets and looked into his wallet, holding it open for me to see for myself. Unfortunately, Jake was fresh out of tenners; there was only a fiver. He was completely out of loose change too, a truth he proved by turning his trouser pockets inside out. 'I'll have to owe you guys five pounds, I'm afraid. Really sorry, John. Nice gig, though.' Judging by the size of the audience, Jake must have coined in a couple of hundred that night. I argued with him for a bit, then I gave up, we paid for our own pints at the bar and drifted home to Deptford. Jake was good enough to pay up about ten years later when I ran into him at a massive outdoor concert we were headlining, and I reminded him he was still in our debt to the tune of a fiver. He gave me twenty, what with all the interest that had accrued.

Johnny told us he had taken a lot of phone calls from a guy called Ed Bicknell, then working around the corner from Park Street for an act-booking agency called NEMS, one of the biggest in the UK and bringing over a lot of the big names from the States. Ed knew his music, apparently, played the drums to a decent standard and had shown early signs of entrepreneurial flair and hard deal-brokering. As an undergraduate and entertainments manager at Hull University in the late sixties, he somehow managed to book massive acts like Jimi Hendrix, The Who, The Kinks, Muddy Waters, John Lee Hooker and Pink Floyd. Anyone who could persuade artists of that calibre to take a detour off the A1 and head into Kingston-upon-Hull was certainly worthy of an audience. He had listened to our demo tape, liked what he heard, and Johnny invited him to come and see us play at Dingwalls on Camden Lock, early in January 1978. At this stage, he was probably only interested in booking us as a support act on one his tours. As soon as we had finished playing, so Johnny told us shortly afterwards, Ed turned to him and said, 'I want to manage this band, and I'm going to.' He was never short of confidence, Ed. He had never managed a band.

After the show we were in the dressing room, towelling down and necking beers, when a man came in with highly coiffeured, swept-back blond hair and wearing a suede coat with a fur collar in the style of Arthur Daley, the slippery conman from the TV series *Minder*.

'Who's this spiv?' someone muttered. He walked across the room and his coat caught Mark's red Stratocaster, which was leaning against a chair, and sent it crashing to the floor.

'Hi, I'm Ed Bicknell,' he said, putting the guitar upright and offering his hand.

Turned out very quickly that Ed was every bit as amusing a character as his comic entrance had promised. He reeled off a stream of anecdotes and banter. We got on with him from the off and, behind the repartee, you could see some steel and hear some sound sense and sharp business acumen. Hardened by his time at NEMS negotiating with many different species of shark and jackal, he was obviously not a man to be brushed aside with ease. His passion for managing us was clearly sincere. As with Johnny Stainze and Phonogram, that's what we wanted to hear. We wanted people who believed in us. He may have been a bit eccentric, but we liked his style, we liked his steel.

Not long afterwards, we went to meet Ed in the NEMS office in Audley Street. It was very fancy. They were representing some big acts at that time so, clearly, he wasn't desperate for the cash. Ed was sitting behind a huge desk looking every bit the professional booker, his fur collar up. The secretary showed us in, and Ed barked that he was not to be disturbed under any circumstances, that this was a very important meeting.

After no more than a minute the phone rang and Ed swung his legs off the desk, exhaling with exasperation.

'Well, I don't care if Bryan Ferry's people need to talk to me,' he snapped. 'I'm in an important meeting. Tell them to call back this afternoon.'

He slammed down the phone and smiled. 'Sorry about that, lads.'

We talked for a while and the phone rang again.

'Well, you can tell Wishbone Ash to stick it up their arse. I told you I'm busy and not to be disturbed.'

And so the meeting continued. Virtually every major act in Britain and a few from the States were sent packing by Ed so he could focus on us. Each time the phone rang, Mark and I threw each other glances and side-of-the-mouth smiles. You had to hand it to Ed, it was a great act. He has since written about his performance that day, so I'm not giving anything away.

What came across to us was that we were dealing with a very colourful character who had something about him. He was very outspoken, frank and, as an added bonus, highly amusing. We liked him.

He railed and ranted about the name Dire Straits. 'Fucking awful name, that!' he said. 'You sound like a shit punk band!' No one seemed to like the name. Phonogram were keen we changed it too. We didn't really care, but it was the name we'd had since after our first gig on the 'lawn' outside Farrer House and we had a bit of a sentimental attachment to it. 'What's in a name?' was our attitude. If the music was good, people wouldn't care less what you were called.

At the end of a very lively meeting or, rather, the 'Ed Bicknell Show', Ed said, 'Anyhow, how do you guys fancy going on a UK tour with this new lot from the States called Talking Heads? I think they're going to go big.' Adding hastily with a grin, 'Just like you guys.'

The tour was scheduled to start in two weeks. We told him we'd get back to him the next day and that we'd have a good think about taking him on as our manager.

Chapter 10

Off with the Heads

We met Talking Heads for breakfast at the Portobello Hotel in Notting Hill, a discreet boutique establishment that has been patronized by many big-name rock stars and actors over the years. Alice Cooper was said to have lost his boa constrictor there and never found it. A plate of posh bacon and eggs was literally our first taste of success but, frankly, it was no better than our daily plate in the Star Café on Deptford High Street — and no side of lamb's liver. The record company were paying, so we tucked in, only to discover when the bills were added up at the end of the tour that it had been deducted from our royalties. We were learning: no such thing as a free breakfast.

If any of us were fooled by the fancy surroundings into believing that our record deal and first tour had introduced us to a life of glamour, we were soon disabused of that notion when the two bands climbed into the Transit van and set off for Sheffield University for the first gig. The Transit would be our limo over the coming weeks, transporting us from one decaying hotel to the next. Not that we cared. It was a great little tour that took us up and down the country, the map of the UK clearly having been lost in the planning, so it seemed: Manchester one night, Brighton the next and back up to Birmingham the following day. The Heads had just come over from Europe and were already pretty whacked out, owing to an even more eccentric route over there. Someone must have failed their Geography O level. Ed?

From the off, we knew we were in for some fun. The lead singer, guitarist and songwriter David Byrne, was quiet, quirky, highly intelligent and inscrutable, preferring to keep his own company but always friendly and interesting to chat to about world music, about which he knew a great deal. The other three were Chris Frantz on drums, Jerry Harrison on keyboards and guitar, and that rarest of all musical species, a woman on bass guitar: Tina Weymouth, great player, fantastic person, entrancing to all who met her. The Heads couldn't have been better, more encouraging company for our first tour, and they were certainly preferable to our second, when we supported the American progressive rock band Styx in Paris — but more of them later.

The Heads liked our music and we liked theirs, which helped the camaraderie. A few weeks earlier, they had released their first major single in the UK, 'Psycho Killer', a cracking song brimming with energy and drive, fusing punk, art rock and funk to make a highly original sound, one that would define them. It was little wonder the Heads had been voted the most promising band of 1977; they were clearly a very talented bunch and, in David Byrne, they had a true leftfield creative who thought deeply about his music. We played about two dozen gigs in all, pretty well back to back, most of them to packed audiences at universities and polytechnics. On average, there were upwards of five hundred people, but a couple were much larger, such as the one at St Albans Civic Hall, where there must have been about two thousand, by far the biggest indoor crowd we had appeared before and about ten times greater than in the pubs we had played in. The health-and-safety rules weren't so strict then, and the unis were pretty relaxed, so if there was demand, it was met.

We had taken on a roadie by now, a gentle giant of a Glaswegian, Pete Murdoch, the ex-roadie for the bassist in Jethro Tull. Pete was strong as an ox, walking around with amps, speakers and booms as if it were no more effort than bringing in a bit of light shopping. More importantly, he was a top bloke, and from day one he fitted into our little touring family like an old friend. He stayed with us for over a year before going his own way. You won't meet a better man. In an extraordinary coincidence, kicking back after some post-show beers, it transpired that he had grown up right across the road from where the Knopflers were born and had spent the first few years of their family life in Glasgow, before they moved to Newcastle. They had thrown stones at each other, apparently. Small world.

It was a very cold winter and we shivered our way up and down motorways, the van heater being effective only for the two in the front seats. Some of the hotels and boarding houses were hilariously low quality, all unwashed sheets and rattling water pipes. In one, there was such a large hole in the wall connecting adjacent bathrooms that we could stick our heads through and brush our teeth in each other's room. We couldn't have cared less about the lack of comfort or the miserly fifty quid we received for each gig, enough, just about, to pay for fuel, food, fags, beer and Pete. It was like a working holiday — and, coming from Farrer House, we weren't in a position to start moaning about the living arrangements.

The problem with recalling tours is that all the shows tend to merge into one hazy blur. One cheap hotel is much like another, one long motorway likewise, and when you're playing, the inside of a venue looks much like the last: stage, equipment, lights, sea of faces, noise, beer, same set list night after night. Sometimes you play somewhere spectacular and you never forget it; other times something out of the ordinary occurs and it becomes branded on your

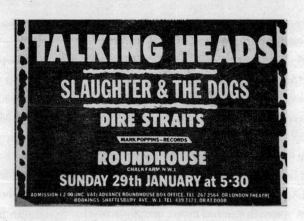

What a line up for £2!

memory. A couple of performances on the tour with the Heads stand out vividly.

About a week in, at the end of January, we played the Roundhouse, a famous venue in Chalk Farm, north London, built in the mid-nineteenth century as a railway turntable to swing engines around so that they were facing the right way at the end of the line. It's a great venue and we were act number two, on before the Heads and after a truly grotesque punk band called Slaughter and the Dogs. So, three bands with entirely different musical styles, each with very distinct followings. The Heads attracted the arty new-wave student crowd, we had our own following and, well, Slaughter and the Dogs had their own, very committed admirers too.

Slaughter were reasonably big news back in the day, a proper full-on, gob-your-guts-out punk band. My God, did they like gobbing at their fans, and my God, did their fans like gobbing back at them. Gobbing was central to the punk experience, and we watched in horror from the wings as the greenies flew back and forth between stage and floor, along with bottles and glasses and pretty well any projectile that came to hand. It was all a bit of an act, a dark panto-mime, as so much of punk was. After the gig, we were surprised to find that the boys from Slaughter were in fact a really decent bunch of lads, polite and respectful even, just like the punk bands we had hosted at Farrer House in the summer. On stage they were wild and, before we went on, the stage crew had to mop the floor to clear it of all the gob and change the mics, because they were dripping.

The three sets of fans made for an uneasy human cocktail and when Slaughter had finished, their lot retreated to the rear and ours moved forward. Plugging in our instruments, we received a parting shot from one of the punks. As Pick settled behind his drum kit, a golf ball flew from the rear, crashing into his cymbals, damn nearly hitting him square in the face.

On the subject of hygiene, we were amused and surprised to dis-cover that the Heads never cleaned their guitars and only changed their strings when one broke. Even then, they would replace only the broken one, not the whole lot, as was standard practice. Mark and Dave changed theirs every other day. I was an exception to this custom because, on bass, I had grown to like the soft, slightly dead sound produced by the sweat absorbed on very old strings. If you listen to that early Heads music, you can hear the strings pinging from time to time and it added to the uniqueness of their sound. Whatever works. (The strings on the bass I was to use for the *Brothers in Arms* tour of 1985–6 have been in situ ever since.) The dull thud of old strings better suited the sound I was after than the bright, sharp pinging of new ones. Pete Murdoch was a bass expert and, bless him, he thought he was doing me a favour when he put some new ones on for me before one gig, only for me to tell him to take them straight off and put the beloved old ones back on.

We had our own instruments, of course, and Mark brought a cou-ple of pedals, but otherwise we shared the equipment with the

Heads, walking on and just plugging in. The Heads were very gracious and generous about us using their kit and also in their appreciation of us as their support act, always clapping and slapping our backs as we came off. Remarkably for a support act, we were getting encores from the first gig. Ordinarily, the audience can't wait to get you off and get into the main act, so it was flattering to be called back on. That could have been awkward with other, less charitable bands than the Heads, but they were genuinely delighted for us. On a couple of occasions, they even asked Mark and me to come on and play 'Psycho Killer' with them.

Probably the most important moment of the tour, in terms of our development as a band, came midway through, when we were invited to play live on *The Old Grey Whistle Test*. It was hosted by 'Whispering' Bob Harris, who, I must report, is every bit as kind and lovable as the reputation that has followed him around has it. The show went out from Manchester live on BBC2, reaching an audience in the millions, all of them music lovers, and a great many from the industry and the music media, no doubt. Thankfully, I tend not to suffer from nerves going on stage, and Mark is cool about it too, whatever the crowd or circumstances, but we were definitely a little apprehensive as we set up. It was live; we couldn't screw it up. I watched a YouTube clip of it the other day and I was amazed by how skinny we were, unhealthy almost. Clearly one Full English a day was not quite enough to meet our calorie requirements.

In the event, we made a good fist of it, and the effect of being on TV was instantaneous. The crowds were way bigger after that and we started getting quite a lot of press interest. Ed Bicknell was great at dealing with that, managing the reporters and making sure we weren't ambushed, hassled and misquoted on the fly. We were moving from one venue to the next day after day, and there was barely time to take it all in and reflect on the experience, but it was extraordinary to take on board that just a few weeks earlier we had been playing in half-empty boozers.

Ed didn't join us for the whole tour, preferring to manage it remotely from his big desk in Audley Street and just dropping in for a gig here and there. The unheated Ford Transit van was not Ed's preferred mode of transport. All the same, our bond with him grew over the tour and, if we learned nothing else about him, he was certainly very entertaining company. *Why let the truth get in the way of a good story?* has always been one of his mottos. He lived for entertainment as a career but also in his attitude to life. He is a born entertainer, a great storyteller with an elephantine memory who collects anecdotes and tales like others collect stamps or butterflies. He was sharp too, still is, and he took no nonsense from anyone. He could be bracingly frank and bullish. You want that in a manager, someone to protect you from the sharks, bullshitters and spongers, someone to show the balls to drive a hard bargain. He openly admitted to modelling his brash management style on Peter Grant, Led Zeppelin's outlandish and formidable manager, who became his friend. By the end of the tour, we trusted in our gut instincts and decided we could work with him. Bringing Ed on board was one of the best decisions we ever made. He was to perform wonders for us.

We were on the road only for about three weeks, but a great deal was going on below the surface in that short period. It was an entirely new experience for us, and we were having to learn fast, adapting to rapidly changing circumstances and pressures. It's interesting how people respond to pressure, and we were starting to discover how our personalities bore up under the force of it. Ed Bicknell has been quoted as saying that he noticed some cracks appearing even at that early stage, but I didn't. We all got on great and, as a band on stage, we were tight. Without Mark, there was no Dire Straits, but each of us brought something to the collective effort. We didn't have a tour manager at this stage, so I took over the admin and business side of it, sorting out the hotels and the expenses. Not exactly taxing work and, having quite an organized mind, I slipped into the role without any fuss. Mark and the boys were more than happy with the arrangement.

A band is a team and, in a good one, a happy one, everyone contributes. It's not just about the music, playing your instrument well, it's how you contribute away from the stage and the studio. What I learned from that Heads tour is that all of you have to be pulling in the same direction, adding what you can to maintain momentum and good feeling. You have to know that everyone else is heaving their weight in some way, otherwise resentment starts to rear its ugly head and divisions appear, and they only get wider with time. I suppose it's a little like any team, be it on a football pitch, in an office or in the armed forces. You're in it together, and one person's failure to make an effort and play their part can jeopardize the entire joint endeavour. Touring is tiring, and nerves get frayed. But you have to stick together, do your bit, be mindful of others. What you don't want is a Jonah character bringing a sense of doom to the rest of the ship's crew. So far, so good for us. The tour had gone as well as we might have hoped.

On our return, we went into the recording studio to put down the first album. This also took about three weeks, and it was just as intense and enjoyable as the tour, only in an entirely different way. The tour was hard work and great fun; recording was hard work too, but all the fun flowed from the creative process. We were determined to get it right and, Basing Street being a very grown-up studio with state-of-the-art equipment and a highly skilled production team, we had to focus, be serious. At times, it got tense, but that's a good sign. It showed we meant business.

Basing Street Studios, just off Ladbroke Grove in Notting Hill, was owned by Chris Blackwell of Island Records, champion of reggae music and one of the great names of the British and world music scene. It was housed in an old church, which had also once been used as the storeroom and workshop of Madame Tussauds. The area back then certainly wasn't the fancy Notting Hill of today. It was rough and raw, brimming with Irish and West Indians, as well as a whole bunch of petty criminals and junkies, artists and bohemians. It was fun, buzzy and edgy, but you wanted your wits about you after dark. There are way too many to name, but dozens of great bands and artists have recorded some of the biggest singles and albums of all time at Basing Street: The Stones, Bob Marley, Led Zep, Queen, The Who, Madonna, George Michael . . . the list really does go on and on. A couple of years after we were there, it was bought by Trevor Horn of The Buggles, and it was in the same old church that the Band Aid track 'Do They Know It's Christmas?' was put down.

The studio equipment was so sophisticated it made Pathway look like the homely basement operation that it was. Pathway was great for a demo, but it didn't have the space or the kit to record a serious album. Our producer was Muff Winwood, former bassist with The Spencer Davis Group, and brother of Steve, one of the greats of British music. Basing Street had as good as become the house recording studio for Phonogram, and Johnny Stainze knew Muff well and rated him highly. Lovely man, Muff, and, as it turned out, a brilliant producer who commanded the operation with a kindly authority. He was more than ably assisted by the engineer, Rhett Davis, one of the finest in the business.

It took a few days to settle into this new environment and learn about the technological possibilities offered by the kit. At Pathway, we played and played until we were happy with a version. At Basing Street, we did the same but we were able to make more changes afterwards and the sound quality was so much finer. Rhett and Muff had all the expertise to mix and edit our sound, taking out what didn't quite work and overdubbing it with a sequence recorded separately after the event. Muff was committed to keeping 'space', which can be as important as sound in a song. That first album has a lovely simplicity to it, just two guitars, bass and drums. It was clean, and the songs could breathe with ease. It was a hard but happy enterprise putting it down in that famous studio, and Muff kept saying, day after day, as it came into focus, 'Tell you what, you guys stick together, you're gonna be all right, you're gonna be all right. Just stay together. Just stay together.'

We loved our time at Basing Street with Muff and Rhett. We were fresh to the studio experience and there was a child-like excitement in putting down a first album. For years, we had been listening to records on the radio and on our record players. Now we were going to have one of our own that was going to be played on the radio and in the bedrooms and sitting rooms of people all over the UK and — who could say? — maybe overseas too. We'd soon be holding the product of our efforts in our hands, seeing it in record stores and hearing it on the radio. Whether people took to it or not, we'd have the satisfaction of knowing we were going to leave a little something behind.

Johnny Stainze was coming in every day, getting more and more excited. We were his baby and you could tell he was proud of his signing. Thanks to Muff and Rhett, it was going down well. We were working long days and there wasn't much action in the pubs and bars of Notting Hill afterwards, just a couple of pints on Ladbroke Grove and into a black cab to be spirited back to Deptford. Towards the end, we were visited by two guys from Phonogram's marketing department to discuss the album cover. The film *Spinal Tap* hadn't been made by then, but what followed was a scene that might have been slotted straight into it, no editing required.

They were quite sure of themselves, but we most certainly did not feel the same way about the mock-ups for the cover they scattered before us over the baize of a billiards table. We looked at them, silent and aghast. Picking up on our horror, one of them piped, 'Obviously, we've been doing this for a long time. Just pick your favourite. You take care of the music, we'll take care of the rest.'

Mark and I threw each other another one of those glances, both thinking the same: *No, you really won't be taking care of the rest if this is the best you can come up with.* Each offering was pretty appalling. It was obvious that the art department had never heard our music and had based all its creations on our name. They read 'Dire Straits' so assumed we were all about disaster and gloom, possibly a punk band or a Satanic heavy-metal band. One of the mock-ups showed a passenger jet heading nose down into the sea, but the biscuit-taker was the red stiletto with the heel impaling a hand. We told them to leave it to us and we'd find something more suitable.

We didn't completely neglect it, but we were by no means obsessed with our image. In the days before music videos, before MTV and the growth of public relations, record companies were not quite so interested in image either. I remember us all being in a terrible mood, maybe hung over, when we had to assemble for a photoshoot in an old warehouse in south London. We had no press pictures to use, and I'm afraid we weren't looking our best. This was all new to us. You can see the results of that flippancy in the final images on the artwork of the first album. We look like comedy versions of something out of *Crimewatch UK*.

This album cover, however, was a big wake-up call, and we realized we needed to take control of our identity before a couple of our friends from the marketing department, without even listening to our music, turned us into a parody of Black Sabbath. The cover image used in the end was hardly ground-breaking, but we liked its uncluttered simplicity, which reflected the music inside: a hazy, impressionistic picture of a girl leaning against the pillar in an empty, brightly lit room. I believe it was taken from a photograph, and all the other details of the room were edited out. I would become more interested in the artwork of our albums later on, but this was one or two levels up from 'fine'; it didn't say too much, didn't make a grand, pompous statement and, best of all, it wasn't a stiletto heel nailing a hand to the ground or a jet crashing into the ocean.

When it was all over, Phonogram laid on a small party in a restaurant on the Portobello Road, with lots of record company people there with their partners. I'll admit to a feeling of some pride as we celebrated with a glass of champagne and some cheese twists. Johnny Stainze was buzzing. He kept reassuring us that we were all in it for the long haul, that they were going to build us over the coming years. 'If you sell five thousand copies,' he repeated, 'we'll be over the moon.' I never got around to asking him what planet he leapt over once it had passed the 20 million mark.

Chapter 11

Wolverhampton Woe to Marquee Magic

We were to set out on way bigger tours a little further down the line, three of them running for twelve months or more and leaving us shattered, but 1978 was by far the fullest, busiest year of our career at that time. There was so much going on and it was coming at us from all sides. This was the schedule: Talking Heads tour . . . recording of album at Basing Street . . . residency at the Marquee Club . . . British tour with Climax Blues Band . . . 'Sultans of Swing' released as a single . . . short, miserable tour to Europe with Chicago prog rockers Styx . . . UK tour . . . *Dire Straits* album released . . . gruelling autumn tour of Europe and then touring more of the UK . . . Ed Bicknell to the States to get a US album deal . . . fly to Nassau in the Caribbean to record our second album . . .

Throw in a bunch of media work in between and during those events, and there was barely time to sit down for a cup of tea in the flat, let alone a quiet pint down the Oxford Arms. Catapulted out of Deptford, we were up and flying, and the momentum rarely slackened. We had met Ed Bicknell in his office in early January; the next minute it was Christmas. The whirlwind of activity swept through our quiet little world, a life lived for years in smoky old-man pubs, greasy-spoon cafés and a run-down council flat, and reconfigured it beyond all recognition, changing our outlook, altering our horizons — and, beneath the surface, altering us too. Imperceptibly and inevitably, our characters were adjusting to a new and ceaselessly changing environment, to new and intense pressures. It would be a while, however, before that transformation manifested itself in our behaviour and in our relationships with one another. We were too busy to process it or to reflect.

While we were putting down the first album, Ed had booked us a residency at the Marquee Club in Wardour Street, one of the most prestigious small music venues in the world. We played there three Tuesdays in March and a Saturday in April. Virtually every great name in British rock music has played the Marquee; it has the same kudos as the Roxy in LA or the Bottom Line in Greenwich Village, New York. It was great, but with no record out there, no one had heard of us, so people dropped in more out of curiosity and because it was the Marquee than from an avid desire to see us. It was to be a different story when we returned there in July.

In early May, we started a two-week UK tour, opening for the Climax Blues Band and kicking off at London's Lyceum Theatre. No fault of the Climax Blues Band, but it was not the best experience. They were a friendly group and we got on fine, but there was nothing like the buzz and camaraderie we had enjoyed with the Heads, who, like us, were a new band trying to find some traction and revving with energy. We were driving ourselves around the country in a hired Ford Granada, playing venues with a capacity of about a thousand, but the atmosphere was always a bit flat, partly I think because Climax had been on the circuit for a while and had quite a long-standing following. The audience had little connection with us, there were certainly no encores, and we'd head back to our basic hotels feeling a little deflated. It was all good experience, we told ourselves.

With the album down and 'Sultans' about to come out as a single, it was true that our minds were probably elsewhere. All that excitement and dynamism generated in the previous months was slowly dissipated by the tedium of travel and the inertia of the crowds we played before. There was a good deal of discussion about which version of 'Sultans' we put out there. It was widely and rightly felt, very much so by us, the band, that the album version did not have the vibe of the Pathway demo version. As we were the ones who had recorded the tracks, we noticed the subtle differences more than anyone and instinctively knew that the first effort was the superior one. That was the one we wanted people to hear. Johnny Stainze agreed, and when Phonogram suggested we go back to Pathway to try to re-create the demo tape sound, he pointed out the futility of trying to top that first effort. He understood that, like good sex or a fine meal, you can't repeat the magic on demand.

In the end, the album version was released here first, but over time I think I am right in saying that Phonogram fed the Pathway recording into the radio station network. We saw ourselves as an album band, but there was of course mounting excitement about our first single hitting the shops and the airwaves. You take the vinyl from its sleeve and feel like an explorer about to set out on a voyage around the world. All that hope and trepidation, that first step into the unknown. Every band will have experienced the exhilaration of that moment.

So out it came, we held our breath, drum roll and . . . pretty much nothing happened. First time out, 'Sultans' barely troubled the charts, peaking at number thirty-seven. The length of it, the version of it — who knows why it failed to make a splash. Of course we were disappointed, but there was the album to come and the tours to promote it, so we got on with preparing for our first UK tour with us as the headline act. Rejection and public indifference are part of the experience for an aspiring band, just as they are in the book world. Both industries have produced countless tales of famous bands and authors who were turned down or ignored for years before breaking through. We were mature enough to understand and weather these harsh facts of life.

First up, though, was a nine-gig tour of Europe with US stadium rockers Styx. We were a strange choice to support this flamboyant prog rock act, but they were huge in North America and had booked in to play some big venues. I was excited too, because I had never been to Paris, where we started, and as it was May all the blossom would be out and we'd see the famous city in its full splendour. What could go wrong? Quite a lot, as it turned out, and fairly quickly.

I think Ed sold the mini-tour to us as an opportunity to get some experience working with different bands. He was probably right, and it definitely was an experience. A lot of American bands back then never bothered to tour outside the States. They didn't need to when there was such a big market at home and they could keep going round and round, selling out big stadiums. ZZ Top didn't leave the US for about ten years.

This was Styx's first big foray overseas, and they really didn't enjoy it. Used to screaming adoration back home, they were surprised and put out by the tepid interest shown in them by continental Europe. We were booked into the same hotel as them, La Trémoille, behind the Champs-Élysées, by far the glitziest hotel I had ever set foot in. It was so expensive we couldn't even afford a cup of coffee, presented on silver trays by liveried staff, so we ate our meals around the corner, slices of pizza served in a piece of wax paper from street vendors.

Struggling with the lack of attention, Styx were not overly welcoming to us and pretty much ignored us from the off. At the first show at the Mogador, a famous old theatre in the heart of the ninth arrondissement with a capacity of sixteen hundred, we didn't even get a soundcheck. It was a seat-of-the-pants gig for us, but it went well. The contrast with touring with Talking Heads could not have been greater. When they got a somewhat cool reception from the Parisians, Styx left the stage looking miserable and sullen. Another problem for them was that the Straits were on good form and, as they waited to come on, Styx would have noticed that the lead singer of their warm-up act was also a very fine guitarist. No one likes being upstaged, least of all by a new kid on the block. We played two more gigs, at The Hague and in Hamburg, before one of them feigned illness. The remaining six gigs were cancelled and they hurried off to the airport. We didn't go and wave them off.

We felt no sadness, just massive relief, but we had learned a valuable lesson that week: treat other musicians with kindness and respect. It's so difficult to get anywhere in the music business so, as part of a community, bands need to offer support and encouragement, no matter where you are in the musical hierarchy.

We kicked off our UK tour on the first Tuesday of June with a show at Club Lafayette in Wolverhampton, for the grand sum of fifty quid. When we came on stage, there was precisely nobody in the crowd, unless you counted the security guy leaning on the barrier below, having a lazy smoke. We started tuning up, laughing at the absurdity of it, when the rear doors were flung open and our crowd rolled in. All two of them, and both absolutely steaming drunk. We'd already set up, we had a contract to play, so we played.

We were in our third song, treating the gig like a rehearsal, when one half of the crowd went to use the facilities and, almost as soon as he came back, a fight broke out with the other half. It was a proper fight, not the usual shoving and windmilling you see when people have had a few too many. The security guard managed to separate them eventually and we wound up the show to the applause of no one. We moved on to JB's in Dudley, where there were, at least, a few punters, and a week later we discovered the cheque from Club

Lafayette had bounced. That's showbiz for you. Another lesson learned.

Wolverhampton hadn't augured well for the rest of the tour, but things soon picked up and we were playing in front of some large and enthusiastic audiences, especially at the unis and polytechnics. It was a real mixed bag of gigs. Some very small backwater joints like the Kirklevington Club, Yarm, outside Middlesbrough, and the Newbridge Working Men's Club in South Wales. They were small venues, but many of them had hosted some big names over the years. AC/DC, the Sex Pistols, The Clash and Queen, for instance, had all played at Barbarella's nightclub in Birmingham. The Metro club in Plymouth had staged Bowie, Eric Clapton, Pink Floyd, Roxy Music, T-Rex, Status Quo ... These little clubs were the lifeblood and nursery of the British music scene. They weren't flashy or huge venues, but when you play them you're aware of the history and of treading the same boards as so many great acts who went on to higher things. Everyone played them when they started out.

Word was getting out about us and the crowds grew to capacity as we travelled up and down, back and across the country in our rented Ford Granada, the glamorous executive car of the day. Someone had bought the full set of cassettes of Dylan Thomas's *Under Milk Wood*, read by Richard Burton in his beautiful, rich voice and, maybe to take a break from music, we played it over and over. Chas Herington, our sound engineer at Pathway, had come on board as our lighting man for the tour. He had just twelve lights, six on either side of the stage, and all he had to do was turn them on and off. From these modest beginnings, Chas would create something far more spectacular over the years to come. For the time being, the money tight, he had to make do with his village-hall set-up, and he and roadie Pete Murdoch travelled ahead from gig to gig in Pete's comically decrepit old van, its rear bumper held in place with pieces of old rope.

Another small, iconic venue was the 76 Club in Burton-on-Trent, so called because it was located at number 76 High Street. You'd think that would make it easy to find, but that was not the case. There was no sign of the place and we drove up and down the street and all over Burton. Finally, we stopped and asked some teenagers and they pointed us to the Jolly Fryer fish 'n' chip shop, like we were stupid. The 76 Club was in the back of the shop and, to get to it, we had to lug our gear past all the people queuing for fish suppers and saveloys.

There was a memorable night at the Newbridge Working Men's Club, the communal heart of the Monmouthshire mining town. It wasn't our usual crowd, and because of a big night of sport on TV, people were pretty thin on the ground: a few dozen middle-aged and red-faced old men supping on bitter, or pints of cider with whisky chasers — a combination we'd never heard of — and tabbing on their cigarettes, sitting on stools at round tables and on benches against the walls. It was cold in there, and the atmosphere was mildly unnerving because there was not a flicker of response on anyone's face as we played, and never any applause at the end of a song. We did a good set but, when we finished, there was silence, so we trooped off to the little storeroom that was our dressing room, muttering about packing up fast and getting the hell out. Then there was a knock on the door and in marched the club manager.

'Come on, you boys,' he said in a strong Welsh accent. 'You can't just slip off like that. We want our money's worth.'

'But they don't seem to like us,' we protested.

'Oh, yes, they do!' he insisted. 'They just keep it to themselves. They're not showy people. Come on, out you get. Everyone does an encore here. Tom Jones did two, and he didn't get any clapping either!'

We downed a beer, went back out and played a rousing version of Chuck Berry's 'Nadine'. Still nothing. Not a smile or a twitch.

We were seeing a side of British life that we otherwise would have no reason to experience. Once again, we stayed in the most basic hotels and there was no money left over from the gigs once we paid the crew, filled up with petrol, ate our meals and drank our pints. I loved every minute of it. We all did. Except perhaps the gig when a guy was sick into my bass bin just a few feet from where I was playing. Not wanting to make Pete do it, Mark and Pick gallantly cleared up the vomit at the end of the gig.

Towards the end of the tour, in the first week of July, we were back in London, playing two nights at the Marquee. We had played to decent crowds there during our residence in spring, but this time the place was absolutely jumping, so full that they had to open the doors at the back and use the car-park area as an overspill. There must have been a thousand people there, adding to the heat of one of the hottest days of the year. Up under the lights, we were sweltering; it was as hot as any gig I have ever played. The sweat was pouring off us, down our faces and arms and all over our instruments. Stage lights in those days threw out a tremendous heat, so intense sometimes that it could affect your performance.

This was the night Mark wore a headband for the first time. The rest of us had wristbands, but Mark, singing and playing, was probably feeling the heat more than the rest of us. It was simply a practical measure to stop the salty sweat running into his eyes and making his guitar slippery. It did the trick, so he wore it from then on and it became something of a talisman for him.

The Marquee pocketed a packet those two nights. It was a pound on the door and everyone was drinking like heroes owing to the incredible heat. The tills were ringing. We were paid eighty quid and, when you took off the cost of the PA, that left us with a tenner. Then take off wages for Pete and Chas, and we ended up well out of pocket. We knew we were going to get fleeced, but playing to so many people this time, it was so outrageous it was almost funny. Afterwards, the manager just gave me a small roll of twenties and tens and

walked off, saying, 'That's what you get. We've got overheads too!'
We didn't really care. We were on a roll. It was a prestigious place to
play and the crowd had turned up to see us, not just for a night out.

Sid Vicious was in the crowd that night, totally off his face. But it
was Keith Moon who really distracted us and took our minds off the
money. We were backstage, drenched to the skin and necking beers,
when The Who's drummer crashed through the door, drunk as
you've ever seen anyone. He mumbled, 'Fucking brilliant!' and fell
over. His minder picked him up, then stayed very close, ready to grab
him, his job for the night being to pick him up off the floor.

Keith kept on muttering, 'Fucking brilliant! . . . Fucking marvellous gig! . . . Fucking, fucking . . .'

Dear Keith, he must have fallen over six or seven times before his
minder took him out. The last and only time I had seen Keith Moon
before, I was a teenager and he was happily smashing up his drum kit
at Granby Halls, Leicester. That was when The Who were on the
rise, shaking up and redefining rock music as they went. It was sad to
see this icon of British music, one of the great drummers, in such a
state. A couple of months later, it was even sadder to hear that he
had died.

The Marquee — and a few of the other gigs on that tour — showed
that there was some growing interest in us out there, but we were a
long, long way from being a household name. We were one of many
bands on the circuit at a vibrant time for new music.

Late August 1978, and we were back in the flat in Deptford. Ed had
been to the States to try to sell the album over there, but he was finding it hard. America is a tough nut to crack for any British band. They
have so much home-grown talent it's very hard to elbow your way
in; you have to offer something doubly special. That said, after the
Beatles phenomenon, the US labels were always on the lookout for
next big UK band.

I wouldn't say we were feeling down when the phone rang that morning, but we certainly weren't battling to keep our feet on the ground and our heads out of the stars.

I took the call. It was Johnny Stainze.

The album *Dire Straits* wasn't being released until early October, but Phonogram had recently put it out in the Netherlands to sample the reaction. Apparently, the Netherlands was regarded as a litmus test for the wider market. If the Dutch went for it, a record company could feel more confident about its chances. We knew nothing of the country's special status as the arbiters of world music taste and had forgotten the album was out there.

Johnny was in a state of high excitement. 'It's sold twenty-five thousand copies!'

'What? What are you talking about?'

'The album — it's selling like clogs. The Dutch have gone mad for it.'

I shouted through to Mark and Dave, 'The album's sold twenty-five thousand copies in the Netherlands!'

Mark shouted back, 'Yeah, right, and I'm a Dutchman!'

But it was true. This was incredible news. Twenty-five thousand copies in a couple of weeks in such a tiny country. That was five times more than the total sales Phonogram had been estimating and hoping for over the life of the album. To them, the first album was just the baby step.

A couple of days later, to the bemusement of our neighbours in the council block, a black stretch limo pulled up outside the flat next to my old Rover. We were taken to Heathrow, flew from there to Amsterdam and were put up in a very smart five-star hotel. We were fawned over by the staff on our arrival and a knot of photographers snapped away as we made our way from the lobby to our rooms.

It was our first taste of media attention and we were walking on air as we made our way up in the lift. But that was when the fun and the glamour stopped. The rest of the weekend was a bit of a nightmare.

*1978. Our first gold album in Holland. All smiles
with Ed Bicknell, our manager.*

There was a constant flow of journalists and photographers to each
of our rooms — Dutch, Belgian, German and French. After a few
hours our rooms began to feel like prison cells. It was weirdly claustrophobic and there was no escape, it seemed, and no one monitoring
our needs. It all got a little crazy and intense. As we were offered no
food or refreshments, the minibars took a big hit, and were cleared of
all snacks and the few beers they held. By the end of the first day, it
was pitch black outside and I was sitting on the bed, dizzy with
hunger and fatigue.

Released from captivity, we were all of the same mind and mood as
we headed out for some fresh air and a drink. Someone needed to
take control of the situation. Phonogram had arranged this media

bonanza and just left us to it. We got Ed on to it, and the next day was a bit better. We were even fed. The whole weekend was a mixture of exhilaration and exhaustion. Another lesson learned — the wet behind the ears had dried a little by the time we flew out. Any number of comments the four of us made might have been taken out of context or distorted in translation. But more than that, if we were going to be a wider success, we really needed our management team to step in and take control. We couldn't be thrown to the wolves like that again.

There was time for a short scoot around the city to see a few sights — including a quick peek at the famous red-light district (only a look!), before a bizarre and troubling couple of days ended on a fittingly crazy note on 1 September. We had been booked to appear on the Netherlands' main music and entertainment show, *Top Pop*, a show that had more in common with *The Banana Splits* than *The Old Grey Whistle Test*. The show liked to use wacky, fun sets and backdrops and, performing on a diamond-shaped stage, we found ourselves miming 'Sultans' and 'Water of Love'. It was the first time we had mimed, and it was a weird sensation. We were flattered that the Dutch were so enthusiastic about the album, but it was a relief to get back to Farrer House.

We had a couple of months at the end of the summer and in early autumn before the album came out and we started the European leg of our tour. Pauline and I managed to get away to Crete for a week and we stayed in a simple room in the tiny fishing village of Agia Galini. Early on, we met an American painter called Raphael Pollock, and I formed a strong friendship with him over endless glasses of ouzo that holds strong today, over forty years on. But at that point I didn't know just how important art was going to become in my life.

Back home, we spent much of the time rehearsing down the road at Wood Wharf Studios, at the mouth of Deptford Creek, where it spills into the Thames. A remote spot, far from the hubbub of London, set amidst the scrap metal and decaying debris of a once thriving dockyard area and overlooking the broad flow of the Thames, it was a perfect retreat for us. After a frantic seven or eight months, we relished the time and space, the opportunity to gather ourselves and work on the music for the next tour.

Mark had been writing fresh material out on the road for the second album, and we had played a few of the songs at our gigs. It was amazing that he had the time, energy and inspiration when there was so much going on. I just wanted to go bed. He was getting close to having a full complement of songs for the second album, which was to be recorded at the end of the year, including 'Single-Handed Sailor', 'Lady Writer', 'Where Do You Think You're Going?' and 'News', a particular favourite of mine.

Wood Wharf was a very basic studio, the only equipment a primitive tape recorder, but it was sufficient for our purposes at that stage. It was great that it was within walking distance from the flat, cheap and, as it looked out over water and big skies, it provided us some sanctuary where we could work without distraction.

By the time we set out for Belgium, the leaves were falling and the new album was coming into sharp focus. The tour was to run for five weeks, three in Belgium and the Netherlands, with a couple of nights in Germany and one in Paris, then back to the UK for two weeks on the student union circuit. The first album came out a few days before we left, and it didn't exactly take the UK charts by storm. But it was early days and one of the reasons any band tours is to promote an album.

In Belgium we based ourselves in the beautiful old university town of Leuven. Its central location meant we could drive ourselves to all the gigs and save on hassle and hotel bills with a long-stay deal. We were scheduled to play some big venues in big cities and there was an air of excitement as we unpacked our luggage and settled into a simple hotel. It was late by then and the only place to eat was a dubious-looking pizza joint by the railway station. I chose the one with the seafood topping. Major mistake. By lunchtime the next day I was very sick. At first I thought it was just a quick dose of food poisoning, but it must have been some kind of microbe infection because it didn't clear up completely for about six weeks. I felt heavily drained by it and I'd lost about fifteen pounds by the time I got back to the UK – weight I didn't have spare to lose.

It was frustrating to be sick because the tour was going from strength to strength, the album was getting more attention over there than back home and all the shows were well attended, sometimes with over a thousand in the audience. Driving around Flanders in our hire car, with Pete and Chas going on before, it was a thrill to hear ourselves on the radio for the first time and, encouragingly, they were playing several of the tracks, not just 'Sultans', but 'Down to the Waterline' and 'Wild West End'.

The Paradiso in Amsterdam is the gig that lives most vividly in the memory, partly because Pauline had flown out for a few days so we could celebrate her birthday on 19 October.

The renovated church close to the Rijksmuseum is one of the great venues on the world music scene. Back then, the security was run by the Hells Angels, probably because no one was given a choice in the matter. It was a scary crew of lads who met us when we rolled up in the car to join Pete and Chas, but they were polite and helpful and all of them spoke perfect English. When we had finished setting up, they announced they were going to sit on stage as we played. Who were we to argue? At first, it was quite unnerving to play with six huge blokes in chains and leather waistcoats, giant tattooed forearms folded over their bellies. But at least there wasn't going to be any trouble, and afterwards they came backstage for some beers – in fact, most of our beers – and they turned out to be really decent guys.

The European leg came to an end with shows in Hamburg and

Berlin. We were a bit nervous about Germany. There had been no official interest in us there and the major radio stations didn't want to play 'Sultans' or the album – a fact we found weird, when their neighbours in the Netherlands were going mad for us. We were indebted to a couple of rogue DJs who loved it and played it on their shows, and in the end it was this that encouraged the record company to release the album there. We soon became as popular in Germany as anywhere in Europe, way more than in the UK at that time. The two shows were packed, and the Germans were to maintain their enthusiasm for us right the way through. We were learning that there is no rhyme or reason to musical taste and that success varies wildly from country to country. You can have a smash in Germany and a flop in France. Mark's songs have the great virtue of universal appeal and the success to come our way was fairly evenly distributed around the world.

We had played to packed houses, to *our* audience rather than for people who had come to see an act we were supporting, and we returned to the UK on a high. We were doing something right, but in Britain the album, like 'Sultans', was met with only passing interest at best, fretting the lower reaches of the charts for a short period and then sliding even from that pale limelight. There was a lot of competition around, but we still thought it was curious. Why were we gaining so much traction on the continent, and apparently in Australia and New Zealand too, but so little at home? The shows at the unis and polys were all well attended, we felt good feedback from the audiences, but still the album languished. We were more perplexed than anything. But we needn't have worried. America was coming.

Chapter 12

Sessions in the Sun

There are many reasons why it's hard to sell an album to a record company, and especially in the States, but the main difficulty is that you are not courting and wooing an entire market or audience but just one or two people in an office. If they don't like it, that's pretty well the end of the talks, possibly the end of a promising career and the extinction of a great talent. To make matters even tougher, not everyone in the music industry knows a great deal about music. Many of the people you are dealing with, the ones who are calling the shots, are executives, businesspeople, sales teams, money people. The ones who really know their music, like the A&R people, tend to be lower down the food chain. They may find the band, push it to their label, but the decision to sign them won't be theirs.

Ed and Robert found themselves up a lot of dead-ends over in the States. They were looking for a separate US deal because we had a clause in our contract allowing that. Phonogram, so strong in Europe, were not so strong in the States, unable to break the market dominance of the big American companies like Warners, RCA and CBS.

They just didn't have the muscle or the hustle to work the radio stations and get them to play their music. The industry was still a little corrupt when we got started, the big recording companies dominating the scene with a mafia-style grip over the industry. Money was often passed to radio stations to ensure a song was played and a label could effectively buy a top-ten hit.

It was towards the end of summer 1978, while we were at Wood Wharf, getting ready for a tour of Europe, that the breakthrough was made. Ed and Mark flew out to Alabama to meet Jerry Wexler of Warner Records at Muscle Shoals Studio — legendary man, legendary label, legendary recording studios. Warners was the deal we wanted above all others. Ed and Mark didn't need to sell it. Jerry Wexler loved the songs and the sound of the band. To be admired by Jerry Wexler was a serious compliment, Jerry being one of the most respected names in the US music industry. A journalist-turned-producer, he was said to have invented the phrase 'rhythm and blues', and he had produced or signed many of the greats, including Ray Charles, Aretha Franklin, Led Zeppelin and Bob Dylan. We came to Jerry's attention thanks to the persistence of Karin Berg, Warners' chief A&R expert on the East Coast, an impressive, charming woman in an industry heavily dominated by men. Karin was very keen on us and stayed with us right the way through.

Record companies expect most bands to fail, to make them a loss, so they sign up a dozen or so acts in the hope that one wins through and covers the losses of the others. 'We throw ten at the wall, and hope one sticks,' they tell you. We were one of the ten, but with Jerry Wexler eager to produce and oversee the album himself and, with the brilliant Barry Beckett as his engineer, we knew we had a good chance of breaking America, the biggest market in the world.

As part of the deal with Warners, Wexler wanted us in the studio to put down a second album — which we eventually decided to call *Communiqué* — as soon as our Europe tour was done. None of us were keen on this because the first album was barely out and we wanted it to have a decent crack at the market. We didn't want any overlap with the second going out while the first was still in the charts and being played on the radio. The *Dire Straits* album was already starting to gather momentum in the States and around the world. Jerry Wexler was a powerful man, not easily persuaded against his judgement, and we didn't want to jeopardize the deal so, reluctantly, we agreed.

So, at the end of November we flew to Nassau in the Bahamas to get down to work in Chris Blackwell's Compass Point Studio.

We were to spend four weeks in Nassau, fly back for Christmas, then head straight off to Muscle Shoals to mix the album. Think Bahamas, you think holiday, but that's not why Compass Point was chosen. We were there to work hard, free of all distractions. Talking Heads, who had recorded there, recommended it to us. Officially, the island is called New Providence, but it is known to most as Nassau, the name of the Bahamas' capital, because the only town on the island dominates all else. In 1978, the rest of the island was almost undeveloped, and it is small enough that you can cycle from one end to the other in a couple of hours. Not that we did that. It was what they call a 'paradise island', but there was very little to do outside the capital but sell exotic fruit from the side of the road, go fishing or lie around in the shade. The bulldozers and property developers were poised to invade but, when we visited, the island was about as removed from jetset cosmopolitanism as you can get.

Apart from Mark making his flying trip to Muscle Shoals, none of us had been anywhere more exotic than northern Europe and Newbridge, South Wales. We arrived via Bermuda, where we ran into a chirpy Max Bygraves in the transfer lounge, an amusing diversion during our long wait. It took the best part of a day to get there and, touching down, the Nassau airport terminal told us all we needed to know about the delightful remoteness of our home for the next four weeks: it was a wooden shack. We drove along rough, winding tracks flanked by thatched food and drink shacks, through the lush vegetation, alongside the palm-fringed bleach-white beaches, the silver-blue ocean glistening under the hot sun. It was going to make for an enchanting change from Deptford High Street, and we took in the landscape in reverential silence.

Jerry Wexler was not the sort of character to slum it, and he had hired one of the most luxurious residences on the island. 'Capricorn' belonged to the widow of an oil tycoon and was one of very few villa-style houses on the unspoilt coastline. When we met Chris Blackwell later in the week, he told us that he was attracted to the island because it was still raw, honest and undeveloped, just as his native Jamaica used to be.

We stopped at Compass Point Studios on the way from the airport, and there was a bunch of guys in chairs out front, enjoying beers below a cloud of ganja. It was a smell that would barely leave our nostrils over the coming month. We'd come to check the amps we had ordered from Miami had arrived; apparently they hadn't, but we weren't to worry. So, we had our guitars, which had been flown out earlier from the UK, and Pick had his drumsticks, and that was it.

It was ten minutes to the house, and there were muffled gasps as we drove through the gates into a stunning tropical paradise being worked by a small army of gardeners. We pulled up in front of the colonnaded façade and, swerving past the marble statues, made our way around to the front of the house, past the seawater swimming pool, and marvelled at the picture-postcard white beach fringed with palm trees. Inside, we were greeted by four members of staff, including a delightful chef with the most infectious laugh you've ever heard and a figure that suggested her cooking was so good she was unable to resist it.

Mark had been given the owner's suite, a room the size of our entire flat in Deptford, complete with white grand piano. The other rooms were not too shabby either. We hadn't come very well prepared for paradise, just one bottle of sun lotion for our four very white bodies. After supper under a domed ceiling of stars, we sat by the pool working our way through a bottle of rum, slightly overawed but enjoying our new environment. We ate and drank like kings while we were there, waited upon by the fantastic staff. The last time any of us had been in a pool, it was down at the municipal sports centre for swimming lessons as kids. A greater contrast with the Crossfields estate was hard to imagine.

We were in a good place in every sense. By now the first album was starting to sell well in a host of countries, and we were about to begin to go to work with a bunch of great new songs we had been playing on tour. We hadn't sought out paradise; we had been parachuted into it and we treated the privilege with respect throughout our stay. No one drove a car into the pool or threw a piano out of a window.

Jerry and Barry flew in from the States the next day, followed soon after by their luggage and half a dozen aluminium cases that I assumed were full of musical equipment. But no, it was mostly food supplied by Jerry's butcher and deli in New York: pastries, pastrami, strip sirloins, chickens, salt beef and a lot of grits, a sort of porridge made of boiled cornmeal. Every Wednesday and Saturday Jerry and I would drive to the airport to collect fresh supplies. The provisions must have cost more than the villa, and we figured that this expense was probably going to be coming off our deal. Learning yet again about the culture of the music industry.

'You guys gotta eat properly when you're working!' Jerry kept saying.

Ernest Hemingway — that was my first impression on meeting Jerry Wexler — but a whole lot friendlier. He was a big, cuddly bear of a man, and in between mouthfuls of food — he loved his food — the

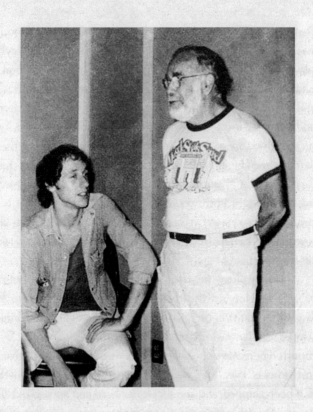

Mark with Jerry Wexler, who produced Communiqué *in Nassau.*
Jerry flew out most of the food we ate from his favourite New York stores,
which then went on our recording bill, of course.

stories flowed out of him, keeping us royally entertained every meal around the big table under the painted stars. His daily breakfast of eggs and grits appeared to be his favourite meal of the day, the grits flying over the table as he regaled us with stories and roared with laughter.

Barry Beckett was a gentle giant, one of those guys you just take to straight away. Mark had met him with Ed in Muscle Shoals and they'd hit it off at once. He was something of a gourmand too, his favourite food being a 28-ounce ribeye. Barry was a fine keyboard player, a member of the fabled Muscle Shoals Rhythm Section, who had played with, produced and engineered many great musicians and bands. It was a privilege to be working with Barry and Jerry. Ed and Mark had learned in Muscle Shoals that Jerry was no fool when it came to business. Trying his luck in the negotiations for the deal, Jerry claimed he should be entitled to a percentage point of the sales for the first album *and* for the third, the one after *Communiqué*, arguing that sales of both would be boosted by the fact that he had produced the one in between. Ed was having none of that, and I'd love to have seen his face and heard his response when Jerry laid out his reasoning.

Work began the next day. The schedule Jerry had set up was breakfast at nine, into the studio for a ten-thirty start, break for lunch (very important), finish up at seven, back for a swim and a drink and supper (even more important). That was our Groundhog Day for a month. There was only one problem: we had no kit, apart from our instruments. Every day, we asked the girl on reception whether it had been shipped, and she shook her head and apologized. Three weeks in, another girl was sitting in for her and we asked again. 'Sure, it's just down that corridor,' she said, beaming.

'Brilliant! When did it arrive?'

'A couple of days before you guys.'

So, most of the album was made with jerry-rigged equipment, begged and borrowed from a couple of reggae bands — a speaker from here, an amp from there, one of them from Robert Palmer, who lived in a little house opposite with his wife. Robert lent us his Fender twin reverb amp, and we got to know him quite well. (If nothing else, the ad hoc arrangements showed that you don't need a mountain of equipment to make a good album.) Robert dropped in to the studio from time to time and we'd go over there for a drink some evenings, and he'd boom insanely loud music at us through his new Bose studio speakers. He was very proud of his new system but, as they were even louder than the speakers in the studio, they made conversation quite tough.

The studio, unpretentious and simple, had been set up about a year earlier by Chris Blackwell, mainly to record Caribbean reggae bands. Talking Heads were one of the first bands to use it, but plenty of big names from both the States and Europe would follow, among them The Stones and The Police, before it went into decline following the death in a car accident of the house producer/engineer Alex Sadkin and, apparently, a steep rise in crime on the island. There was certainly no evidence of crime when we there. It all seemed very innocent and gentle.

It takes a while to get used to working in a new environment, but there were few distractions on Nassau so we got our heads down in the studio day after day, marshalled by Jerry, who was a stickler for time-keeping. Jerry had a strong presence and, even if he hadn't been intervening, you noticed it when he wasn't there. There was an authority about him, part of it natural, part of it earned through his incredible work in the past. He was one of those people you wanted to impress. He truly loved the sound of the band and the music's understated simplicity. A good producer allows a band to be true to itself and just nudges things along when necessary. That's exactly what Jerry did. The first album was getting a lot of airplay now and he was eager to emulate the feeling and sound of it on *Communiqué*. He let the music breathe and wanted nothing added, no strings or brass. When he did contribute, it was always valuable.

For example, one time I was in the control room with Barry, who was doing most of the production hard graft, and Pick was working on some percussion for the song 'Single-Handed Sailor', about the yachtsman Sir Francis Chichester sailing around the world. There was no shaker in the studio, so Jerry took a film canister down to the beach and put some sand in it. Pick was trying to re-create the sound of the sea; it worked perfectly and he did it in one take. That's what you're hearing on the record — sand being shaken in a film canister.

There was certainly no shouting or confrontation in the studio. It was all very professional and positive. Jerry had a reputation for being tough with musicians in the studio, but there were no clashes with us. He could not have been less authoritarian or more encouraging. He spent a lot of time on the phone, checking on the sales of the first album, and we got daily updates on its progress. It was going down really well in the States and around the world, as well as in Europe, but especially in Australia and New Zealand. It was quite weird being marooned on a tiny island while our music was being played all over the world, but the good news was inspiring us in the studio.

We'd been playing most of the songs on the road and at Wood Wharf, in total for about six months, so they were pretty polished and we were pretty tight. We changed bits and pieces, but no more. That's the beauty of a recording studio; you can analyse everything more closely. The only song that hadn't been written was the title track, 'Communiqué'; Mark would complete it while we were there. Jerry wanted to call the album after one of the other tracks, 'News', and I think that would have been just as good. He imagined people asking, 'Have you heard the News?'

The album came to be overshadowed a little by later ones and, inevitably, it was compared to our first. That's just the way it is. You can't avoid comparisons. Very few second albums are considered to have trumped the first, and although the critical reception — and the sales — would be very positive overall, some of the criticism, I felt, was a little unfair. You have to see each album as a unique stand-alone piece of work, not as an extension of what came before. I have always loved the feel of this record and it never fails to trigger happy memories of our time at Compass Point.

*Outside Compass Point Studios, 1978. I can highly recommend
making a record where the sun shines.*

The album was a unique sound for the times, a little different from
anything else around then – not disco, not punk, not new wave. That
was not intentional; it's just what came to Mark naturally and how
we interpreted it. Where you make an album affects the sound and
feel of it. Had it been made in New York, it would have probably
sounded very different.

It was a very happy month, helped by the steady flow of good
news about the sales of the first album around the world. Every
time Jerry got off the phone, there was more of a spring in his step.
It vindicated his decision to sign the band and it augured well for
Communiqué. We had battled away in pubs and little clubs for so
long, this was heartening news. But we looked at the whole enterprise with detachment, soaking up the experience rather than
revelling in it, never striving after success for its own sake.

There wasn't much socializing or partying while we were in Nassau. It was all very laid-back. Other than seeing a bit of Robert Palmer, we had supper with Chris Blackwell a couple of times, down at his modest little house nearby. Jerry took us out for a lobster barbecue in town one evening. The restaurant was just a shack, but the memory of the blissful evening, the sun sinking on the picturesque fishing harbour, has stayed with me. We ate freshly caught lobster in garlic butter, as delicious as anything I have ever eaten, washed down with a few beers. It was one of those rare moments, insignificant in itself, but it was that feeling you get when all feels right with your world.

A few people from the record company came out, one with a journalist or two in tow, one of whom was more interested in the local fauna than our music. He was obsessed by snakes and other reptiles and, apparently, he smuggled some back to the UK in his luggage and clothes, including a lizard in his pants. Ed came out too, even though, like Dracula, he hates the sun. He loves the heat, but his skin is so pale he can't venture out of the shade. Pauline, and Dave's girlfriend, Chris, came out together too. It was great to see Pauline, but she was mindful that we were working hard so she kept out of the way, happy hanging out by the pool and reading. Ed was busy organizing a short tour of the States for when we had finished mixing the album at Muscle Shoals. It's not often in life that you hit a period when everything is going well and you can see nothing but good news on the horizon. But Nassau in the winter of 1978 was definitely one of them.

December 1978 was the start of what came to be known as the 'Winter of Discontent' in Britain, a turbulent period of widespread strikes, trade union militancy, severe snowstorms and a mood of national despondency. We were not completely cut off from current affairs, of course, but we were living in a somewhat self-contained world of tour vans, studios, hotels and music venues. We heard no British radio, watched very little TV and rarely read a newspaper during this time. It's weird how even a major event of history can pass you by when it has no direct bearing on your daily life. We were recording in New York in 1982 when the Falklands War broke out. We had no idea about it at all for days. We were in a windowless recording studio for twelve hours, then back in the flat after a few beers in a bar or a bite to eat in a restaurant.

I'm afraid we weren't sharing the mood of national gloom when, still slightly tanned from Nassau, we flew out to Alabama in festive mood, ready to mix the album. It was my first trip to the States, that semi-mystical land that had rushed into my imagination while I lay in bed at Stonehenge, listening to Elvis and R'n'B tracks on Radio Luxembourg as a young teenager. We were going to be in Elvis country too. The United States is a very diverse country, as it's so huge, and rural Alabama was by no means representative of the whole, but I couldn't help but feel the excitement when the aircraft touched down.

We could have taken the album to be mixed in New York or LA, but Muscle Shoals was Jerry and Barry's patch, where they had produced a good deal of their great work. Also, as everyone kept telling us, our sound was very American and, in places, it does resonate a little with an atmosphere of the Deep South, an impression intensified by Mark's distinctive picking style. On arrival in North Alabama, a hop from the border with Tennessee, there was no mistaking that the Deep South was where we had landed. If you wanted to go native, all you needed to do was put on a cap and jump into a pick-up.

There was still some quarrelling going on behind the scenes about the release date for *Communiqué*. Ed was continuing to argue that we should wait until *Dire Straits* had been given a decent run-out and we had finished all the touring to promote it. In the words of one of the Warners people, it was 'really starting to kick some shit out there'. But Ed had to be careful. You didn't want to go upsetting Jerry Wexler, or Warners, and in the end there was a compromise.

The mixing of an album, very different from recording, is an interesting stage of the process when each element of the music is examined in detail. Mixing is a fine art, but we all had the opportunity to contribute to the end product.

It was a pleasure every morning to walk into that historic building, a squat concrete block on Jackson Highway originally used as a coffin showroom. It was converted into a recording studio in 1969 by a group of musicians calling themselves the Muscle Shoals Rhythm Section, known to all as 'The Swampers', who set themselves up in direct competition with their former employer, Rick Hall of FAME studios, just down the road. So many of the great albums in my collection, the songs I had heard on the radio as a kid, had been recorded and engineered in that iconic little building. It was an honour to join a rollcall beneath the names of Bob Dylan, Aretha Franklin, The Rolling Stones, The Allman Brothers, Lynyrd Skynyrd…

The Swampers, incredible musicians to a man, dropped in a few times over the two weeks. Guitarist Jimmy Johnson, drummer Roger Hawkins and bassist David Hood are not household names, not even in the States, but they are the musicians' musicians. I don't think they were just being polite when they said they loved the sound of the album. Praise indeed!

Barry and Jerry were very pleased with the sound of the record, too, and so were we. It was a very laid-back set-up there and the atmosphere was perfect for us. There wasn't that much work to do, just a bit of tidying up, a little dub here and there, but it sounded better and better coming through those speakers by the time we were done. At the same time, good news reached the studio about the growing success of the first album around the world. We were increasingly impatient to get out there and play, and we didn't have long to wait. After a few days back in London, we were back on the road.

Chapter 13

Into the Blizzard

The *Communiqué* tour was to run from early February 1979 and feature 116 concerts over five separate legs, three in Europe and two in North America, ending in London just before Christmas. It was a daunting schedule and it was probably just as well we didn't know that, by comparison with subsequent tours, it was no more than a leisurely stroll. It was a big moment for us, this, our first substantial tour, performing as a 'name' rather than as a band wanting to be known. People wanted to see us. Every show was sold out.

Admittedly, that wasn't very difficult on the first American leg because all the venues were small, booked before the album began to motor up the charts. There was pressure on us from Warners and the promoters to upgrade to larger venues, but we wanted to honour our commitments and so we rejected that plan. Besides, it was no bad thing to stoke demand. To meet the interest, the second leg in the States was added for the autumn.

It was daunting, too, because we were now public property, fair game for the critics. The second album was going to be released in

June, midway through the tour, and by the time we got to the Rainbow Theatre in north London on 20 December, our reputation would either have been enhanced or diminished. Playing live is one thing, but becoming an impressive live act is quite another. We were going to learn a great deal from the experience however the tour went and, as it turned out, by the time we were done, we were on our way to morphing into an entirely different outfit, and the music to come would be geared to public performance as much as to private listening. If you play to big audiences, you need a bigger, fuller performance: more sound, more lights, more projection. You need to put on a show rather than just step out under a few spotlights and play your tracks.

A week of gigs in Germany had been hastily tacked on to the start of the tour because we had become very popular there very quickly. The country that hadn't wanted to know us at the outset was now our most fervent champion. We kicked off with a night in the Dutch port of Rotterdam before crossing the border for six shows played to capacity crowds. In Cologne, on the day the album was released, we performed 'Down to the Waterline' on *Rockpalast*, the biggest music show in Germany, and it went out live to the whole country, fuelling our popularity still further. In terms of exposure, playing on national television was the equivalent of about ten thousand gigs.

In that severe winter, the coldest since the great freeze of 1963, Germany lay carpeted under a thick eiderdown of snow, and snow was falling heavily as we prepared to head north for our final performance in the industrial river port of Bremen. We woke up in Cologne to be told that Germany was experiencing its worst snowstorm in living memory and many roads were blocked, including some of the major arteries. It looked like the show was going to be cancelled, but we were determined to play it because we didn't want to disappoint the two and a half thousand fans who had bought tickets. That was a huge audience for us. The trains were apparently still running — they were fitted with snowploughs — and we decided to go for it, the whole band helping Pete Murdoch, Chas Herington and Pete Granger, the sound engineer, pile the equipment aboard.

When we arrived at Bremen, the snow outside the station lay so thick you couldn't see any of the parked cars and, with the roads impassable, we walked to the hotel through the deserted streets. The manager of the Stadthalle, astonished and delighted we had even attempted to make it, put out announcements on local radio to say the show was on. It was a big venue and the original plan had been to pull the curtains on the rear half, but the tickets kept selling and, when we came out, there was a full house of five thousand.

We kicked off with 'Down to the Waterline' and noticed straight off that Dave was playing but there was no sound coming from his guitar. I saw Pete Murdoch creep on stage and turn up his amp. At the end of the song, I saw Dave fiddling with the controls and, when we went into 'Six Blade Knife', again, you couldn't hear Dave. I looked at him, my face creased in curiosity, and mouthed, 'What's the problem?' Whatever it was, it seemed to be sorted, but towards the end of the set there was another curiosity as we went into 'Where Do You Think You're Going?', a song which grows in speed and power. As the song was pulling away, I felt it slowing down, like a high-speed train nearing a station. The drummer holds the speed controls, but when Mark and I looked back to him, Pick was looking the other way. The song pootled to its conclusion at an unnaturally slow rate and, when Mark and I turned to Pick, enquiring by the expression on our faces as to what the effing hell he was doing, he ignored us and carried on at his own pace.

The atmosphere afterwards in the dressing room was tense. Every band has tensions and rows. That's inevitable in a creative enterprise, especially under the pressure of live performance, trying to get it right night after night. Friction and debate are healthy, within limits, but it depends on the cause behind the tension. We went straight into quite a heated post-mortem and Pick said he had no idea what we were talking about, that he was just playing it as it felt right. Then Pete Granger, the out-front sound engineer, came in, absolutely steaming with Dave. Poor sound reflected badly on him, so he was probably anxious that we'd thought he'd screwed up somehow. There was a bit of a ruckus, Dave claiming he didn't like the sound coming from the amp, to which Pete said, 'How would you know? You couldn't fucking hear it, let alone listen to it.' Pete could be quite direct.

It was soon forgotten – or at least, parked – and we walked back to the hotel through the deep snow, because there were no cars or taxis, for a few beers, and packed our bags, ready to head home in the morning. Bremen was a massive step up for the band, a seminal moment in our growth, playing to five thousand people, all of whom had battled a severe snowstorm to come and see us. There was a great deal of media interest too, most of it landing on Mark, inevitably. It was our first experience, too, of autograph hunters. We'd signed the odd one here and there, but in Bremen there was a whole wolf pack, clutching pads and pens and pushing them under our noses. Autograph-hunting, we were to discover, was something of a national sport in Germany, so it wasn't quite as flattering as we might have felt in the moment. Even today, forty years on, I get about a dozen items a week in the post for me to sign, and there's always a German stamp on two or three of them.

Like the snowstorm, this huge surge in popularity came out of a blue sky and it was something of a shock. We realized that we were entering the chaotic maelstrom of success. The pressure was on, but though it had only just begun, it was clearly already being felt. By slowing down that track, Pick was maybe sending out the message that he wanted some control, to exert some influence. Bremen showed us that we all needed to be on the same page, singing from the same songsheet, so to speak; otherwise, the performance would go off track.

As for Dave, it was impossible to know what he was playing at. It was weird. Turning your own sound off in the middle of a huge concert was a very curious thing to do, and cutting himself out like that reflected on all of us. Back in London, we were too busy preparing to fly out to the States to give it much more thought, but Bremen was an alarm call. It was going to be different from there on. In the raucous clamour of that five-thousand-strong audience, a question had been shouted loud and clear: now that we had found success, did we have the steel and cohesion to handle it? We were about to find out. The States was next on the agenda and the anticipation was high. Both 'Sultans' and the first album were riding high over there.

It's worth reiterating what it's like on the road. Over the years, we were to play over a thousand major shows around the world, a few of them at the same venue twice, three, four times ... The set lists changed as new songs and new albums were added, but the experience was roughly similar each time, whatever the size of the audience. Each show is lived intensely in the moment. That engagement with the crowd, who have flattered you by paying good money to come along, is like nothing else. But the last chords die away, the lights drop and it's gone, spirited away into a giant, swirling, happy, misty ball of memory. From time to time, a show returns to me, but that'll be for extraneous reasons, or because it was somewhere iconic. Performing live is very much an experience to be relished in the here and now, like a great party, or a firework display, or an incredible evening with friends, or a walk through the woods on a perfect autumn morning. It's a concentrated, trance-like experience, and you know as you troop off stage, sweating and buzzing, happy as a skylark, that it's over, but that tomorrow you'll be doing it all over again, just in a town with a different name. It's what happens in between the shows that lingers in the memory.

So it proved on this, our first tour of the States, an almost impossibly exhilarating prospect as we touched down in Boston, knowing we'd be playing from sea to shining sea, border to border, and taking the stage at venues where so many great bands had performed: the Roxy, the Bottom Line, the Old Waldorf . . . You couldn't see or hear the nerves, the excitement, the tension, but you could feel them. Logistically, this was going to be our most complicated tour to date, with so many shows spread over thousands of miles. Ed had brought in a tour manager, Paul Cummins, to handle all that, and his choice was a masterstroke. We all took to Paul immediately, and not just because he was doing all the hard thinking and organizing on our behalf. He was smart and good fun — smart enough, at any rate, to wait until we had finished with Club Lafayette in Wolverhampton and Talk of the East in Lowestoft before coming aboard.

A brilliant organizer, superb man-manager, with a memory like a computer and an accountant's gift for figures, Paul was to be quartermaster general, reconnaissance commander and cavalry captain of the marching army that Dire Straits on the road was soon to become. He had worked with Andy Fairweather Low, XTC and Talking Heads, had seen us play at Hitchin College in November, apparently, had liked what he saw and wanted to get involved. (He remembers a bunch of punks at the front gobbing at Mark, and Pete Murdoch grabbing the mic and threatening to get down and sort them out, but he was beaten to it by the rest of the audience, who gave them a mighty thrashing and threw them out.) Paul was very good news indeed. He quickly became a great friend, and remains so today.

We started in the north-east, playing the big cities — Boston, New York, Washington, Buffalo and Cleveland — and crossed into Canada to play in Montreal and Toronto. But there were also places new to our geography: Willimantic, famous for its textile mills, so we learned; Providence, capital of Rhode Island, and one of the oldest settlements in the States; Upper Darby Township, Pennsylvania, where the folk-rock singer Jim Croce grew up . . . America shot by like the

Our first US/Canadian tour in 1979. Fifty-one shows
in thirty-eight days. Quite tiring but huge fun.

reel of a film gone berserk on fast forward. They were cosy, intimate gigs, most of them, the venues having the same vibe as somewhere like Ronnie Scott's in Soho, often with the audience sitting at tables, eating or being served drinks, the sound and lights excellent at all of them. It was all very civilized, the far end of the spectrum from the giant stadium show, and a far cry from Club Lafayette, with its two brawling drunks and no one else.

Often when we arrived at the club or theatre there'd be a small crowd out front looking for spare tickets, and there was always some press, reporters eager for an interview. It was incredible how many DJs claimed to have been the first in the States to have played our music. Sometimes we were doing two gigs a night to meet demand — fifty-one shows in thirty-eight days — making it even harder to disentangle one show from the next in the memory. Had we opted to upgrade venues and played to half-full floors, it might have been dispiriting. These little hothouse locations, with a small throng out in the cold pressing to get in, generated great atmospheres. It was the perfect introduction to a tour that might otherwise have felt overwhelming.

We had hired two giant Chevrolets and a small truck for the equipment to transport us around up on the Eastern Seaboard. In the depths of a frozen winter, there were some hair-raising moments driving through blizzards and trying not to slide off icy roads. At Wilimantic, we had time to kill and thought it a sensible plan to fill it by smoking some weed and racing around an empty ice-bound car park outside the Shaboo Inn, where we were to perform later in the day.

At Buffalo, in upstate New York, our dressing room out the back was, I think, some kind of a caravan and the temperature inside was about minus four, well below freezing anyhow, and it played hell with tuning the guitars. We got them sounding about right and crossed the car park into the venue, but it was so stiflingly hot in there the guitars went out of tune straight away and we had to spend a few minutes sorting them out. It was not the most heart-stopping start to a show, to be sure. The *Spinal Tap* theme was maintained throughout the performance because a massive artificial wall of flames had been installed between the stage and the audience. We could barely see the crowd, and they could barely see us, a surreal experience.

With a rare day off before the Buffalo show, we took ourselves to Niagara Falls, about twenty miles to the north. It was a breathtaking sight in the frozen landscape, every twig frosted, icicles hanging from every roof and branch and, in the middle of the falls, a giant ice sculpture formed by the water freezing as the raging torrent splashed up at the foot. Even more arresting was bumping into DJ John Peel, who was enjoying a short holiday with his wife. I don't think the Straits featured regularly on his playlist but he was very friendly and engaging and wished us well in 'this crazy country'.

It's part of the joy of touring that something eventful, dramatic or amusing occurs at every stop, breaking up what otherwise might become monotonous. The singer of our support band the previous night at the Bayou in Washington DC strutted on stage and hollered into the mic: 'Good evening, Chicago!' and someone hollered back, 'You're in Washington, you fucking idiot!' But the most memorable episode of this section of the tour was not quite so funny. Dave and I always shared one Chevvy, me at the wheel, him on the map. We were driving down to New York from the north, both quite excited because neither of us had ever been there and it was one of the world's great cities. Distracted, too, perhaps, because a few minutes earlier we had heard 'Sultans' on the radio. We were in the outskirts heading towards Manhattan, the skyline ahead a forest of skyscrapers, their windows lighting up as the sun headed down.

Almost as soon as we pulled off the freeway, we realized we had taken a wrong turn and driven into the Bronx, a byword for crime and violence, a no-go zone regarded as one of the most dangerous parts of NYC in the late seventies. There was no getting back on the freeway, so we had to keep going through a dozen sets of traffic lights, all of them red of course, and past lots of street corners where groups of young men were gathered. It very quickly became apparent that two fresh-faced lads in an expensive hire car was not an everyday sight in the Bronx, a poster district for inner-city deprivation and neglect.

When the street-corner group at the second set of lights spotted us they ran over to check us out, pressing their faces against the windows. We were fair game. Dave was shouting at me to jump the lights, and I could feel my heart rate breaking any previous personal bests. By the time we reached the last set of lights we were nervous wrecks, and it was a relief finally to cross into Manhattan and reach our hotel. It was good to be reminded there was a real world outside the little bubble of our band on the road.

We were staying at the Gramercy on Lexington Avenue, a hotel favoured by a lot of musicians which has since become quite luxurious. Back then it was cheap and we liked its bohemian vibe. We were to play two nights at the historic Bottom Line in Greenwich Village and, to our huge embarrassment, the record company sent over a limo to ferry us there. The Bottom Line is a cool little venue, and you really don't want to rock up there in an absurdly over-the-top stretch limo with a peaked-capped chauffeur opening the doors for you. Madison Square Garden maybe, but not the Bottom Line. We didn't want to play the swanky big shots, especially with Oxfam as our couturier. None of us ever felt that way. Success — yes, please; fame — no, thank you. As the traffic crawled along, the street thick with honking yellow cabs, we were alarmed to see a crowd under the awning entrance, our name on billboards either side. Quite a big crowd had gathered because the album had risen to number four and 'Sultans' was being played all over the radio. The driver was about to park up and as, luckily, no one could see us through the blacked-out windows, we told him to pull up around the corner. We jumped out and walked round the front. After the show, Warners had arranged for a presentation to mark the album going gold in the US, which meant

Our first visit to Texas. We discovered how huge and varied the US was, and it was a real thrill.

we had sold 500,000 units. It was our second gold; our first had been in the Netherlands, not long before. It was all moving very fast.

The next phase of the tour covered the big cities of the country's heart, so we headed further and further west, hearing 'Sultans' on the radio everywhere we went — Detroit, Chicago, Milwaukee, Kansas, Denver, Dallas, Houston and Austin — before, like the early American settlers, we finally reached the promised land of California, the Golden State. Pauline, and Dave's girlfriend, Chris, were flying out for the week, adding to the air of anticipation.

If you're an aspiring band, to be given the chance to play the Roxy in Hollywood and the Old Waldorf in San Francisco really does feel like the fulfilment of some sort of quest, a dream become reality. California was about six thousand miles from London and Deptford High Street, but it was an even longer way, figuratively. It had been a very long journey for all of us and, even if we were to fade into oblivion shortly after, pulling up at the fabled Sunset Marquis Hotel, our album at number four, no one was ever going to be able to take the memory of that thrill away from us. The Roxy is one gig I remember in Technicolor, footnoted detail. It was one of those episodes in life where the living of it is keenly felt, exquisite, rarefied. You experience it but are watching it happen like a great film or theatrical production at the same time, savouring every moment, never to be forgotten.

Chapter 14

The Night at the Roxy

Elbows on the balcony railing, I'm looking down on the Sunset Marquis pool, watching a guy spinning in his inflatable, nursing his Daiquiri, an uneasiness gnawing a little at my guts. My cocktail is different, a heady mix of nerves and exhilaration. I have been living off it for five weeks, night after night, coast to coast in the States. But tonight, the whirlwind tour almost done, there is a double shot of nerves in the shaker, two parts nerves to one part exhilaration, with a dash of fatigue and a twist of disbelief. We're playing the Roxy.

Neil Young, Frank Zappa, The Temptations, Bob Marley, Van Morrison, Bruce Springsteen, Chuck Berry, Lou Reed, Jimmy Cliff, The Ramones, Patti Smith, Etta James, Jerry Lewis, B.B. King . . . and 'Tonight, ladies and gentlemen, all the way from London, England, yes, please give it up for . . . Dire Straits!'

Or, in my head at least, please give it up for four lads from the borough of Lewisham.

That's how it feels anyhow — not quite believing it's real — and I am trying to get my head around the absurdity of it, pretend it's just another gig, like the ones we were doing a few months back. It's not a big gig, the Roxy, just a couple of hundred guests, but it's the Roxy. The Roxy! Tiny, but in its way, in kudos terms, as big as Madison Square Garden, the Hollywood Bowl, Wembley . . .

Right below me, Southern rock band the Ozark Mountain Dare-devils, all bushy beards and long hair, are poolside, slumped on loungers, swilling long-neck beers, bantering with the beautiful Californian babes milling around in their bikinis. A couple of cool-dude waiters are floating between the tables handing out cocktails and clearing the empties. The music is low but amplified in the intimacy of the pool area, a small courtyard overlooked by two storeys of rooms on all sides. The sky over to the west is a deep burnt orange fading to grey and the outdoor lights come on, silhouetting the mini-ature palm trees.

There's a hand on my shoulder. It's Mark.

'You all right?'

'Yeah, great, it's just, you know . . .'

'Weird.'

'Yeah, weird. A long way from Deptford, that's for sure.'

'Embrace it. We could be in the Dog and Duck begging for a mid-week slot after the darts match.'

I picture us around our little wooden table, four pints of brown ale, rolling our fags, moaning about the band on the little stage in the corner labouring through their set of Beatles and Stones tracks, a few old guys on their bar stools reading the *Racing Post*.

Below me, a guy with an afro is walking into the shallow end with a beer in one hand and a smoke in the other.

Mark says, 'Come on, we've got to go. Reception just called — the limo's here.'

'Limo!' This time it felt right. We were in Hollywood, for God's sake. You didn't take the bus.

We knock at Dave's and Pick's room and make our way down, past the pool, Pick playing the air with his imaginary drumsticks, the real ones sticking out of his back pocket. One of the reclining Ozarks, a hot beach-babe sitting on his lounger now caressing his chest hair, raises his beer bottle by the neck.

'Way to go, guys!' He smiles. 'The Roxy — you made it, man. Enjoy!'

In the air-chilled lobby, the doorman nods and stands aside, pulling open the door to the street, and we are back out in the soft, dry heat, making our way down the carpet under the long golden awning. Spring, like autumn, barely exists in LA. The temperature hovers between 60 and 70 degrees and I am overdressed in my charity-shop DJ jacket and heavy Levi's. A smiling chauffeur in his peaked cap has the rear door open for us and we disappear into the huge interior of the shiny black Lincoln, bigger than the kitchen back in Deptford.

We pull away, swing left into Sunset Boulevard — downtown Los Angeles behind us, Beverly Hills up ahead. We are all silent, staring out of the windows, taking in Hollywood's neon bar signs, the roller-bladers and the lightly stirring palms. Our second time in a limo in as many weeks. (We find out back in London the record company has put them on our bill, like breakfast at the Portobello, and the sirloins and salt beef in Nassau.)

A small crowd of a few dozen is hanging outside as the chauffeur eases the limo to the kerb. The Roxy looks like a detached family house, minus the stacked logs and plus double swing-doors. Right outside, there are two Hells Angels-style bouncers and a lamp post with a big orange neon 'R', like a giant lollipop, planted in the sidewalk between the towering palms. We climb out, a few heads turn our way and a guy with a boogie box on his shoulder shoots through us on his skateboard, trailing the smell of weed.

The owner, Lou Adler, record producer of The Mamas & the Papas and Sam Cooke, greets us in the lobby — Pick playing air drums probably the giveaway that we must be the band he'd booked. You can't mistake Lou, in his beret, beard and shades. He's very friendly, and none the worse, it seems, for his recent kidnapping and split from Britt Ekland. We shake hands, thank him for the honour of playing his venue and, yes, we promise to come and find him in the bar after the show.

'Hey, man, no idea you guys were English. That's so cool. The music sounds so, you know, American. Rock 'n' roll with a touch of the blues.'

Mark says in Geordie, 'Yeah, we've had that a lot since we've been here.'

The dressing room backstage is no bigger than the ones in the village halls back in England and, if we were lucky to get one at all, in the pubs too. We can swing a kitten, but not much more, and we're bumping into each other, cursing and apologizing as we get ready, heading out into the open of the passageway to neck a few beers before the guy comes and tells us it's time. 'The Roxy is full, guys, and it's ready to rock.'

When we flew out to the States we were in great shape, tight as a drum skin, not a chord or beat out of place, song after song. You can't hit the road out there unless your performance is at peak fitness. If you're not stage-ready and you're lucky to be playing on the right side of the tracks, they'll groan and shuffle away to the bar. In less courteous places, especially the unis and the hick towns, you'd better have some slick dance moves to avoid the shower of projectiles from the floor.

You probably won't see that in the Roxy, but I'd sooner take a hurricane of Bud bottles in Pig's Knuckle, Arkansas, than a glum silence in Lou Adler's joint. Screw up in the Roxy and influential people in the music world will soon get to hear you weren't up to much. Get the place jumping — and you never knew who would be in the audience any night at the Roxy — and the good news travels fast. These little gigs at iconic venues have a unique atmosphere, and the pressure to perform well was hard to put out of our minds. In front of a small, exclusive audience with big names from the music industry seated below, you really don't want to mess up.

We are on top of our game, roused by the sheer thrill of the experience, and we go straight on stage and into our set, no conferring, and kick off with 'Down to the Waterline': 'Sweet surrender on the quayside/You remember we used to run and hide . . .'

So far, so good, but it's unlikely anyone in the Roxy has heard of our tracks other than 'Sultans', least of all the new ones from

The Roxy in LA. What a night. Hanging out with
Bob Dylan afterwards was pretty surreal.

Communiqué, due to be released later in the year. That's in the back of my mind and the pit of my guts as we move through the set, feeling the heat of the moment — and the heat of the lights. But Mark's on top form and, thanks to all that practice, we are playing tight and seem to be going down well.

It's hard to tell if the audience is having a good time. It's no standing and they're all in the wall booths and the seats and tables on the floor. The stage lights are making it hard to distinguish faces in the darkness, let alone whether the faces are smiling, the toes tapping. The only people I see close up are the ones filing past the stage to my right into the restrooms. There's a lot of traffic heading both ways, like there's been an outbreak of dysentery or the pope's in there signing autographs. Then I notice most of the ones coming out are running a finger under their nose and I twig. Of course, we're in Hollywood.

When we finish, shirts drenched from the effort and the heat, we get a good cheer, the lights come up a little and one or two of the crowd are on their feet, applauding over their heads. Which is impressive for such a tough crowd who'd seen it all. We bow and hold up our hands in thanks. From their reaction, we seem to have passed the Roxy examination. But there's no time for a debrief and back-slap because one of the stage crew is leading us upstairs. The arm-crossed bouncer guarding the entrance looks us up and down — he's wearing better clothes than us — then he works out from the sweat we must be the band.

'Way to go, guys!' And he holds the door open for us.

I don't stop in my tracks but it's an effort to keep moving forward. The small bar is packed and all heads turn to us, a ripple of applause rolling around the room. But it's not that that's arresting my attention. It's Rod Stewart propping up the bar, saluting us with a finger and a big grin and waving us over. Rod Stewart — one of the biggest acts on the British music scene right then. And was that Britt Ekland with him? And there's Stevie Nicks! Stevie Nicks of Fleetwood Mac. And is that Linda Ronstadt?

Lou Adler sidles out of the crowd, tilting his bereted head, arms open, palms up, grin splitting his beard.

'Boys, what can I say? That was sure something. Magnificent. Loved it.'

He turns and taps a guy on the arm. The guy is dressed smart-casual, good-looking, tanned, late thirties.

Lou says, 'You guys know Jerry?'

'No, we don't know Jerry. Hi, Jerry.' We all shake hands with Jerry.

'Jerry is governor of California, probably the next president but one, we reckon.'

The penny drops. He's that politician who dates Linda Ronstadt. Jerry tells me he and Linda are going to be in London next week, en route to Africa. He's passionate about animals and the environment.

I'm only half listening. Because I am staring right at him. He's twenty feet away.

Bob Dylan.

Bob Dylan, hero of my teenage years, and now. Bob Dylan right there, at our gig, sitting at the other end of the bar. I feel a jab in my ribs. It's Mark.

'I know.'

'What do you say to Bob Dylan?'

'Good question.'

Dylan looks our way and taps the brim of his black felt hat.

'Okay, he's coming over.'

Dylan slides off his stool and through a posse of women, his backing singers, I guess. Mark and I walk towards him. We're shaking his hand. Bob Dylan's hand.

'That was great, guys,' he says. 'Congratulations. It's some sound you got going.'

Or words close to that effect, because I'm talking to an icon and

I'm in one of those trances where it feels like I'm under water, not taking it all in. For some reason, I'd imagined Bob Dylan would be a little aloof, looking down from his Olympus at the lesser mortals on the lower slopes. But not a bit of it. He's very friendly and laid-back.

We all drift back to the bar, we get beers and we start talking. He's very interested in Mark's songs and his distinctive playing style. In spite of being the heart of the band, and quite literally centre stage, Mark isn't crazy about being the centre of attention. He's shy and modest. But who's going to mind the spotlight if it's being beamed by one of the great figures of the twentieth century, the crown prince of sixties counterculture?

After a time, I leave them to it, to talk guitar and songcraft, and I work my way along the bar and find myself taking a shoulder-slap from Roderick David Stewart and having a beer thrust into my hand.

Towards the end of the night, the party starting to break up a little, Bob Dylan's still there, still talking.

He says, 'They put you up at the Sunset, I guess.'

We nod.

'Me too — why don't we hang out back there?'

A few minutes later we make our way downstairs — the pope still doing brisk trade in the restrooms — and they've got the limo around the front for us and we're cruising back down Sunset Strip, Bob Dylan and his chauffeur-cum-bodyguard following in their own.

Pick's got the biggest suite, so we head there and the man comes in, hat down over his eyes, a couple of wide-eyed Ozark Mountain Daredevils in his train. We get a crate of beers and some Jack Daniels sent up.

Dylan says, 'Hey, I've got some new songs I'd like to play you. Anyone got a guitar to hand?'

I go to my room along the corridor and fetch my Ovation acoustic and Mark goes to get his. I give mine to Dylan and the two of them start playing, the rest of us just hanging out, smoking and drinking beers. During the night, Dylan invites Mark — and later Pick — to go to Muscle Shoals, after our US tour, for the recording of his next album, *Slow Train Coming*.

We, the band, catch each other's eye from time to time and exchange grins. It's a far cry from a lock-in at the Oxford Arms and back to Farrer House for beans on toast, that's for sure.

The sun is crowning over the roof when the music stops, a pale pink light slanting over the empties. We sit back in silence, draining the last of our beers. Dylan is almost horizontal on the sofa, hat right down over his eyes, boots up on the coffee table.

Pick looks at his watch and says, 'Hey, it's April Fool's Day.'

Mark says, 'You don't say.'

Chapter 15

Into the Arena

The Germans were stalking us across the globe. A crew from Bavarian TV were there to film us at the Roxy and at the Old Waldorf in San Francisco, cutting it with grainy footage from back in Deptford and broadcasting it as a mini-documentary about our rise from deprived Deptford to the sun-kissed glamour of California. It was very well put together, but a strange experience to see us in our sink estate talking shiftily to camera, as bemused as anyone by what was happening. Half a year earlier, the idea of a European television crew knocking on the door of our council flat would have been met with gales of laughter.

Back in England, we had six weeks before the next leg of the tour began — two weeks in Europe, mainly in Germany and a month in the UK — and there was a little time to kick back and put our feet up. Mark and Pick went back to Muscle Shoals at the end of April to work on *Slow Train Coming*. Dylan was going through his heavily Christian period and Mark and Pick were slightly taken aback by the religious nature of the music, but they returned in buoyant mood from the experience of working with this semi-mythical figure of world music.

Our world was changing fast. At the same time as Maggie Thatcher was preparing to move into Downing Street, we were making plans to move out of number one Farrer House and into our own houses, in very slightly more upmarket areas of south London. Pauline and I were setting up home in Forest Hill. Everything was getting bigger. When we hit the road in Europe, Pete's decrepit van and the band's hire car had been replaced by a couple of trucks and a tour bus, the crew had gone from three to about a dozen, and we had our own catering unit, run by Lorraine, quickly and inevitably dubbed Quiche Lorraine. She was another much-loved stalwart who was to stay with us for many tours.

The venues we played were all roughly three thousand capacity, including Circus Krone, a massive indoor big-top tent in Munich. They were all full — we could have sold at least double the tickets — and the autograph hunters descended on us like General Blücher's Prussians at Waterloo. Not all of them were innocent, wide-eyed fans, we soon discovered; some were professional collectors on the hunt for signed albums and pictures to sell.

We played four festivals, in Dortmund, Munich, Berlin and in the Loreley Valley near Frankfurt, our first experience of massive out-door gatherings. Set on the bend of the Rhine, the Loreley Festival was the most spectacular we had played up to that point, sixty thou-sand fans against a picture-postcard backdrop. The other bands in the line-up included The Police, who we shared a dressing room with, and Talking Heads, Whitesnake, Dr Feelgood and the Tom Robinson Band, all of us warm-up acts for Barclay James Harvest, the English prog rock band, who were massive in Germany. It was both flattering and daunting that Dire Straits had been chosen to come on just before the headliners, ahead of all those big names, proof that we were working our way up music's food chain at an alarmingly fast rate. Twelve months earlier, we had been squinting through the smoke from the corner of a small London pub, but now we were looking out over a vast sea of swaying faces. The biggest indoor gig we played — had ever played, probably — was staged in Paris before about five thousand at the Palais des Sports.

Communiqué came out in mid-June, and it was generally well received, climbing to number five in the UK and going straight to number one in Germany, leapfrogging the first album, which was still at number three. Both stayed up there for months and it was the only time in German chart history, up to then, that a band had had two albums in the top three. It went gold or platinum in twelve countries, selling heaviest of all in France, which was weird, because we had barely toured or promoted it there. The first album had also reached number five not long before and it was to stay in the charts for two and a half years, dispelling our fears that there would barely be time for it to bed in before it was trumped by the second.

In early September, we went back to the States for a month, this time to play large venues and travelling not in Chevvies but in a tour bus. We played a gig every day but two, moving by night across the country. It was as tiring as it was invigorating, and inevitably there was tension around, more felt than seen or heard. There were a great deal of publicity demands this time, with interviews for radio and press at every stop, most of them fielded by Mark. He was under huge pressure, off stage and on it, but he was handling it in a characteristically phlegmatic and composed way, and the band was playing well, not a dud gig among the twenty-two.

It was now that Paul Cummins came into his own, commanding the crew, the itinerary and dealing with every hotel and venue. His smile was as broad as his shoulders, and he was loving the challenge. It was an impressive effort because this was his first experience of a tour on that scale. Having a much bigger crew was a boost to our morale. Now we were part of a wider effort and the strains were shared, the tension dissipated. We could see that we, the musicians, were not the only ones under pressure to get our jobs done, and done well. And to time. All of a sudden, we were part of a very big family, a band of travellers, all looking out for each other, all pulling in the same direction to achieve the same end: put on a great show.

They are a worldly lot, a road crew, and most of ours were veterans of global tours with a stack of tales to regale us with. The communal meals were a great way to bring us together and for the band to hear about what was going on behind the scenes. Our bubble had been blown way bigger and it was uplifting to be part of this huge, daily collective effort: arrive at the venue, unload, build the stage, set up the equipment, build the lighting rigs, uncoil miles and miles of leads and cables, prep the instruments, do the soundcheck, walk on stage at eight-thirty, go straight into the set, drink beer, grab food, conduct post-mortem, pack up and hit the highway for the next city. Our crew, most of them Welsh, were as good as any attached to any band on the road at the time and a great many of them stayed the course with us.

A top crew, well marshalled by a highly efficient generalissimo like Paul Cummins, is the golden key to a good tour. In almost a thousand gigs, our guys never screwed up once. We never missed a gig, we were never late on stage, nothing ever collapsed, caught fire or suffered a catastrophic breakdown. People remember the band, not the crew, but there was no way we could have become the huge live act around the world that we did if our crew had been even three quarters as professional as they were. We went on stage, everything ready to roll, knowing that Pete Granger, out front, was going to squeeze the best sound from every song, Chas Herington would put the lights in the right place at the right time, Adrian Fitzpatrick would be a wizard on the monitoring desk. Within a couple of hours of the last chords fading out, we'd be packed up, on the road, crashed out with a beer on the buses.

We had a couple of weeks off before we crossed the Channel for the third time since February, the convoy even larger now, the itinerary extending into Scandinavia and taking us as far north as Gothenburg. We were on the road for four weeks and on the three days that there was no gig we were ploughing up and down motorways, crossing border checkpoints to get to the next location. With just a few hours' sleep a night, we were soon running off adrenaline generated by the reception that greeted us at each venue.

They were big shows, up to about five thousand people at each gig — a fact I mention not to boast about our growing popularity but to underline the enormous pressure soon bearing down on the band. The twin pressures of rapid success and the exhaustion of long back-to-back tours have broken hundreds of bands over the years. For us, as with other bands, the problem was that there was no time to take stock, to adjust, to share and discuss how we were all coping. You just bang on from one show to the next, go home, crash out and decompress for a few days, put in some TLC with your long-suffering wife or girlfriend, and then you're back in the studio or on the road. That is not to invite sympathy but to provide an insight into why it is that some bands, or band members, just can't hack it. I flag that up here with sympathy, not censure.

It was a similar story back in Ireland and the UK, where, after two shows in Dublin and two in Belfast, we finished with four in London, two back in our old stomping ground at the Lewisham Odeon and two at the Rainbow Theatre in Finsbury Park. When we had toured the UK back in the early summer, there may have been one or two autograph hunters at the stage door; now there was a crush of about fifty to a hundred. It's flattering when a fan wants you to scrawl your name in a notepad or on a picture, but it was becoming difficult to satisfy the new demand. You could spend an hour scribbling away when you needed to be doing a soundcheck or, at the end, when you're shattered and just want to go to bed. As a band, we were not

*About as close to Deptford as we could get to play
in 1979 following the US tour.*

interested in the limelight and we filtered out as much of the publicity as Ed and the record labels would allow us to get away with. For me, the interaction with the audience when playing live is the greatest of all experiences to be enjoyed in a band. That connection with so many people, a seething, happy mob, all of you moved and united by the shared experience of the music, is a magical phenomenon. But by the end of 1979, we were keen to leave the joy of that reciprocal love inside the auditorium and flee the additional attention before and after.

Christmas was four days away when we arrived at the Rainbow, pretty shattered, partly from month after month on the road but mainly from the two full years of remorseless effort, the constant daily demands on our time. The physical exertion of touring, all the attention and the need to be helpful and charming, not seeing our girlfriends, not sleeping in our own beds, the pressure of playing live night after night, not living as healthily as we might at home . . . The aggregate of all that took its toll and we went our different ways for Christmas, all of us exhausted.

We were all suffering one way or another, and that came across in a documentary about the band made by Alan Yentob, future Director of Programmes at the BBC, for the corporation's *Arena* series. Watching it today, you can see how frazzled we were. This was partly because we hadn't been looking after ourselves physically, even though, being young, we look like we're in good shape. Refuelling with the usual after-gig refreshments may have given us short-term, nightly relief but, over a long tour, you pay the cumulative price, the compound interest of late-night snacking and pints and any other self-medication of choice. It was around then that I gave up smoking and, although there had always been an unspoken agreement not to drink before a gig, from there on we got a bit smarter about how we unwound afterwards too. No one had anything like a serious problem with drink or drugs; it was just a case of how we unwound, dulled the post-gig buzz, and the lack of sleep that entailed. The main problem was exhaustion and tensions inside the band and with girlfriends, who were always having to compromise. Ed remembers this period as the lowest in the band's experience.

Our relationships with our partners had inevitably suffered after a year or two away from 'normal' domestic life. How could they not? I can't speak for the others but, for me, there was one time I dropped my guard. I loved Pauline very much, it was a dumb mistake, but frankly, you had to be a kind of saint to resist all the temptations all of the time. You could pretty well have whatever or whoever you wanted, any night of the tour, and there were plenty of people hanging around the band to indulge you in your moments of weakness.

I won't forget a night in a German hotel bar after a gig when Dave and I were at a table enjoying a beer and trying to decompress before heading up to bed. The promoter came over and, talking like a waiter reading off the specials menu, gave Dave a full range of options: black, white, fat, thin, old or young. Dave's face was a picture. He thought it was a joke at first. When he realized the man was deadly serious, he politely declined. That's how easy it was to stray. You didn't even have to get out of your chair. Then you had all the fans milling around, and many of them were gorgeous and very open-minded. You had to be really strong. I wish I could say I learned my lesson that first time. Partnered with a gorgeous and intelligent woman like Pauline, why would I go looking elsewhere? The only answer I can give is that after month after month in an all-male environment, I felt a growing need for female company – and that's not a euphemism. If you spend a year on the road like that, it gets to you. The only saints are dead.

I watched the *Arena* documentary again recently to remind myself of our state of mind at that period. The documentary filming was done in April, by which time you'd think we might have recuperated and rediscovered our zest, having downed tools at Christmas. Not so. We come across as quite a gloomy bunch, with the exception of Pick, who is chirpy – and amusing about his youth as a drummer in the Boys' Brigade marching band in Leicester. Mark, as ever, is philosophical and darkly humorous about new fame and its demands. I'm fairly candid and a bit downbeat about the tensions emerging in the band. Dave comes across as pretty miserable, admitting that he finds the strains of touring intolerable, that his relationship with Mark is in serious trouble and that he cannot foresee how we can survive another album and a long overseas tour. Yentob did not need to be Sherlock

Holmes to pick up on this as the principal theme and the programme ends with Dave talking to camera and predicting doom in the near future.

By then – late spring 1980 – Mark and Ed had been to New York to check out studios and a producer for our third album, then untitled, but to become known as *Making Movies*. One of the suggestions was Jimmy Iovine, hot news at the time after great work on Patti Smith's album *Easter* and Tom Petty and the Heart-breakers' *Damn the Torpedoes*. Mark was impressed by the production values on both and he and Ed came back convinced that Jimmy was the one to work with to help us develop musically. Our experience at the huge Loreley Festival on the Rhine and many other big gigs had convinced us that we needed to bridge the gap between a mellow studio sound and one more suitable for live perform-ance before large crowds. That meant more instrumentation – keyboards, above all.

On his return, Mark and Paul Cummins, who had struck up a good friendship on tour, took a break in Brittany with their girl-friends. Mark had been under constant pressure and he needed a quiet pause before tackling the next album. The band was contrac-tually obliged to have songs ready for a third album to be released in October and, even though he was coming off the back of that gruelling tour, he had written most of them before heading to France. His ability to work under the pressure of these deadlines, with so many other demands on his time, was very impressive. It was a good idea to take himself off somewhere remote, away from all the publicity, noise and attention, with Paul. Ed Bicknell was a brilliant band manager and businessman, but he was not a man you shared your problems with. Paul had different gifts, among them the ability to empathize, an essential skill when dealing with the army of a road crew and the inevitable stresses that emerge in any band on the road.

Before we headed to New York, we went back to Wood Wharf to work on the new songs Mark had written, which included 'Tunnel of Love', 'Romeo & Juliet', 'Espresso Love', 'Solid Rock' and 'Skateaway'. It was an exciting moment, as it always was when you were presented with a collection of songs in the raw and you set to work on them.

I had already heard 'Romeo & Juliet' and, if the other songs were of similar quality, it was looking very promising. Mark had come over to my house in Forest Hill with his guitar and said he wanted to play me a song he had been working on. It was about a failed love affair, he said, and started plucking the first chords — so familiar now — and then he started singing it and there was an instant thrill, an immediate recognition that he had written something very special. Mark had been struggling in his private life, and I was astonished that he was able to produce something so beautiful while being so distracted. But, thinking about it afterwards, I realized it was precisely because he had been troubled and anxious that he was able to be so creative. I doubt whether much, if any, great music, art or literature has ever emerged from the souls of the complacent. A soul in a state of agitation has a better chance of producing great art than one at ease with itself.

The last tour could not have ended soon enough, and we were all delighted to have had the chance to take a break from music, and from each other. It did the trick. The contrast in mood and attitude could not have been greater. It's a completely different experience, but studio work can be just as thrilling as playing live. You're creating, and there's a deep satisfaction to be taken from giving a song form, structure and energy. We were a happy group again, playing music, working on some great new songs, back in our first musical home. Wood Wharf was very rudimentary, but it was our haven and we loved it. Its very location, just down the river from the *Cutty Sark* at Greenwich, literally up the creek and figuratively away from the flow of daily life, created a cocoon where we could work without distraction. There wasn't even a phone in the studio.

By the time we were ready to head out to New York in June, we appeared to be in a far better space than six months earlier. There was a fantastic album there for the making, in a great studio, our private lives had been squared away — at least for the time being — we had lived clean and slept well, we had two highly successful albums behind us and, for the first time ever, we each had a few quid in the bank and a car in the drive. What could possibly go wrong?

Chapter 16

Grim Fairytale of New York

This is going to be a tough chapter to write, and I have to be careful about it. Two brothers falling out is no one else's business but theirs. But, inevitably, it had become the band's problem as well. As a great friend to both, it was painful to witness and to have to deal with. I remain friends with both, one more than the other, partly because I live down the road from him and he has probably become the greatest of many friends accrued over the years. But you're all brothers, of sorts, in the tight-knit, sometimes claustrophobic, family-style unit of a band. The pain of a bust-up is felt by all, shared by all, and it doesn't go away. There were no winners in New York. Once the bell for the final round rang and the struggle played itself out, as it had to, there was just an aching sadness, an emptiness.

I say there were no winners but, as far as the band went — and it's quite a big 'but' — the storm was to leave behind fresh air and blue skies, a better kind of emptiness. Parking the personal here, in terms of getting on with our profession, it was a positive development. Free of friction, unburdened by heavy tension, we pushed on as a happier unit for having put an end to an awkwardness that had been under-mining our progress. Mark had written a bunch of great songs and there was a strong sense that we were about to produce something very special. We were at a high point of creativity, under a deadline to produce a new album. The pressure was high as it was. Perhaps it was the subliminal awareness of this that triggered the bust-up, the knowledge that the next album and tour were going to dwarf in scale the two that had gone before; another year on the road, another year away from home, even more media attention, bigger crowds, more pressure.

Who knows — maybe Dave sacrificed himself for the greater cause without even knowing that was what he was doing? There was definitely a sense of pre-ordained destiny about what happened and, in a way, Dave probably did fall on his own sword. With pride at stake, the pressure on, it was the only way it could be done. A quick hand-shake, an exchange of best wishes and a taxi to the airport would have been worse, in a way. Dave couldn't just get up and say, 'Guys, I'm not sure about all this. I'm going to go and chill and think about it in London for a bit,' then casually slip away. To see the deed done, it had to be dramatic and spectacular.

There is no doubt, as Dave freely admits and admitted at the time, that the stress of success and the exhaustion of touring had taken its toll on him way more than it had on the rest of us. A few like it, some tolerate it, many can't stand it. Dave loved it and hated it. There is nothing shameful in shunning the limelight. We're all built differ-ently, temperamentally, one character no better than the next; some are more suited to centre stage, others to the shadows. Problem was, Dire Straits had now become very successful, so there was going to be even more exposure, attention and pressure.

I may be talking out of line here, but maybe it was partly a case of one sibling living in the shadow of another. It is easy to understand how hard it must have been for Dave, a talented musician, to have to play second fiddle, musically and publicly, to a great songwriter and guitarist. But on the other hand, what was Mark to do? Chuck it all in to make his brother feel okay? Of course not. This was the stuff of Shakespearean tragedies: the collision of two mutually exclusive goods — or at least two mutually exclusive positions — that could end in no other way but misery; two brothers who loved and admired each other blown apart by circumstance. And thus it came to be written, this dark fairytale of New York.

The Power Station, so called because that's what it used to be, was a fairly new recording studio, situated on West 53rd Street between Ninth and Tenth Avenue in an area of midtown Manhattan known as Hell's Kitchen. It had been gorgeously refurbished, with wood panelling on the walls and big sofas everywhere, a very far cry indeed from Wood Wharf, but the areas were similar in history and, both down by the water, in appearance too. For decades, Hell's Kitchen was home to thousands of poor Irish immigrants, attracted by work on the nearby wharfs and docks of the Hudson River, just as the people of Deptford had once been drawn to work on the Thames. We felt at home in the Power Station. It was still fairly rough around the edges. We made the twenty-minute walk there every morning after a massive breakfast at a restaurant called Woolf's, but we always got a cab back or walked in a group of four or five. No sober or sensible New Yorker would have walked alone through Hell's Kitchen after dark. No sober or sensible New Yorker would eat — could eat — for at least twelve hours after breakfasting at Woolf's. No kidding, every day we each ate a huge pile of eggs, bacon and hash browns, tomatoes and mushrooms on a plate the size of Central Park.

We arrived in June for a two-month stint, and to save on hotel bills we rented apartments on a block overlooking Central Park. It was not just the Bronx, the whole of New York was still edgy and dangerous then, yet to be cleaned up by a massive law-and-order campaign in the nineties after a crack epidemic led to an even higher spike in crime. Central Park, in spite of the wealth that overlooked it, wasn't much safer than Hell's Kitchen once the sun had sunk. Murders and rapes took place in the park while we were there, just a few hundred yards from where we walked or slept. Heading to the studio in the morning was like walking through the set of a *Starsky & Hutch* or *Kojak* episode. Tramps filled the doorways, unshaded lightbulbs hung in the grimy windows of dilapidated apartment blocks, gangs hung out in caged basketball courts and sirens wailed 24/7.

Why is it that a down-at-heel, menacing area is so much more inspirational than a comfortable, leafy one? I guess the vigilance heightens the awareness of your environment, makes you feel plugged in. No doubt, had we recorded our third album in the genteel comfort of the Hamptons, for instance, it would have been a different album. The vitality of Hell's Kitchen, life in the raw every way you looked, stirred us up and absorbed that tension.

The studio was dominated by the personality of Jimmy Iovine, co-producing with Mark and a man so plugged into the mains you could see his bones through the glow. If he spoke to you for an hour, which he'd be very happy to do, the transcript of it would make a small novel. He was wired, a true 'New Yoiker', of Italian ancestry. When Mark and Ed had met him earlier in the year, he had been wearing a canary-yellow zip-up jumpsuit and a bright red baseball cap, and his dress sense tells you everything you need to know about the character within. Jimmy spent an astonishing amount of time on the phone and he was no sap as a businessman, so Ed had had to put in some hard negotiating shifts to get his fees down. Jimmy was great, very organized and born with the gift of a great ear, but a lot of the hard work in that studio was done by his sound engineer, Shelly Yakus.

Shelly was a strong personality and a perfectionist. Never before had we undergone such a fierce examination of our equipment in order to achieve the sound Shelly was after. Many hours were spent trying out different bass strings and drum skins. I liked the slightly deadened sound of the old strings on my '59 Fender Precision, but he wanted me to use fresh ones. I must have changed them a dozen times, but none of them seemed to please him and, eventually, I was allowed to use the ones I felt comfortable with.

Pick had it even worse and Shelly was especially obsessive about the sound of his snare drum. The studio was a big room and this search for the perfect sound ended one day with the entire floor carpeted in discarded drum skins. Towards the end of the day, Pick got up, walked over the sea of skins and said, 'I'm not hitting that drum one more fucking time. If you don't like it, get an assistant in to hit until you're happy.' A studio assistant was called in to finish the experimentation, and all was well.

Jimmy and Shelly wanted the best sound possible before we put the music to tape. We were working long days, putting in a massive effort to get the best out of the new material. As always when recording, it was a process of trial and error.

Keyboards were going to be an important element of the music, and Mark had asked Jimmy to seek out a good player. We got better than that — we got Roy Bittan from Bruce Springsteen's E Street Band. He made an instant and sublime impact on the songs, especially 'Tunnel of Love' and 'Romeo & Juliet', and the introduction of the keyboards opened up a whole new range of possibilities for all our music to blossom. He had provided the missing link in our development. He was only with us for a couple of days, but his contribution had a transformative effect and he was an absolute delight to work with. Today, when fans of Dire Straits dwell on the music, they think of keyboards as well as guitars. It didn't redefine the band, but it certainly added richness and diversity to our music, and that would

One of the first Music Man basses I bought in the early eighties, used on the Making Movies *tour. I still use it on stage today.*

have a big impact on our performances on the upcoming tour. The arrangement possibilities of each song became boundless.

We were always looking for ways to move the band forward. *Making Movies* was a major departure for us, but we never strayed too far from the original sound. We just added layers. Mark was forever interested in new equipment, new instrumentation, constantly searching for something fresh to add.

The Fender Stratocaster guitars were the hallmark sound of the first two albums, but in New York Mark discovered Rudy's Music Shop, recently established but soon to become a favourite haunt when we were in the city. If you're a guitarist, Rudy Pensa's musical emporium is like Santa's grotto. Like legions of other professional musicians, Mark and I have bought many beautiful guitars from Rudy over the years. On this occasion, searching for a different sound, Mark went for a red Schecter with Seymour Duncan vintage pick-ups. Schecters are beautifully made guitars, used by big sound proponents like Prince and Pete Townshend.

In spite of what was to unfold, it was a wonderful experience putting down *Making Movies* in the Power Station. I am not sure I have ever felt so alive, musically or creatively, as I did there in the summer of 1980.

So, we'd already be there in the studio, having covered a dozen blocks and walked off our enormous Woolf's breakfast, when Shelly arrived with his beer cooler rammed with vitamins and supplements. Many New Yorkers seemed to be paranoid about their health and I don't think I ever saw him eat what the rest of us would recognize as 'food'. He seemed to just live off enormous health shakes, made in his mixing contraption, which made the walls shake when he pressed the button.

It was usually late morning when Jimmy rocked up and it was never long before he'd get off the phone and bark at Shelly, something along the lines of 'Shelly, that snare drum sounds like shit.'

Shelly used to shout after him, 'Asshole!' After a while, you realized this was just a bit of New York street theatre; no hard feelings. It was intense, but it was great fun and we got on well enough for Jimmy to invite us back home one evening for his Italian mother to cook us some truly fine food. That was one of the rare good meals I ate while I was there. Our diet was poor, mainly takeaways. The monster breakfast in the morning was followed in the evening by pepperoni-heavy pizzas or half-pound burgers sent up to the studio, followed by a bunch of beers on the way back to bed. Pick and Dave often used to head off back to the apartments, and Mark and I would call in at a cellar bar called the Possible 20 and have a few drinks to unwind. Halfway between Hell's Kitchen and Central Park, it was a bar well known to musicians living in or visiting New York, and one night we ended up having supper with Thin Lizzy's Phil Lynott, who Mark had done some studio work with. Phil was clearly struggling with the lifestyle.

It can be hard to look after yourself when you're not at home, when you're working long hours into the night, often eating on the fly. I had already given up the smokes, but the unhealthy lifestyle caught up with me in New York. It was probably all the breakfasts and burgers, but my guts were complaining, so badly that I sought help. It being the music industry, and it being New York, I didn't get recommended to a gastric expert or surgeon but to a very small Asian shiatsu master who walked up and down my back and put me on a diet of seaweed.

Bad guts looked like they were going to be the least of my health problems the night I took a cab back home from the studio by myself. It was only a ten-minute ride and, it being so late, there was virtually no traffic around, so when the cabbie took a strange turn, back towards the dock areas, I leaned forward and said, 'Where are you going? I think it's the other way.'

'Hey, buddy, I know where I'm fucking going!'

'But you're going in the wrong direction.'

At which point he pulled over into a side-street and — there was no glass or meshed barrier in cabs then — he spun round, flashing a very large knife at me, barking, 'Don't you fucking tell me how to do my job.' The words were barely out of his mouth and I was out the door and running as fast as I'd run since my schooldays.

The album was to feature just seven songs, and only one of them — 'Solid Rock' — was shorter than four minutes. It was no surprise that the best-loved tracks turned out to be 'Romeo & Juliet' and 'Tunnel of Love'. They are beautifully crafted songs, songwriting at its best. I have never tired of playing them, even today, forty years on, in my solo career. Today, 'Hand in Hand' is not as well known or played, but that deserves a place on the top shelf too, and 'Solid Rock' is great to perform live. The track 'Les Boys' is something of an eccentric anomaly, a light comic song inspired by a gay cabaret act from Birmingham which we saw in our hotel bar in Munich late one evening after a gig. Gay Brummie cabaret acts were not a staple of pub or hotel entertainment back in the UK in the late seventies, and these lads had come to Germany, which was way more open-minded, to seek work. For us, but not for the dozens of portly middle-aged German executives in the bar and a smattering of hookers, it was bizarre and very amusing to watch them talk and sing in their heavy Midlands accents. They came and joined us after their performance and they were highly amusing company.

The light comedy of 'Les Boys' was certainly not an appropriate soundtrack for the mood in the studio that developed over the first few weeks of recording. Dave's growing unhappiness was manifest in his body language, his muttered complaints and his reluctance to do what was being asked of him. It created quite a negative, tense atmosphere. There was an incredible, thrilling energy in the creation of that album, but the tension was eating away at it. As his old mate, I tried to speak to him about his mood, openly, frankly and sympathetically. (Thank God, Ed wasn't around too much. His advice to Dave would have been very short and to the point!)

'It wasn't meant to be like this,' Dave would say, meaning the scale of the success and all the pressures that it entailed. To which I could only say, 'Well, it is! It is what it is, so we just have to get on with it. It's irreversible. We can't turn back the clock and go back to the Hope and Anchor.'

But he was not a happy man. There was only one way it was going to end — and it wasn't with the band folding or going back to the pub circuit and a quiet life in Deptford. He and Mark were not talking much and, to avoid an open dispute, it was easier to let Shelly and Jimmy tell him what to do and for me to encourage him. There was no single event that led to the rupture. It had been building for at least a year.

Mark was very much the band leader, and rightly so, and for Dave, the younger brother, that was difficult. I got that, but the resentment and the gloom were dragging us all down and it all came to a head one day in the studio. There was a pretty simple guitar part for Dave to play on 'Romeo & Juliet', and when Dave came into the studio having not worked on it, Jimmy, as producer, told him quite sharply to go away, learn it and we'd put it down the next day. The argument erupted when Dave came back the next day still not having done so. We were all going, 'Come on, Dave, we need to move on.' It was banter, but with an edge of impatience and anger that our efforts were being held back because he was not pulling his weight like the rest of us. We were all tired and a little fractious.

Mark had held his tongue throughout but was getting more and more frustrated — there was more at stake than just the recording of the album. They were family, with the same loving mother and father, and a bust-up would be a cause of despair for all. But now he snapped and gave Dave both barrels. There was quite a lot of storming in and out and, eventually, Dave went back to the apartment to be with his girlfriend, Chris. Back in the studio, we all agreed that the situation had become unsustainable and we had to give Dave an ultimatum – and I volunteered to do that and set off for Central Park.

There was no shouting. It was just very sad. We sat and talked. He unloaded, saying how hard he was finding it and admitting that his demons were becoming demons for us all.

I said, 'There are two ways to resolve this. Come back to the studio, bury the hatchet with Mark and we crack on – or you go home.'

Dave said, 'Well, I'm going home.'

As I walked back to the studio, the anger I had been feeling morphed into a deep despondency. Dave was a mate and his friendship had set me on this thrilling musical journey. Of greater significance, he was Mark's brother and there was no way their row was going to be patched up over a pint back in London.

'Dave's going home,' I said, walking into the control room. The news was met with blank faces, and for ten minutes or so we milled around the studio in silence. Then Jimmy said, 'Right, let's get on with it!' and we picked up our instruments and went back to work.

The few small contributions Dave had made to the recording were taken off, and Mark re-did them. Sid McGinnis, a very accomplished session musician who has worked with a number of top bands and artists, was brought in by Jimmy. It was distressing but inevitable, the way it had panned out, but from a professional point of view, frankly, there was a great deal of relief in the studio afterwards. Mark is a very private person and I am sure he was having great difficulty dealing with what had just happened. We knew to leave him alone to do that. He's a consummate professional, and we all got back to the music, the perfect diversion. A great album was some sort of consolation, but the emotional cost was high.

To his eternal credit, after some time out Dave threw himself back into music, working hard on the piano as well as the guitar. Already a good player, slowly he turned himself into a fine musician and in 1983 produced his first solo album, which I played on. Since then, he has released an album every two or three years and toured all over the world. Like the Straits, he did well in Germany. I have stayed in touch with him, but we never mention 'the war'!

Chapter 17

The Big Wheel Keeps on Turning

When we got back to London at the end of August 1980, there was certainly no time to dwell on the ructions in New York. We had to crack on — fast. The American leg of the *On Location* tour, as it had been dubbed, was just seven weeks away and we were short of a guitarist and a keyboard player. Paul Cummins went on the hunt as soon as we landed — and it was more than just an excuse to use his giant car phone, because whoever came in was going to have a lot of songs to learn, very quickly. Paul had acquired one of the early models of the satellite phone and he was very, very proud of it, like a kid at Christmas with an Atari computer game. It was so big he almost needed both hands to hold it to his ear, but it made his job much easier. We needed to get into Wood Wharf with a full band as soon as possible. They needed to be the right musical fit, but the right characters too. We really didn't want any more friction.

Paul's first call was to keyboardist Alan Clark, who he knew from his friendship with Scottish duo Gallagher & Lyle. Alan had also played with Lindisfarne and Newcastle rock outfit Geordie in a line-up that included future AC/DC frontman Brian Johnson. Alan, a free agent at the time, was lying in bed when the phone rang, but it took some persuasion by Paul to get him down to Wood Wharf. Alan liked the band, and the Newcastle connection was an influence, but he feared we were too guitar-based and that he might end up no more than a bit-part player, with no musical space for him to indulge his prodigious talents. When he turned up at the studio in Deptford, he came more out of curiosity than in high hopes, but when he was played the new tracks from *Making Movies*, he liked what he heard. He never left. We had bagged ourselves a very fine keyboard player.

Good guitarists are easier to find, but whoever came in had the tough task of stepping into Dave's shoes and he had to be the right fit on all counts. Paul placed an ad in *Melody Maker*, which, in hindsight, seems an extraordinary thing to have done, like we needed a cleaner or someone to cut the hedges. One candidate was turned down, time was running out, and Paul was scratching his head furiously when the phone rang late one evening. There was a mellow Californian voice on the other end of the line and a guy called Hal Lindes announced himself. Hal who? Paul had never heard of him and, it turned out, he had never played with a band of any note. A lover of British music of the sixties, Hal had come over from California and had played the pub circuit for a few months before joining a post-punk band called Darling, but it had not been a happy experience. The band split straight after the release of its only album and he was on the hunt for a fresh challenge. You had to admire Hal's chutzpah. It took some balls to put yourself up for a band plated with gold and platinum when you'd never played a venue bigger than a boozer.

Hal told Paul he played a '59 Strat in the raw rock 'n' roll style of players like Keith Richards. Well, thought Paul, we're going for a harder rock sound, so what was the harm in giving the kid a try-out? He certainly wasn't short of the confidence he was going to require.

Paul told him to work on a few songs from *Communiqué* and come down to Wood Wharf in the morning for an audition. Hal didn't have a copy of the album so he rang around his mates and, having finally got hold of one, sat up all night working on the songs.

It took him time to find his way to the studio and things didn't bode too well when he rocked in half an hour late, an apologetic grin on his cherubic face. Paul was fuming. Mark handed him a Walkman and told him to listen to some of the new tracks before we got to work. The boy could play, no doubt about it, and over the next couple of days he worked really hard on refining his raw style to suit the songs – 'taking some sandpaper to smooth off the rough edges', as he put it. He was a fast, eager learner, and he came with the added bonuses of being an incredibly good-looking guy with a gentle soul. The question you have to ask yourself when a new band member is being considered is: can I face this guy at breakfast for 250 mornings a year? We knew by the end of the first day that Hal would fit right in. We had our band.

Hal and Alan integrated themselves quickly and we soon left together for a short promo trip to Europe, miming our way around TV studios and doing hideous amounts of press. For the next few weeks we worked on songs and set lists for the tour, all variations on the same theme: start with a bang, take it right up, bring it down, raise the tempo and go out with a bang. Getting the ebb and flow of the set is crucial. You may have fifteen great songs, but if you knock them out randomly, with no structure, they don't really add up to a satisfying experience. There has to be a narrative. With the new material and a harder rock sound, we had more options than ever, and Alan's keyboards gave us not just a richer sound but more flexibility in the arrangement of tracks because, rather than just ending one song, pausing and starting up another, we were able to link them up, slide from each one to the next and create some flow and cohesion in the performance.

By the time we flew out for our warm-up gig in Vancouver, we were stage-ready, our spirits higher than they had been for a couple of years. We had fresh, original material, a new, bigger sound perfect for live performance, a happy band — and our private lives were in good order.

The album, out to coincide with the start of the tour, was very well received pretty much universally. It would stay in the UK charts for almost five years. The general consensus was that we had taken several steps up since *Communiqué*, recognition that the songs and the music had evolved. The review in *Rolling Stone* saying that Mark as a writer, and the band as musicians, had emerged from our shells and come of age is, I think, spot on — though I find the comments regarding the first two albums a little mean. Many Dire Straits fans regard the first album as our best. The review said:

> *Making Movies* is the record on which Mark Knopfler comes out from behind his influences and Dire Straits come out from behind Mark Knopfler. The combination of the star's lyrical script, his intense vocal performances and the band's cutting-edge rock & roll soundtrack is breathtaking — everything the first two albums should have been but weren't. If *Making Movies* really were a film, it might win a flock of Academy Awards.

The American leg of the tour was only a month long and the itinerary was slightly different from the last, taking us on a horseshoe-shaped, anticlockwise route, sticking close to the borders and the coasts and leaving out the heart of the country. We began in Seattle and Oregon, then moved down to California, into Texas, along to New Orleans and Baton Rouge, Atlanta and Nashville, then up to the big cities of the Northeastern Seaboard. That's a lot of asphalt, but this time we had the luxury of a state-of-the-art touring coach for the band and a separate one for the crew, each fitted with beds, a shower, fridges, TVs and video players, a revolutionary bit of technology then, yet to hit the mass market.

We travelled by night, the crew following in a convoy of three or four big trucks behind the coach, unwinding with a few beers and maybe a smoke, the ghostly landscape of America streaming past the window. Our driver, Richy, was small in stature but big in character, with a very impressive love life on the go. He had been driving bands and artists across America since the early sixties — Duke Ellington and Dolly Parton were his favourites — and over the years he had managed to establish a girlfriend in almost every city we visited. It became something of a joke at breakfast in the hotel to see who Richy would be coming downstairs with that morning.

Richy was full of great stories and Mark and I got into the habit of taking it in turns to take a drink up front to chat with him as we ploughed through the darkness down the long, arrow-straight highways, the dark silhouettes of cacti, mountain ranges and skyscrapers, motel signs, neon-lit diners and backwater hick gas stations offering a spectral kaleidoscope of that huge, diverse country. Back then, there was a strict speed limit of 55 mph and, perhaps keen to get to his next woman, Richy had installed a CB radio to talk to the truckers up ahead and find out where the cops — the 'smokies' — were waiting so that he could speed up to eighty or ninety in between. Sharing that front seat with Richy and talking about his time in Vietnam as a professional soldier was a real highlight.

The coach was Paul's idea, and it was a good one. It avoided all the hassle and exhaustion of air travel and, once you had reached a region, all the driving around in cars, getting stiff backs and no sleep. To pull out of Nashville and Elvis country in the Deep South and wake up in Washington DC to see the Senate building outside the window was pretty cool. With his giant phone, Paul could call ahead to hotels and venues rather than having to wait to use a landline at the other end.

The Making Movies *tour. Where has all that hair gone?*

Seeing him jabbering away on his phone, us hammering through the night in our posh coach with its video screens, from one great city to the next, created a powerful sense of mission. At the turn of the decade, it really felt like we were moving out of one era and into another, as a band and as a society. The rapid advances in technology which, thanks to Mark's restless curiosity and lust for experimentation, we were starting to embrace compounded this sense of being on a journey, an adventure into the unknown.

The labour unions in the States were still very powerful at the time and the Teamsters, as they were known, demanded that visiting bands employ mostly US crews and hire mostly US kit. A show could not go ahead unless a band complied, so we had only a skeleton crew of our own. The stage crew was twice as big as it was on the *Communiqué* tour because we were putting on more of a spectacle at the larger venues, Chas starting to work his magic with the lights. Ed had been clever again in not booking us into vast auditoriums, thereby generating a sense of unrequitable demand.

He was aware, too, that the States had gone into quite a steep recession and there was less disposable income washing around the economy. So most of the venues were in the thousand- to two-thousand-capacity range, and we also played a number of the small, iconic venues, including the Exit Inn in Nashville, two nights at the Old Waldorf in San Francisco, three at the Roxy in LA and one at the Bayou in Washington. (One of the nights at the Old Waldorf was recorded and produced as an LP, but only for radio. It was never sold on the open market, which is a shame.)

It was great, very flattering, but mildly unsettling to have all these VIPs and well-known faces from music and showbiz staring up at us from the tables right in front of us. I had to pinch myself sometimes, seeing people whose records I used to buy now coming to see us play. The one I remember most vividly was Jerry Garcia of the Grateful Dead, who turned up at the Old Waldorf and came backstage afterwards to celebrate his birthday with a giant cake in the shape of a guitar. You've never seen so much hair on one man, but he was the gentlest and most laid-back of souls.

It's really very strange coming to terms with rapid success, but I don't think we were ever seduced into becoming arrogant or complacent, an easy temptation when, daily, you are surrounded by a posse of eager autograph-hunters and hotel staff look at you and serve you with expressions of nervous awe. We were feeling the same awe ourselves about the experience and, in fact, that creates a kind of humility and gratitude. Mark has never sought out the limelight but, unfortunately for him, he was in high demand. If you watch interviews with him from around that time, his awkwardness with the flattery comes across very strongly. He looks slightly bemused when the interviewer tells him he's a great songwriter or that such and such a song is a classic.

The album was already selling pretty well in the States when, while in LA, we performed 'Romeo & Juliet' and 'Skateaway' on *Fridays*, a new comedy sketch show featuring future big-name performers like Larry David (who co-created *Seinfeld*) and Michael Richards (who played Kramer in the series). Launched on ABC to rival *Saturday Night Live*, *Fridays* had a big reach in its early days and our appearance on it had a real impact on the sales of *Making Movies*, helping it on its way to becoming multi-platinum over there. It wasn't quite The Beatles appearing on *The Ed Sullivan Show* and triggering Beatlemania, but it gave us a massive boost in profile in the States. Certainly, at every gig of the tour after that, there was always a bunch of people outside the entrance trying to get tickets. At this time in the US, there were limited media outlets compared to today and you grabbed the opportunities, so we were doing radio and press interviews in every city and town.

The album was doing very well all over, selling 900,000 copies in Italy alone, which would have been an incredible feat for any band, and even more incredible because we had never toured there. Touring raises your profile hugely. There are posters and adverts everywhere and you end up doing a lot of media, so to have sold so many copies from a standing start really was remarkable. It was nine months before we'd tour Italy, and we had no inkling of the craziness that awaited us there.

Back in the UK at the end of November, before starting that leg of the tour, we appeared on *The Old Grey Whistle Test* again and made our one and only appearance on *Top of the Pops*, playing 'Romeo & Juliet'. It was eventually broadcast on 5 February 1981 after its release as a single. We were visibly miserable about the experience. We had nothing against *TOTP* as a programme; it just wasn't our scene and, like many other bands, we hated having to mime. I am not allergic to pop music, but we were not a pop band. We were old romantics, not New Romantics. We did not wear make-up or girls' clothes (fashionable as it was then becoming). If ever we were haughty and sniffy about anything in our music, it was the obligation to go into a studio and mime our way through a song for an artificially excited rent-a-crowd Broadcasting House audience, who shortly afterwards would cheer, say, 'There's No One Quite Like Grandma', with exactly the same fervour with which they had greeted your performance.

We played bigger venues in the UK than in the US, all to capacity audiences, but once again Ed had been clever in not over-egging it, stoking demand and limiting supply. The Apollo, Manchester, and Civic Hall, Sheffield, held about three thousand, so they were big enough for us to make a bit of money, unlike the last two tours, where we had barely broken even.

A week before Christmas we headlined an indoor festival at the Westfalenhalle in Dortmund alongside Roxy Music, Talking Heads and Mike Oldfield, the world still not quite having finished its love affair with *Tubular Bells*. It was great to see the Heads again. It had only been two and a half years ago that we had toured together, but so much had happened to both bands since, it seemed like a decade ago that we had all been shivering our way up and down the UK in our clapped-out Transit van. We came back for three nights at the Rainbow in north London, then went off to Ireland for a brilliant week over New Year. It was there, before very large and ecstatic crowds, that we realized we must be doing something right. The Irish were great and, with a shiver, today I can still recall the incredible warmth of their reception. It was very moving.

It was the height of the Troubles in Northern Ireland and we were given a taste of the dangers facing the people there every day when we played Belfast and the promoter who met us dropped in casually that there had been 'no bomb threats yet, but there probably will be'. We were staying at the Europa, then the most bombed hotel in Europe, and heading to check in was like crossing a small war zone, as you had to pass through rings of barbed wire and concrete barricades. Inside, we were all body-searched. We played two nights at Ulster Hall, and there were bomb threats on both. The first came before the doors had opened, so we could sit that one out, but on the second night the call came when the house was full and the whole building had to be evacuated into the freezing January night.

Back from Ireland, Pauline and I set off for a few days' holiday on the Greek island of Hydra. It was our last opportunity to spend some proper time together before yet more travel. Pauline was about five months pregnant and the hope had been to have a quiet time of it. It turned out to be anything but a relaxing break. Staying in a white-washed windmill above the harbour, Pauline had to take a donkey up the steep hill, so it was not an ideal location to find ourselves in when her waters broke. The hospital on the island was unable to cope with such an emergency so we had to take the fast boat to Athens. From the port of Piraeus, a taxi delivered us to one of the city's big hospitals, but that did little to calm our anxiety. The hospital was filthy and the doctor was smoking as he examined her. He was quite upset when I asked him to put his cigarette out. Pauline, of course, was in a state of some distress and so I called the tour operator, who arranged for her to be transferred to the American hospital. It made no difference. She had miscarried. It was unspeakably sad.

We had a couple of months off touring before heading off for the Australasian leg of the tour. *Making Movies* was selling hard there. It wasn't much of a break because we spent a great deal of the time doing promotional work on the continent — but miming doesn't feel like hard work and it was difficult to take it seriously. We made our way from studio to studio and, it all being a bit silly, we ended up eating and drinking too much and generally misbehaving ourselves, our punishment for the degeneracy being a severe bout of food poisoning in Italy.

We were the star turn at the annual Sanremo song contest in Liguria, the coastal area just along from France. It was an event, so we were told, that was fixed in advance by the Mafia, who got to choose the winner of the 'competition', the prize being a slot on television at peak viewing time. We were just guest performers, not contestants, and I am very glad that Ed's conscience was not troubled by having to consider coughing up a bung for the mobsters.

From there, we jetted off to Madrid to appear on a programme called *Applauso*, a huge deal over there and a brilliant way to push our cause in Spain. In those days, before the advent of the video and the satellite link, you had to turn up in person. It was very flattering, but a bit of a bore too, all that travel hassle just to mime away for half an hour. We had no control over the production of these events so we ended up in some slightly embarrassing sets that we most certainly would not have chosen ourselves. We did a show in Cologne called *Bananas*, and it was exactly that — bananas. We felt a little like primary-school kids in an end-of-year show for the parents. On this occasion in Madrid, the filming turned into a farce when the dry-ice machine went into meltdown. A row of buckets had been placed along the foot of the stage, but it soon became obvious that the stagehands had used far too much of it and we quickly became engulfed in a very deep fog that crept up our legs and over our torsos until we completely disappeared from view. By the end, Pick, whose drums had been raised on a small platform, was the only one of us left on view, and we giggled our way through the songs, trying not to breathe in the harmful vapours. But the reason we did them was because TV shows were the only way to get exposure to a mass audience.

It all felt a little tawdry, like we were selling out somehow, being thrown on TV like a brand of baked beans. The bizarre sets added to the dreamlike, surreal nature of the experience — a feeling that reached its peak when, at the end of the promo tour, we appeared on the BBC's *Kenny Everett Show*, Kenny being the king of 'wackiness' and hugely popular in Britain at the beginning of the eighties.

In March 1981, we flew out to Australia and got back to doing what we loved — playing live. My word, did the Aussies like us. I think *Making Movies* was number one by the time we arrived and, giving us a taste of things to come out there, they couldn't get enough of us. Once again, Ed and the promoters there had kept the venues reasonably low-key, no more than two or three thousand, but they were all packed out.

Most of Australia's population is to be found gathered in the conurbations around its great cities and, as would become the norm, we played a number of gigs at each venue. After a tour opener in Perth, we played five in Melbourne, four in Adelaide, six in Sydney and two in Brisbane. It was my first time in Australia and I fell instantly in love with the place. Being engaged to Pauline, an Aussie, perhaps influenced my feelings about the country. Her family were farmers a couple of hours upcountry from Perth on the west coast, and it was great that she was able to come out so that we could spend a week up there before the tour began. It was a world far, far removed from that of a band on a global tour — and equally far removed from the farming world in which I had grown up. Unlike the rich soil and green acres of Leicestershire, the natural conditions of Western Australia offer little help to the farmer. The soil is poor, the sun and wind are harsh, the land will yield a decent crop every other year at best and one sheep needs a whole acre to itself. Pauline's family farm covered 20,000 acres — a vast area in England, but considered a small concern over there and barely enough to make a living. I have no knowledge and little interest in farming, but it was a fascinating week, out there in the middle of nowhere, witnessing a small community trying to eke out an existence in a landscape not much more promising than the surface of the moon. I was given a steak with my eggs for breakfast every day, and I enjoyed it all the more, knowing how hard it had been to produce.

Australia in the raw made a big impression on me, but there was not a city or an area over there I didn't enjoy. Flying for hours over that wild, baked, orange outback to arrive in a sophisticated European-style city, the people so friendly, was a true privilege in a job that can be gruelling and repetitive. Under the beating sun, surf rolling in on the beaches, the colours so vivid, the restaurants buzzing, the crowds so enthusiastic, this was touring at its best. We weren't getting much sleep, but it was so invigorating we never felt tired. We finished up Down Under with a massive outdoor show at Western Springs in Auckland — ninety thousand people, the biggest we had ever played and, I think I'm right in saying, the biggest outdoor gathering in New Zealand up to that time. The roads around were so clogged with traffic that we had to delay the show for an hour and a half.

After a short break back in the UK, we embarked on the final leg, forty-one gigs over two months across Europe, and this time we went all over — including up to Finland and over to Poland, then in the thick of a struggle to overthrow Communist rule, but we were in and out of both countries before we had a chance to take them in. We kicked off with fifteen shows in Germany and headed up to Scandinavia, all brilliant, raucous atmospheres, but the shows that stick most vividly in my mind are the stunning one we played in the French commune of Orange, down in Provence, and then five absolutely crazy ones in northern Italy.

At Orange, we had the privilege to play in the magnificent Roman amphitheatre, which was built early in the first century AD in the reign of Emperor Augustus. It was very difficult to get my head around that: playing electric rock music in a huge building constructed just a few years after the birth of Christ and still looking much as it must have done then. The sun setting to our right, the giant exterior façade behind us, we looked out over five thousand faces crammed in along the tiers of stone seating that appeared, from below, to rise so steeply as to be almost vertical. The theatre was declared a UNESCO World Heritage site that year and we were one of the last rock bands to have the honour of performing there. They only stage an annual opera festival there now. The crew probably did not feel the honour as keenly as the band, toiling in the baking sun to set up the stage in very confined spaces without the usual fixtures and fittings or the decent power supply they enjoyed when working in auditoriums built twenty centuries later.

And so to Italy and a week of utter madness. Dire Straits had gone massive there, 'Romeo & Juliet' becoming one of the country's best-selling singles, *Making Movies* one of its bestselling albums. We had been booked to play in huge sports stadiums, but not without some painful arm-wrestling. Ed had been driven to the edge of despair trying to organize the gigs and, unable to extract any hard figures out of the all-powerful promoter Franco Mamone, there was even some doubt as to whether we'd go. He settled on $25,000 a show, in spite of us playing to crowds of between thirty thousand and a hundred thousand – a sum that barely covered our costs. Ed warned Mark and me that it was going to be an organizational and administrative nightmare, and he wasn't wrong. Ordinarily, playing gigs of that magnitude would bring a very broad smile to your bank manager's face, and it was absurd that we might even make a loss. But we had such a strong following there, and the fans would take a no-show as a snub, so we felt morally obliged to perform. So it went ahead – and we got out of there alive.

From the moment we arrived we realized we were in a wildly cha-otic, dangerous environment, a world as far removed from the calm order and efficiency of Germany and Scandinavia as might be imag-ined. In Milan, we were to play in the Vigorelli Velodrome and all twenty-five thousand tickets had long sold out. On the day, ten thousand more people, maybe twenty thousand, began to mass in the streets around the stadium, looking to find a way in.

With growing alarm, Paul had seen the mayhem developing throughout the afternoon and asked for us to be given security to get us through the mob to the venue. Mamome was making an absolute fortune out of us, though presumably much of it was being passed on to the men in dark suits and dark glasses. You'd think Franco might have access to some decent heavies, but what we got was two Mercedes saloon cars and two 'security guards', both in their sixties. They were a pair of charming old men with silver hair, but they could no more guarantee our safety than swim to the moon. So it was with some trepidation that we set off from the hotel, with our security detail fiddling with their pacemakers and hearing devices. There was an air of brewing violence in the crowd, but our drivers managed to crawl through it and we hurried backstage. 'Backstage' is something of an exaggeration. It was as open as any area in the stadium and, as far as we could see, totally unpoliced.

Paul was becoming increasingly anxious about the situation, and with good reason. There was even a historical precedent to support his fears. When Led Zep played the Vigorelli in 1971, the concert descended into a brutal riot, fans fighting police in a pitched battle. The clock was ticking down, an ominous atmosphere was brewing nicely outside and the crush of fans trying to get in grew ever more alarming. The Carabinieri decided it was our problem and kept out of it. Maybe they were in their civvies and had come to see us. What police there were just walked away and left the scene to the mob. Paul was left calling the shots and trying to control the situation. He found the most senior policeman in the arena, who insisted we opened the doors to avoid a riot or a life-threatening crush, but there was no guarantee that in doing so a disaster would be avoided. There still might have been a stampede or a riot inside. There were twenty-five thousand fans inside and about the same number outside.

Poking our heads out from backstage, we watched the mayhem in horror as the flood of bodies poured into an already full stadium. Our merchandise guy was forced to abandon his gear and flee the bedlam. It was all very rough and the counterfeit merchandise guys wanted shot of him and to get their hands on his goods. (No wonder. One of the crew saw a fake T-shirt in circulation emblazoned with the words 'Sutlans of Swim'.) He came to shelter backstage with the rest of us, but there was no security there either — unless you counted the two pensioners — and soon we were surrounded on all sides, like a medieval castle under siege. When I went looking for a bathroom, I came upon the first-aid room, and it was as if I had stumbled into a field dressing station in a war zone. It was packed out with casualties, several with broken limbs but most with head wounds from airborne bottles. We went on to play as soon as possible, hoping the music would calm the scene, but there were still bottles flying and fights breaking out all over. Many of those flying bottles had been pissed in and it was spraying everywhere.

The crew were worried the stage would be stormed from the rear, where punters had been forced in by the crush, and, as we played, a posse of roadies plus the merchandise guy had to keep the mob at bay by swinging baseball bats and any other suitable weapon to hand. We had little choice but to play on. Had we not, none of us was in any doubt there would have been a full-blown riot and we might well have been lynched by the angry hordes as we tried to make our escape. It was a war zone in peacetime.

After the gig, which went fine, if a little nervously, Paul reported that the medical facility had been overrun by casualties all evening and the medics were struggling to cope with the influx. Lovely city, Milan, but we were very happy to see it in our rear-view mirror the next morning. Bologna, the next stop, was a little more peaceful, but that wasn't very difficult. The most alarming moment came when Paul had a gun put to his head by the local promoter. But he was the only one that was alarmed. To everyone else in the room, so it seemed, this was just how business was done.

The final show took place in Turin, at the Stadio Comunale, home to Torino football club. Here the crowd was allowed on the pitch as well as in the stands and there were roughly a hundred thousand people inside. It was our biggest audience to date, bigger by far even than Auckland, but we wouldn't see a single lira of the huge takings. With tickets costing the equivalent of £10, that was £1 million pounds on the door, a vast sum today, let alone back then. We got $25,000 to pay our crew. Everyone involved had done better out of it than us.

But at least there was no mob of ticketless fans ready to riot or die in a crush outside. The anger was reserved for inside the arena. We had the Irish singer Paul Brady as our warm-up act, and we wished him the very best of luck as he headed out on stage by himself with only his acoustic guitar as accompaniment and weapon of defence. Paul played music more suited to a large tavern than a giant sports stadium, and soon the abuse was rolling off the crowd and the bottles were flying. But the hordes were reckoning with the wrong bloke. Paul was a tough character, and he was having none of it. He returned the abuse with interest, hurling profanities back at them: 'Shut the fuck up!' We watched him bellowing into the microphone, the projectiles filling the airspace. 'I'm going to play these fucking songs whether you like it or not!'

And he did. And, incredibly, he won them over and left the stage to applause. A truly heroic performance. We feared a catastrophe at every gig we played in Italy and, as tour manager, Paul was beside himself much of the time. You don't want deaths or riots at your concert. It doesn't make for great headlines. We feared the worst when a fire broke out in the goal mouth below us, a bare-topped gang of about fifty having created a bonfire of debris, including their own shirts. Apart from that, it all passed off swimmingly — not quite like an evening at Glyndebourne, but at least no one died. As far as we know. We didn't hang round too long to find out.

Never in my life have I ever been so delighted to arrive in Belgium. We played two big but peaceful festivals — Torhout and Werchter — before bringing the curtain down on a lively few weeks in the civilized surroundings of Luxembourg. It was good to get back to the UK.

Chapter 18

Electric Power

It had been over four years, way back in the spring of 1977, since the band had had a true break, been allowed to enjoy our private lives and, if we so chose, do absolutely nothing. We'd had a few weeks here and there between legs of a tour, but that was always more recuperation than rest and relaxation. It takes months, not weeks, to decompress truly. The analogy between a soldier coming back to civvy street from the front and a musician coming home from a long tour is absurd on one level, but there are similarities. I think now of my dad's experience in the Second World War. It is dislocating to switch from a frenetic, intense world of noise, nerves and adrenaline, constantly on manoeuvres, to a life of domesticity and idleness sitting in the same location every day, free to do what you like. To go from playing before a broiling crowd of eighty thousand people to fixing the broken tap in the bathroom is a peculiar transition. It's hard to find your rhythm and it takes weeks for the adrenaline to subside and to be able to turn your mind from one very specific mission to a vague, pleasantly mundane and general one.

The returning-soldier analogy is perhaps more appropriately ascribed to the experience of the partner and family back home. They, too, have had a rhythm to their lives and it's probably harder for them to adjust to the new domestic arrangements. For a few days, I felt something of a stranger, not remembering where the coffee mugs were kept and finding myself sitting on the sofa at eight-thirty in the evening with my body clock telling me it was time to step out on stage. For your partner, too, while you're away, there is the constant anxiety about what you have been up to in all those bars and hotels, whether you have managed to resist the manifold temptations presented in every city visited. The anxiety is justified. Many stray at some point on a long tour, usually towards the end, when memories of hearth and home have dimmed and the lack of intimacy has built up into a need. It's not really about sex, but intimacy.

I had been a good boy on the *On Location* tour, mainly because I was very much in love with Pauline. I missed her very much, and we had been able to see each other from time to time, in Australia, and also on the UK legs and in the breaks in between. Now, we had the rest of the year to ourselves while Mark worked on songs for the next album. Knowing it was not until January that we would return to Wood Wharf to work on them allowed me to immerse myself in home life — and I dived in.

I had forgotten the joys of a quiet, domestic life, the simple satisfactions of working on the house or going out to the shops, the cinema or the pub with Pauline. There was no social media, of course, and, as the band spurned publicity rather than stoking it, never hiring a PR company, all of us apart from Mark could go about our daily lives without fear of being pestered for an autograph or putting up with a long inquisition from a stranger at the bar about the chord structure of 'Romeo & Juliet'.

The feeling of happy domesticity was sealed in the late summer when Pauline and I were married. Her folks flew over from Western

Australia and mine came down the A1 from Leicestershire, and we kept it a small, low-key, intimate affair, the formalities taking place at Lewisham Town Hall and the celebrations, with about thirty guests, in our back garden in Forest Hill. Back from his many extracurricular musical enterprises, Mark acted as best man. I had known him only five or six years, but perhaps it was because of the intense heat of forging the band that our friendship had been fashioned so much faster and harder than others.

The honeymoon was equally low-key, a week in Fowey in south Cornwall, walking along the beautiful estuary and coast. It was a slightly unorthodox honeymoon, insofar as we had Pauline's parents with us, but it was no less happy for that. There are times in your life when you have to recognize that life is unlikely to get much better. This was one of them. I was keenly aware of my good fortune in this period: I had a lovely wife, the music was going well, and there were bags of fun waiting for me out there, travelling the world, playing live. In September, Pauline announced she was pregnant. If you find yourself in a dream, let it run as long as you can. Don't pick holes in it, relish every moment, because you never know what lies in wait to ambush you. That has always been my very simple attitude to life.

We had a bit of cash in the bank now, not heaps of it, but enough for me to donate my trusty old Rover to the scrap merchant and treat us to my first new car, a black VW Golf GTI, with a little golf ball on the gearstick. I loved that car. I have developed a minor interest in cars over the years, but that one remains my sentimental favourite. Transporting Pauline and me on many happy excursions out in the country, visiting friends, I see it as a symbol of the happiness of those times.

One Sunday morning that autumn we set out for a drive and a pub lunch, heading in the vague direction of the South Downs over towards Brighton and Lewes. Pauline was flicking through a magazine as I drove and saw an advert for the sale of a house in a tiny village called Telscombe just in from the coast, about seven miles from Brighton. It was pure chance we were only a few minutes away, so we drove down into the hamlet, which was nestled in a fold of the Downs and, apparently, untouched by the progress of time since the eighteenth century. There was a church, a scattering of cottages and a couple of houses, including the Old Rectory. We pulled up outside and both of us knew instantly that this was where we wanted to be as a family. We couldn't resist knocking on the door, which was opened by a very young kid with a yapping dog at his feet. The kid kicked the dog so hard, it yelped and scurried away. The owner of the house turned out to be a Tory MP whose business had been struggling and I could sense my long hair was not a style he would have chosen himself. 'Are you a musician?' he asked.

'How did you guess?'

We explained we were interested in buying the house, so he let us in and showed us around. He turned out to be a very charming character and it probably helped our cause that his two late-teenage daughters were mad Dire Straits fans. Over a gin and tonic in the lovely flint-walled garden, we shook on a deal. Hard-pressed for cash, he included most of the furniture, and a month later we moved into what was to become a very happy retreat. Like the Golf, that house remains a reminder of joyful times. Life was certainly moving at a dizzying pace and it was hard to take in the fact that just three years earlier I had been single and eating beans out of a tin in a council flat, with no idea about what the future might hold.

After a quick break for Christmas at Telscombe — Pauline's bump now visible — the band gathered at Wood Wharf for our next major challenge, putting down a new album followed by another marathon of globetrotting. I was intrigued to find out what magic Mark had conjured this time. Before we had gone our separate ways for the break, I knew we would come back to work on an epic song, 'Telegraph Road', a metaphor about the settlers heading west in their wagons and the building of modern America. The very length of the song (fourteen minutes and eighteen seconds) is a metaphor in its own right. We had been working on it during soundchecks before concerts on the tour, but it was far from ready for public consumption. Mark had also been playing with the song 'Private Investigations', so I had an inkling that, once more, something highly original was in the offing, yet again a sharp departure from what had gone before.

Making Movies was a great piece of work and the songs were fantastic to perform live, but this album, *Love Over Gold*, was different again.

One song that didn't make it on to the album in the end was 'Private Dancer', mainly because, Mark rightly decided, it should be sung by a woman. The lines 'I'm your private dancer, a dancer for money, I'll do what you want me to do' just didn't sound right coming from Mark's mouth! He ended up giving it to Tina Turner – with spectacular results, but more of that later. Another, 'The Way It Always Starts', with vocals by Gerry Rafferty, ended up on Mark's film soundtrack album to the Scottish cult movie *Local Hero*, which he would work on after we had recorded *Love Over Gold* and before we hit the road again.

Wood Wharf had become a cramped environment, and much louder than when we had used only guitars. We spent about a month there, putting in long days, and it was one of the most intense and creatively demanding of all our album rehearsals. We flew to New York at the beginning of March and returned to the Power Station to put the songs down. We would not leave there until the second week of June. There was no Jimmy Iovine this time; Mark was going to produce it himself. He had very clear ideas about the sound and shape of the music he wanted the band to achieve. He brought in sound engineer Neil Dorfsman, who he had worked with on *Local Hero*. Together, they made a great team. Neil had only been working as a sound engineer for a few years but had already worked with top names like Diana Ross, Bob Marley and Bruce Springsteen, and has since gone on to work with scores of leading bands and artists. He was an amusing man, too, and he made all the hard work an absolute delight to look forward to each morning.

There was a very fine grand piano at the Power Station, but we had a problem with a section of 'Private Investigations' that left everyone scratching their heads. When Alan lifted his foot off the pedal, there was an audible thump in what was meant to be a pause in the music and, for reasons beyond my technical scope, it was impossible to edit out. The only answer was to get in another grand piano, not an easy task, unless you are working in a hangar, and so we had a day of Charlie Chaplin filming as one piano after another was humped and shunted in and out until a suitable one was finally found.

There was a great deal of space in the music on this album and the sound quality had to be spot on. This is where Neil came into his own. When it was all done, the clarity of sound, and the silences, were so perfect that 'Private Investigations' came to be used by electrical shops up and down the UK to show off the quality of hi-fi systems and speakers. It was described by the people who specialize in these things as one of the purest pieces of audio recording up to that time.

It being the fourth album, we had learned a bit about recording along the way and the whole band felt confident to add their views to the mix. It was a truly collaborative effort. Some critics were to describe the composition of Love Over Gold as being similar to classical music. They were referring not so much to the sound but to the arrangement. It was certainly a very different studio undertaking to anything we had experienced up to then, and all the more satisfying for that.

Ordinarily, you'd put a song down in one uninterrupted take, or rather, over and over in uninterrupted takes until you got some just about right and created a good range of options to choose from. But on 'Telegraph Road' Pick's snare drum started to lose its tension after being hit for seven or eight minutes. That didn't matter when we were playing live, but you'd notice it on your hi-fi at home. It was lucky Neil Dorfsman relished a challenge, because there were plenty to overcome in putting down 'Telegraph Road'. The only solution was to split the song in half and splice the two halves together on the tape. But you'd never know that to listen to it.

Heading to New York, I was a little anxious about leaving Pauline, who was now getting on for seven months pregnant and was feeling it. It was not an easy pregnancy and it was her first since the miscarriage, so she was a little nervous, understandably. She moved in with some friends in Chelsea, which was a comfort to both of us, but still. I was calling whenever I could but, in the studio for twelve hours a day, I was often out of contact. Late one night, word got through that she was having problems and had been taken to hospital in west London.

'Go! Go! Go!' was the chorus from the band, but there were no more flights, and I had to wait for the early-bird Concorde. According to my watch, owing to the time difference, I arrived at Heathrow before I had left. What an aircraft! I jumped into a black cab and rushed to the hospital. By now, the situation had calmed down. It was a false alarm. The baby wasn't coming and Pauline was not in trouble. I stayed for an hour or two and, reassured all was okay, legged it back to the airport and caught the evening Concorde to New York, making me surely one of a very few people to have taken that famous supersonic plane twice in a day.

I had never been on Concorde, and I was bowled over by the glamour of it. It's a very small aircraft, which adds to the impression of exclusiveness, and you got looked after like royalty – or Joan Collins. In addition to its speed, it had two further attractions: you never got jet lag because it flies so high, and it always left on time because of its tight fuel limitations, and so was given priority over all other flights. Or rather, almost every time. There was a ten-minute delay this time and the crew were in a fluster because a passenger was running late. Loads of VIPs, American and British, used Concorde for journeys of urgent international importance, so we were all wondering who the mystery last passenger might be. Prime Minister Margaret Thatcher, maybe? US Secretary of State Alexander Haig, who was busy conducting shuttle diplomacy over the Falklands War, currently raging in the south Atlantic? No, it was Robin Gibb from the Bee Gees, and he looked sheepish when he finally boarded and ducked into his seat.

It had been my ongoing fear that I would miss the birth of my first child but, in the event, there was a decent warning period and I was able to be there at the hospital for James's birth on 18 May. It was a wonderful moment, my first child, but a complicated one for me, a musician on the road for so many weeks of the year. I had to resign myself to the hard truth that I was going to be something of an absent father. That, I know, must have been very hard on Pauline.

It was all going on in our lives at this period. Forest Hill was fine, but we didn't know anyone in the neighbourhood and, with me away so often and for so long, we started the process of buying a smaller house near Clapham Common — just around the corner from Charlie Gillett — so that Pauline could be more central and closer to a community of friends while I was away. To reduce the loneliness and add an extra layer of support and comfort, her great friend, the social documentary photographer Bob Mazzer, and his wife, Jenny, moved into the basement. Their son, Arthur, was born around the same time as James, and they have remained great friends ever since, as — terrifying thought — they head towards their forties.

Bob is one of my favourite people, and we are good friends to this day. He was an old mate of Pauline's and I had first met him when he was living on top of a big hill in a small hippy commune in North Wales. It had snowed so much the car was unable to make it up the hill and we had to leave it at the foot and tramp and slide our way up the icy slope. I don't remember much of that weekend — the entertainment and refreshments being so well coordinated by Bob and his mates — apart from heading out in the snow to milk a goat to get some milk for my cornflakes.

Pauline and I weren't long back from our honeymoon when Ed called to say that Pick wanted to meet Mark and me for lunch. Alarm bells followed the telephone bells. The venue chosen was Blakes, off the Old Brompton Road in west London. Blakes, designed by Anouska Hempel, was a very rock 'n' roll hotel, its black walls the perfect backdrop for the gloomy news that Pick had come to announce. He wanted to leave the band. He'd had enough of the rigours of touring and wanted to work on different kinds of music. Apparently, he'd said to Ed that if he couldn't play with a band like Weather Report, he might as well give up. To which Ed had replied, 'Well, you might as well give up then.' With Mark and me, the immediate exchanges of the conversation went something along the lines of 'Okay, Pick. You've recorded the album and will get your royalties, but you're not going to do the hard graft of touring and promoting the album?'

Mark and I were taken aback, shocked even, but Pick was adamant and there was no use trying to persuade him to change his mind. It's hard physical work being a drummer at the best of times, and I think Pick had found it doubly so once we had turned ourselves into a busier, fuller live rock act. Two hours of playing drums under hot lights is a proper workout, as tough as any session in the gym. Added to that were the exhaustion of touring and the fact that he had just got married, to Linda. We got his point. Pick was a fine, fine drummer and I had learned so much from him in the engine room of the band.

Drummers, like goalkeepers and wicketkeepers, are often slightly maverick, oddball characters, different from the rest of the team, and Pick conformed to this stereotype. He was pretty quiet and withdrawn on the whole but would suffer sudden bursts of manic behaviour, jumping on to the table in a pub or restaurant or playing the spoons like drums. He had been the last piece in the Dire Straits jigsaw and, back when we were rehearsing in the bedroom in Deptford, his playing had pulled us together as a band.

He was going to be missed, but any fears that the engine room was going to start malfunctioning were immediately allayed. We rang Paul from a phone box out on the Old Brompton Road as soon as lunch was over. A few days later, a Welsh guy called Terry Williams turned up at Wood Wharf. We all knew of Terry, a member of the band Rockpile with Dave Edmunds and Nick Lowe, a confident and powerful drummer. For a few days, he sat at home and listened to all our music, including the new material, before appearing in Deptford for a session. Within a couple of hours, it was as if he had been playing in the band from the outset. He also came with the added advantage of being physically very robust, more than capable of dealing with long, hard two-hour-plus sets, and he was a well-seasoned tourer and understood the rigours of life on the road.

His first assignment was to join us in JAM studios in north London over the first three days of October to put down an EP (Extended Play), including the single 'Twisting by the Pool'. It was the perfect opportunity for Terry to bed in to the band. This was a departure for us in both format and content; our first EP, a bit of fun and a contrast to the intensity of *Love Over Gold*. I guess it was a sign of our growing maturity and confidence in our core music that we felt safe enough to release it. It was a little tongue in cheek, but when it was released in January 1983 we knew we'd made the right decision. It reached number fourteen in the UK, number twelve in the US, and 'Twisting by the Pool' became something of a dance hit in Europe.

By then, 'Private Investigations' had been released as a single and had risen to number two in the UK charts, our highest position – an incredible feat considering that even after an edit for the single it was still just under six minutes long. A little of that credit must go to the Radio One disc jockey Dave Lee Travis, who ignored the station's rules about playing songs over three minutes long. He played it often, and always the full length of it, ensuring that it reached the biggest audience out there on radio. It did even better overseas, topping the charts in a few countries, including the all-important, litmus-testing Netherlands. In the UK, the top spot was denied us by Survivor's 'Eye of the Tiger'.

Then came the release of the album itself, just before we entered JAM studios. As with the first three albums, we had no idea how the new music might be received. You never knew. There is no telling with taste, fashion or zeitgeist. As it turned out, it went down even better than we could have hoped, topping the charts in Britain and five other countries. It also reached number nineteen in the US, despite there being no accompanying single to rocket-boost it, and it went platinum in France and Germany and double-platinum in the UK and Canada.

The changing nature of our music demanded a change in the nature of our live performance, and it was on this tour that Chas Herington stepped up out of the shadows and came into his own. Our shows became a more dynamic spectacle. He turned a Dire Straits performance into a *son et lumière* spectacle, his work with the lights perfectly complementing and reflecting the music. We hit the road with a warm-up gig at Guildford Civic Hall, a sketchy performance memorable only for the after-show appearance backstage of Eric Clapton, a guitarist much admired by anyone who has ever picked up the instrument. It was flattering that he came to see us or, more probably, to see Mark in action.

Of our six major world tours, *Love Over Gold* was probably the least draining. We had decided to cut out North America, partly because we didn't have a single out over there, but more because we had toured there so much we felt it was time to give it a break and focus on Australia, where we were as popular as we were anywhere on the planet. Also, the venues we played were way bigger so we probably sold just as many tickets as we would have done in a longer, fuller tour. In the UK, we played two nights at the Birmingham NEC and four at Wembley Arena, which hold 15,500 and 12,500 respectively. So one night in either of those is the equivalent of about thirty shows at the Roxy or the Marquee.

The easier schedule allowed me and Pauline to have a genuinely relaxing Christmas down at Telscombe, much of it spent following James, now eight months, crawling his way around the house. In February 1983 the band members headed to the Grosvenor Hotel on Park Lane to pick up our award for 'Best Band' at the Brits ceremony. You don't set out as a band to win awards; you do it for the love of playing, no more. Truly, it had been a long journey from Deptford, though a very short one in time. It was just over four years since the release of the first album, *Dire Straits*. We must have known in advance we were going to win the category. People who aren't going to win don't show up at these events, on the whole. The award, in reality, was a recognition of Mark's songwriting skills as much as of our success as a band. His star was in a sharp ascendant. In addition to his work with Dire Straits, he also found time to produce Bob Dylan's *Infidels* in the middle of the upcoming tour, and his now famous soundtrack to *Local Hero* was just about to be released. Incredibly, over the next year or so, he also wrote the musical scores for the Irish drama *Cal* and another Bill Forsyth comedy, *Comfort and Joy*. He also produced Aztec Camera's album *Knife* and he played on an album for Scott Walker. I have written a few songs of my own over the years, and it's only when you've had a crack yourself that you are able to acknowledge and respect the efforts of others.

*

You wouldn't want me to describe every single show we played on every tour, which is just as well because, as I mentioned, I can't remember most of them. They swarm in my memory as one giant performance, a sea of faces before me, the heat of the lights, the sweat, the concentration, the roar of a happy audience, then a few beers after and either back to the hotel for a bite to eat or straight on to the tour bus. Besides, this book would have to be broken down into three separate, massive volumes, longer than Edward Gibbon's *History of the Decline and Fall of the Roman Empire*. And who ever finished that?

So I tend to think in highlights. The most significant part of the tour, not for the band but for me, came when we arrived in Sydney. I was lying in my hotel room, the Sebel Townhouse in the Kings Cross area, when the phone rang.

The Sebel was a famous Sydney landmark and the unofficial hotel of the Australian music and film industry in sleazy Kings Cross, home to hookers, pimps and dealers. It was colourful and edgy, you might say. A year or so earlier, the hotel had hosted the reception for Elton John and Renate Blauel's wedding. Tales of excess and wild debauchery at the Sebel are legion; the discretion of the staff is one of the reasons why it is so loved by the more untamed celebrities.

On the other end of the line a voice said, 'G'day, mate, Brett Whiteley here. Do you fancy coming to see my paintings?'

The name rang a dim bell. Where had I heard that name before? I couldn't remember. 'Er . . . okay,' I said.

I had nothing better to do but lie around before the first gig the next night, so I hopped in a cab and presented myself at his huge studio-cum-apartment, a former gasworks in the Circular Quay area, on the harbour opposite the Sydney Opera House. Brett was on the phone when he let me in and gestured to me to make myself at home and have a walk around.

Focused mainly on music, I had taken only a passing interest in the visual arts since my days in Don Faulkner's classroom, occasionally visiting an art gallery if we had the time while on tour. But as I took a stroll and looked at Brett's canvases, I underwent some sort of experience. It was the only time in my life, in a studio or a gallery, that I have been so moved by what I was looking at it was almost a physical experience. By the time Brett got off the phone I was almost speechless. I knew enough about art to know that I was in the workplace of a genius. I am sure the effect would have been the same even if I had taken no interest in art. Brett Whiteley was one of the great artists of his generation. I have collected a few of his paintings over the years, including a very large one, *Paris Summary*, which is ten foot square and hangs in our hall at home. I walk past it a dozen times a day, and each time I am reminded of that extraordinary character, artist and friend.

'Do you like chicken livers, mate?' he chirped, putting down the phone.

'Well, sure, lovely.'

'Great, let's get chicken livers and some good Aussie red to drink.'

Brett liked his chicken livers, I was to discover, almost as much as he liked his drink.

So, that's what we did. He ordered up from the French restaurant under the studio, we ate chicken livers, drank wine and became the best of friends. It was an intense and at times difficult but enriching friendship that lasted ten years, until the fateful day he had a heart attack as he was coming off heroin. I could write a whole book about Brett. In fact, a few people have. He was a great inspiration, an unpredictable character who reopened my eyes to art and gave me another way of looking at life. He was both sophisticated and coarse at the same time, wild and dangerous but thoughtful and kind, a drunk junkie angel with the tongue of a viper, the sensitivity of a toddler and the ice-cold heart of an artist on a mission to deliver what he knew he had to deliver, and nothing was going to stop him doing that or from being himself in order to do it. To visit an art gallery with Brett was an experience; his depth of knowledge and insight into art was remarkable. He saw things invisible to lesser mortals.

I have been privileged to know two great artists well in my lifetime, both great friends: Mark and Brett. Some people you meet have a special way of seeing the world and reinterpret it for the rest of us. Brett was one of those. He did the world great favours with the art he left behind — check it out, it's mind-blowing — but he did himself no favours in the execution of it. He was tormented by demons. To achieve what he wanted in art, he'd explain, he needed to 'nudge it along a bit' or 'trick them up' with drink and narcotics. When he was off heroin, he used to throw back three massive whisky and orange juices then hurl himself into his work. He was a very gifted draughtsman but felt he needed the boldness he thought stimulants gave him.

I've met a few characters like Brett in music and art over the years, the ones who can't produce their remarkable work without some help from substances. People laugh at the notion of artists 'suffering for their art', but there is some truth in it. No great art has ever emerged from smugness and complacency, and some of the very greatest work has emerged from some of the greatest suffering. I lost a great friend and artist to that truth. The artist is in the business of re-presenting life, putting it into some sort of altered state so that it's a little strange, to make you look at it, read it or listen to it in a way that will make you stop and think. That's what gives it meaning, being slightly different to the plain truth.

Brett absolutely loved his music, and I know that when he called the Sebel that first time it was Mark he was after, and I am very happy that Mark was out and that he got put through to me instead. He came along to all four of our shows in Sydney, and we loved having him around, entertaining us all backstage. He ended up becoming great friends with Mark too. He got to know many other Sebel guests, including Bono, Billy Connolly and Bob Dylan, and you had to admire him for having the courage to call them up. Brett was obsessed with Dylan, knew as much about his music as anyone, and he was overjoyed when Dylan agreed to hold a press conference in his studio on one visit to Sydney.

The *Love Over Gold* tour was also memorable for our one and only visit to Japan. We went there after sixteen shows across Australia, all pretty big, a minimum of six thousand each night, plus two huge outdoor shows in New Zealand, in Wellington and Western Springs outside Auckland. Japan is a wonderful, weird place. It might just as well have been the moon back in the early eighties. The country was only just starting to emerge from its self-imposed isolation from the world, and not many people spoke English, which added to the strangeness and the comedy. We put on four shows, three in Tokyo, one in Osaka, and the most remarkable and mildly unsettling feature of all the crowds was their extraordinary politeness, bordering on the reverence you'd see in a church congregation. We played every single track to a completely motionless, packed but silent auditorium. And as soon as the last chord was struck, the room erupted into rapturous applause. Then, total silence again. It was, I imagine, similar to being a member of an orchestra playing at the Royal Albert Hall.

Having time off during the day, we made the most of it and wandered around doing the tourist thing, and drawing attention to ourselves without doing anything. It was slightly unsettling that, because I was so tall, and Hal was so blond, people pointed at us wherever we went.

Daily life in Tokyo was no less bizarre to us Westerners than the concerts we played there. On the Sunday we were there we went to Yoyogi Park to kill some time before the show and came across dozens of little gangs of teenagers dressed up as fifties American rock 'n' roll kids with a Japanese twist. I guessed that this trend, like baseball, must have been a legacy of the American occupation after the war. Each little group had its own boogie box playing Buddy Holly and Eddie Cochran, and the lads were wearing leather jackets and brothel creepers, the girls in knee-length bobby socks and pigtails, all grooving to the beat at their feet. I guess the eighties for Japanese youth was the equivalent of the sixties for us: youngsters asserting themselves against their parents, emerging from the austerity and the old hierarchies. It left a big impression, Japan, so different to Europe, Australasia and the United States, and a true pleasure for that.

We returned to the UK and, after a short break, hit the road again in Europe, most of the shows staged outdoors in large sports stadiums. The highlight was another utterly crazy week in Italy, this time with a new promoter, David Zard, which reached the peak of craziness in Naples. The medieval home of the commedia dell'arte, Italy certainly has a cultural gift for drama and comedy that is expressed still today in every area of life. In every activity from serving a coffee to staging a concert, the attitude seems to be 'Why make an event simple and straightforward and free of hassle when you can have some fun and turn it into a something thrilling and unsettling and, in hindsight, quite amusing?' That pretty well sums up our experience in Naples, admittedly the craziest of all Italian cities.

The gig itself, of course, only went ahead, so we were led to understand, with the permission of the Mafia. And, as with the last time in Italy, we stood to make precious little money. In spite of playing before about thirty thousand people, we would cover only the cost of our road crew and our hotel bills. On the night, the hair-raising comedy began when we climbed into the complimentary limos outside the hotel and were given a police escort to the giant Stadio Comunale, about twenty minutes out of town on the motorway. There was absolutely no time pressure, but that didn't stop the cops haring off at breakneck speed, sirens blaring, lights whirling, and soon we were weaving in and out of the traffic in these giant limos. It was terrifying and we clung on to whatever handle or support we could find. Nothing like keeping under the radar and not drawing attention to ourselves.

You're not meant to park up on motorways, the fast traffic posing a mortal danger to those who do, but from about a mile from the stadium the slow lane had been turned into a parking lot and concert-goers were ambling down the tarmac like they were on the pavement of a pedestrianized precinct. We were in a state of borderline shock when, to our great relief, the limos pulled up to the venue and we made our way backstage. But that was only the start of the fun. There had been a huge thunderstorm before we had set out and the stage had been struck by lightning, blowing out much of the equipment. The roadies did an amazing job to get enough of it up and running again in the hour they had before we took to the stage. Half the amps and pedals were still down, and we played the whole concert at half power, although, amazingly, no one seemed to notice.

It's funny looking back, but it was highly alarming at the time when another thunderstorm broke halfway through the show. A bolt of lightning struck the stage scaffolding and the electricity travelled down into the crowd. For a few seconds, one entire section of people was mildly electrocuted, electricity rolling through them. It was like a giant Ready Brek advert. But there is no more excitable, naturally electrocuted crowd than an Italian one and, once again, no one seemed to notice apart from us, as we looked on in horror from above. After the concert, we were driven back, again under police escort and again like we were in a Formula One race, but this time it was even scarier because all the power in the city had gone down and our limos raced after the police down the narrow streets in complete darkness. The Naples council had not paid their electricity bill, apparently.

I should mention Mel Collins here, a wonderful sax player who joined us for the European leg of the *Love Over Gold* tour, because not only was he a great musician but also he had the interesting habit of playing his sax stark naked in the corridor after a gig. Or sometimes he would find the highest balcony wall in the hotel and play his sax to anyone who would listen. He was erratic and eccentric — we did worry about him a bit. But also completely brilliant.

After a stopover in Zagreb (only marginally less crazy than Italy), and a huge show at Punchestown racecourse in Ireland, the *Love Over Gold* tour came to a brilliant climax with three nights at the Hammersmith Odeon, now the Apollo. It's fair to say the Straits had rarely played better than we did those three nights. The second night was recorded and the music put down on the double album *Alchemy Live*, with artwork by Brett on the cover, and featuring a guest appearance by Hank Marvin, another great influence on young British guitar players, and a delightful man.

At the Odeon, you hear a band in complete harmony with itself, every song superbly executed. It's all about feel, music, and we were all on top of our game at the end of that tour. It's difficult to describe to someone who has not had the experience, but when a band hits its stride, everything falling into place, there is no feeling like it. Terry Williams, always powerful, never skipped a beat, and it was probably his virtuoso performance that set the pace and tone. Hal, too, was as good as he had ever been, playing with real confidence. Inevitably, I have forgotten many shows we played, but never those three. There was incredible energy on stage and in the audience both nights as soon as we walked on, and the exhaustion we had been feeling vanished. We had never been better and, home again afterwards to my wife and child, for me, life had never felt better.

Chapter 19

Brothers and Souls

When the bass player of a rock 'n' roll band steps out and says he wants to produce a solo album, most record-company executives pretend not to have heard; they look at their watches and leg it for the emergency stairs. Phonogram had the good manners to indulge me. Dire Straits were getting on for becoming one of the biggest bands in the world at this time, so perhaps they were unable to look the other way, not wanting to upset one of its two remaining founder members.

Egotism was not my motivation. On the contrary, I was every bit as anxious about the enterprise as I am sure the label was. I had been playing other people's music all my life and you can't do that without feeling something of a passive passenger on the magical music bus. If my effort proved a failure, then at least I could not kick myself years down the line for not having given it a go. I believe there is music and art in all of us. It takes labour and craft to write a song, paint a picture or write a story, and after the tour I had the will, bordering on an urgency — as well as the time on my hands — to find out what, if anything, was inside me to offer.

I had forgotten that I had already tried my hand at writing songs. Recently, I was rummaging around in some boxes in an outbuilding at home and found a mouldy old diary from 1978 in which I had scrawled several pages of lyrics. Evidently, the desire to write songs had always been there, but now I had the opportunity to settle down and apply myself to the task.

I was under no illusions. It was a daunting prospect to come up with a whole collection of songs worthy of release. There are more strings on a guitar than good solo artists to emerge from a successful rock band. Sting, Eric Clapton and Phil Collins spring to mind at once, but even some of the greats, like Mick Jagger, struggled to make an impact solo. There is always the suspicion out there that the solo artist is just clinging on to the coat tails of their band. There is also, I suspect, a feeling that whatever is produced will be a pale imitation of the band's work. Inevitably, comparisons with the band will be made and, on the whole, the solo artist's efforts are often soon forgotten. Mark is one of the few to go on to enjoy a flourishing solo career. But my attitude is that if you want to have a go, why not? It's up to others if they want to listen to it.

It's difficult to know where to start with a song — the music, the lyrics, a powerful experience, the germ of a story, a strong image? I found that the emergence of each song was different. Strumming a few chords might set me on my way, or it might be a line in my head that brings its own rhythm and metre and triggers the flow, or an experience or a story that has made an impression on me. For many songwriters, the piano is the working tool of choice, so I invested in a Yamaha baby grand, which I installed in the house at Telscombe. I still use it today and, like many instruments, it has improved with age. So, too, does my youngest son, Harry, at playing it — he has become a far better player than me.

Every day, I sat down at the keys and gradually taught myself to play. I remain a very rudimentary player today, but I am good enough to experiment with song ideas. Learning a new instrument is a wonderful experience. New worlds and creative possibilities open up, and my confidence and excitement grew in step with my technical progress, spurring me on. The piano is often described as the complete instrument, and each day I did feel a noticeable expansion in my feel for and knowledge of music.

I wasn't particularly methodical about the writing and soon my head was full of chords and I had scraps of lyrics, song titles and ideas filling my notebook. Each song has its own life and, over the months, one by one, they came into some sort of focus, assuming a shape and a definition I could almost see as much as hear. Noel Gallagher once described the process as 'waiting for a song to fall into your lap', and he's right. There's no telling from where and when it will come. There is an infinity of options and there is no standard or perfect way to go about it.

A mixture of songs began to emerge, some based on personal experience, feelings and memories, some on observations of the world. 'Boy with Chinese Eyes' was about the birth of my son James, 'Night Café' is a story inspired by the Van Gogh painting *Café Terrace at Night,* the title track, 'Never Told a Soul', is about the break-up of a relationship, and I am particularly fond of 'Northern Land', about the Troubles in Northern Ireland. 'Jimmy on the Central Line' is about a busker, an idea triggered by my friend Bob Mazzer's haunting photo, which we used for the cover of my first solo album. Bob is a highly regarded photographer today, capturing gritty and colourful pictures of daily life in Britain.

Before heading into Parkgate recording studios, in Battle down on the East Sussex coast, I worked closely with Kevin Jarvis, an excellent local pianist. He's a very good player, and when he sat down to play the track 'Never Told a Soul' for the first time, he brought it to life in a way I could never manage. I now understood how exposed you are as a songwriter. You're putting your soul out there, as well as

Above: Mark
and I had a lot
of fun.

Left: 1985. 'Are
you sure that's
the right chord?'

Above: Very sweaty gig on our first US tour in 1978.

Below: With Hal Lindes during the On Location 115-date tour of the US in 1980–81. Who said 'that ain't working'?

Great live action on the Love Over Gold *tour in 1982–3.*

The Hammersmith Odeon, now the Apollo, was one of our favourite gigs. December 1985.

From the On Every Street *tour in 1992. This was one of 229 shows.*

Above: Great to have Eric Clapton playing with us on the Mandela seventieth-birthday concert at Wembley Stadium. He loved letting Mark do most of the solos.

Below: A moment of madness when Jagger and Bowie turned up unexpectedly at a Prince's Trust gig. It was a surreal moment for me at that event to play bass on 'I Saw Her Standing There' with Paul McCartney himself.

The line-up for the Prince's Trust gig in June 1986. A few familiar faces surrounding Tina (the Queen) Turner!

Above: My lovely family at my sixtieth-birthday party. What a night that was.

Below: My four beautiful children: Harry, James, Jess and Dee Dee at Jess and Moses's wedding.

Above: Every schoolboy dreams about joining a rock 'n' roll band and owning a pub – and why not? I bought the East End Arms in the New Forest in 1989.

Below: Dirt bikes and donkeys outside my pub.

Above: When the Straits stopped touring I was able to follow my other passion, painting. From a very early age I've always been inspired by painters and pictures.

Right: Simply the love of my life – my wife, Steph.

your craft, for people to judge. There is no hiding place. Mark and Terry came down and played on a few tracks, and that was reassuring. Chris White, who would become involved with us in Dire Straits, did some sax work, Bobby Valentino from The Fabulous Poodles, who we knew from our Deptford days, provided some violin, and Phil Palmer, nephew of The Kinks' Ray and David Davies, contributed some guitar. Phil would join Dire Straits as a supporting musician on our final tour, and so a great deal more than just an album came from my solo enterprise. Connections were made; reputations and relationships were forged as a result of it. I was lucky, too, to have Jody Linscott, a fabulous percussionist, work on a couple of tracks. Jody has done session work with scores of bands and artists. She is as wonderful a person as she is a musician, and we have continued to work with each other over the years.

Recording turned out to be a very enjoyable experience. The visiting musicians often stayed the night at the studios, so we were able to kick back and enjoy ourselves at the end of a session. With every passing, busy day, I felt more confident about the songs. I managed to secure Phill Brown, one of the top audio engineers in the music business, to co-produce the album. He had worked with Bowie, Bob Marley, Traffic, Led Zep and Talk Talk, among many others, and it was greatly reassuring for me to have his inspiring input and technical skills when we recorded the album. Phill was organized and brimming with creative suggestions — a true master of his craft, fantastic to work with. The mixing was done in George Martin's famous AIR Studios in Hampstead, north London, and we shot a video for the title track in an old chapel nearby. It looks painfully dated now, as most things from the eighties do.

The album was released in the spring of 1984, but by then I was back on Dire Straits duty and there was not much time for promo work. I was happy with the way it was received and it sold about eighty thousand copies, paying its way and making Phonogram a few

Another gold album from the Netherlands, this time in 1982. Some of us still hadn't learned to look at the camera!

quid. It came out at roughly the same time as our live album *Alchemy*, and it was certainly no threat or rival to that. *Alchemy* was a huge success, making the top ten in almost every major record-buying country except the States, reaching number three in four countries including the UK, and number one in the Netherlands, our favourite backyard.

Making a solo album was an adventure on which I had to embark, a mountain looming over me that I knew one day I'd have to climb. In doing it, I felt I had grown up and moved forward a little as a musician and as a writer. I had discovered what I had suspected to be true: it's hard work writing songs. So, rejoining the Straits to work on our fifth album, I was a little wiser about the craft and in a better position to understand Mark's latest achievement. With *Brothers in Arms*, he displayed songwriting of the highest order. The album was to become one of the bestselling of all time, and it was going to catapult the band as far as you can go in the world of music — without being Elvis Presley or The Beatles, that is. We were in for an extraordinary, slightly overwhelming, few years.

When the band reconvened that early summer of 1984, almost a year since the end of the *Love Over Gold* tour, Mark had written all nine of the songs that would end up on the album. They were an interesting mix of styles. We started informally, meeting in Mark's mews house in west London, where he had a piano. Tentatively at first, we worked our way through them, getting the feel for the new material.

There was one new face in the gathering: Guy Fletcher, a highly talented and experienced keyboardist who had toured with Roxy Music and Steve Harley & Cockney Rebel. He came with two additional advantages other than his exquisite playing: he was technically adroit with anything electronic and digital, an essential quality in a world of rapidly developing technology. We were soon to learn that no amount of buttons, dials, sliders and flashing lights could defeat Guy. You could sit him down in the cockpit of a jumbo jet for half an hour and he'd probably work it out and take it for a spin. He was also a delightful, easy-going guy and I knew from our first handshake that he was going to be a pleasure to tour with. We remain great friends to this day. He and Alan Clark were soon to be known to the crew and the rest of the band as 'the keyboard twins'.

Guy replaced Tommy Mandel, who had joined us for the *Love Over Gold* tour and had done a great job, not least in keeping us in high humour with his antics throughout. Tommy is a lovable and excitable New Yorker. Being Bryan Adams's keyboardist is his day job but, luckily for us, he had a gap in the schedule that allowed him to come on board with the Straits. When he first turned up for a pre-tour rehearsal, he was wearing a charity-shop purple suit over a black T-shirt and he had no socks on, and no luggage, just a carrier bag with his toothbrush and a few other miscellaneous items.

Someone had the courage to say, 'Tommy, we're going to be on the road for nine months. You might want to change your clothes, especially your underpants, occasionally.'

Tommy looked nonplussed but eventually agreed that a change of clothes — underwear, at least — made some sense, and someone was sent out to buy him what he needed. He was a very talented player, and quite technically minded too. Tommy's eccentricities were sometimes expressed in his playing. At a concert in Sydney, a weird whooshing noise filled the air during 'Sultans of Swing'. After the gig, Mark asked politely what he had been doing.

'I thought some Siberian wind might add a little something.'

'Siberian wind? Do you mind not doing that again?'

'Yeah, sure, no problem. It was just a bit of fun.'

He was fun, that was for sure, especially after the show, constantly entertaining the rest of us and anyone else who happened to be in his orbit. If there was a piano in the hotel bar or foyer, he'd get on it and play. In other characters, the prankish comedy might have become irritating, but not him. Mad as a box of frogs, maybe, but Tommy was a good guy. We loved our short time with him and he could really play.

Guy took over his role on a permanent basis because he was based in the UK, and the keyboard work, whether piano, Hammond organ or synthesizer, was becoming an ever more important part of our music. The wealth of options opened up by technology meant that we now had more kit than a NASA control room, and Guy and Alan were going to invest many long hours in exploring and perfecting the sound. This was the first album when we didn't use Wood Wharf to rehearse, partly because transporting the equipment was an issue, and also because it was just too small for the expanded band and too unsophisticated for the more involved, multilayered music we were now playing. Mark was constantly pushing the boundaries of new technology, so he hit it off with Guy straight away, and soon we had an enormous machine called a Synclavier, bought by Mark. I do not have anything like the knowledge to explain it to you but, in short, it was an early digital synthesizer capable of almost any sound and, more importantly, it could record what we were doing. Thank God for Guy, because he's probably the only man ever to master all its manifold possibilities.

The album was to be recorded at George Martin's AIR Studios in the Caribbean on the tiny British Overseas Territory of Montserrat. Before we left to go there in October, we spent a couple of weeks fine-tuning in the rehearsal studio of Phil Manzanera, producer, lead guitarist of Roxy Music and a friend of Guy's. The idea was to give the songs more structure and definition in a proper setting before heading out to Montserrat, where we were to team up with Neil Dorfsman again.

It sounds very flash, very rock 'n' roll, to go to the Caribbean to record an album, but the truth is more prosaic. There's a reason why it wasn't done in New Orleans, or even in Kingston, Jamaica: no distractions. Montserrat, like Nassau, is tiny. There's literally nothing to do. There's no great cultural or social scene in which to get lost. The idea was to work, and that's what we did, very hard, for a few months. Sure, we'd unwind with some beers and rum, maybe a few extras, but that didn't happen until very late in the evening, by which time we were exhausted.

It was a cool studio, too, with all the facilities, and some great names have recorded there, including The Stones, The Police, Phil Collins and Elton John. We put in even more hours than we planned because it rained virtually every day, upsetting the keyboard twins, who loved to head out windsurfing whenever we weren't in the studio. The rest of us weren't too bothered by that, we were happy holed up in the studio, but it was a shame for Pauline and James, who came out for a few weeks.

Neil Dorfsman is another perfectionist, one of the reasons why he has become so successful. He feels music in his bones, and he was always determined to get the sound just right. The producer almost becomes a member of the band during recording, as George Martin did with The Beatles. It was no insult to Terry Williams that Neil felt the drums weren't absolutely spot on. The studio recording had to be precise. Terry was one of the best live drummers in the world, but Neil was a little frustrated that he was perhaps a few percentage points short of the precision needed for the recording.

Brothers in Arms was one of the first albums to be recorded digitally, on two Sony twenty-four-track digital tape machines, so the requirement for absolute accuracy was way greater than it had been in the past. It was also one of the first albums ever published in CD format, as well as on vinyl and cassette. Precision was the watchword. When it was discovered, during a break for Christmas, that some of the recording was faulty and several of the drum tracks had been lost, the decision was taken to rework some of them after the break. Omar Hakim, a very accomplished drummer, was flown in. Terry wasn't over the moon, but he understood the situation. Both drummers are credited on the album because Terry's excellent crescendo at the start of 'Money for Nothing' was retained.

I loved working with Omar in the drums and bass engine room. We clicked straight away and it was a privilege to witness him at work. Omar, who has played with scores of the great acts, was only with us for two or three days, but that was all he needed to put down every track to perfection. It was like watching someone patting their head, rubbing their stomach, spinning a dozen plates and negotiating a tightrope all at once. Just watching him arrange his kit was extraordinary. He kept playing every drum and cymbal he had set up while he added the next piece. It was as if he had eight arms and four legs, all playing different rhythms. There are few drummers who can do anything you ask of them, but Omar, schooled in jazz fusion, is one of them. As he was building his kit, Mark turned to me and said, 'Well, I don't think he's going to have much trouble with our stuff.'

There's a big difference between playing live and recording in a studio. A more fluid energy is needed in the febrile atmosphere of a packed auditorium or stadium while, in a studio, all the instruments are recorded separately on their own tracks before being mixed, so it has to be tight — tight as a drum, if you like. The drums first, then the bass, have to be spot on when recording, otherwise the whole song, even if just a few inches out at the base of it, starts to lean. Terry rejoined us for the tour and, as ever, he was outstanding when we played live, a really physical, emotional drummer whose playing always drew the attention and the plaudits. Ask people about a Dire Straits concert in this period and so many of them mention Terry's drumming.

Recording digitally was a first for us. None of us really understood it back then. We learned as we went, but Neil and Guy were loving it because we were able to record a great many more tracks than in the past. With all this technology in use, it was amusing, if slightly nerve-wracking, to watch the state-of-the-art Synclavier and the digital machines being delivered to AIR Studios. Life on Montserrat was beautifully simple, by no means backward but neither was it an advanced and modern country at the cutting edge of the high-tech revolution. Kids ran naked in the dirt roads, girls sat outside houses plaiting each other's hair, there was no more than a handful of shack bars and roadside food joints and certainly no cashpoint machines or any of the other mod cons you saw back home. Life can't have changed much for decades. We were sitting outside the studios when the Synclavier and other equipment arrived and were slightly aghast to see it in the open air, strapped down in the back of a Toyota pick-up, bumping its way up the rutted hillside in a cloud of dust.

To everyone's relief, the machinery was fine, and we settled down to refine the diverse range of songs over the coming weeks and months. I didn't need to be a techno geek to understand that the AIR Studios was a cut above any other recording studio we had worked in. There was a Neve 8078 mixing desk, as good as it got back then. The only issue was space. It was a very small room, about twenty foot by twenty-five, no bigger than the average sitting room, and there were a lot of us and a lot of equipment to fit in. The drums were squeezed into one corner, the piano (left by Elton John) into another, the keyboards in the control room. My bass amp had to go in a broom cupboard.

The studio was in the most beautiful location, high in the hills overlooking the azure waters of the Caribbean to the west. Working into the night, we'd often take a short break at last light, sitting by the pool with a beer, watching the giant sun sinking over the horizon. The production team stayed at Olveston House, George Martin's beautiful plantation-style home, but I took my own place, a simple clapboard house nearby, so that Pauline and James could have some peace and privacy, using the facilities at the villa when they wanted. The cook was excellent – a really friendly guy called George, known locally as 'Daddy George', as he was father, apparently, to a great many children on the island – and there was also a pool set in a stunning tropical garden.

The work of the bass player in the recording studio is always done early on in the process, so I was able to slip out from time to time for a dip or nip back to grab an hour with Pauline and James. The most challenging track for me, as it would be for any bassist, was 'Ride Across the River'. The notes had to fall at exactly the right moment, in sync with the keyboards.

Part of the challenge of the album was switching between so many different styles of songs, from 'Walk of Life' and 'Money for Nothing' to 'So Far Away' and 'Brothers in Arms'. They were all great tracks and they would all be released successfully as singles, along with the fifth and last single, the slightly less successful 'Your Latest Trick' (although in Poland and France, strangely, it went to number one). We all felt in our bones that 'Money for Nothing' would go down well and were not convinced at first that the opening track of the album, 'So Far Away', was the best choice for the first single. I love that song and, being about life on the road and missing home, it spoke to us all about the strains of touring. But its simplicity proved to be its great virtue and it did well pretty much everywhere on its release. 'Walk of Life' is just pure, upbeat, innocent fun. It very nearly didn't make it on to the album, and who knows what would have become of it? It's unlikely we would have released it as a stand-alone single. Neil Dorfsman wasn't crazy about it, didn't feel that it sat well with the rest of the songs, but he was voted down by the band and on it went. I'm pleased that it did because, with its humour, it brought some balance to the album. 'Brothers in Arms', inspired by the recent Falklands War, was a slow, powerful, mournful song about the futility of war, embraced ever since by the Armed Forces as an anthem at charity fund-raising events.

When recording in the studio, mics are often moved around in the hunt for the best possible sound. The distinctive guitar sound on 'Money for Nothing' came about as a result of a happy accident. It was in the morning and no one had noticed that the mic in front of Mark's Laney amp had fallen and was pointing down at the floor. Mark was using his Gibson Les Paul, trying to achieve that slightly distorted sound similar to the one that ZZ Top's Billy Gibbons gets. Neil was setting up the equipment for the session, and he was about to correct Mark's mic when Mark's guitar tech, Ron Eve, burst on to the talkback, shouting, 'Don't touch a thing! It's perfect!' The sound was so close to what they were looking for that none of it was altered in the mixing process afterwards.

There was little opportunity for hitting the town while we were in Montserrat, partly because we were working till about eleven every night and partly because, as I say, there was no town to hit. There was Plymouth, the capital, but the population of five thousand was no greater than that of a small English market town. Market Harborough, say. Some Saturdays we'd head down there to the evening market and go to the only nightclub in town, the entertainment hub of the island, rammed with happy locals dancing their socks off to Peter Tosh and the local reggae band Arrow. Plymouth was a deeply sleepy place, but today it is a true ghost town because in 1995 it was buried by a massive volcanic eruption. The whole town was evacuated and not a soul lives there now, or in the southern two-thirds of the island. Weird to think that we once danced where all that ash and rock now lie.

After work, most nights we'd head down to a nearby shack bar run by a very long-suffering guy called Andy. He was often sound asleep when we rang him to say we were coming, but he never complained and by the time we got there he had the reggae and calypso on and his contraband beers on ice. George Martin and his wife, Judy, were around, but we didn't see many other people other than the friendly locals most of the time we were there. There was some excitement in the studio one afternoon when the most beautiful two-masted sailing ship sailed into the bay. Nothing ever sailed into the bay, so this was quite a moment. The phone rang an hour or so later. It was Neil Young's recording engineer. He was sailing around the world with Neil in his 101-foot Baltic trading schooner. Neil was keen to see the studio and check out the new digital recording machines — he had a real interest in it all. Neil's music meant a lot to all of us, so we were delighted to play host, and he spent some time asking Neil Dorfsman about the Sony tape machine.

The only shadow over our happy period in Montserrat led, very sadly, to Hal leaving the band a couple of weeks after we arrived on the island. The problem was not really of Hal's construction. His girlfriend, Mary, once married to the English musician and producer Peter Frampton, came out with their young son, and they rented their own house. It became an exclusive enclave, and Mary would occasionally invite me and Mark over for supper, but not the rest of the band or any of the production crew. We felt very uncomfortable about setting ourselves apart from the band, especially on an island where there was almost nothing to do. Like the musketeers, the band sticks together. So we always declined and we began to feel increasingly irritated by this unnecessary and distracting source of division.

It came to a head when Mary's friend Twiggy, the model, arrived on the island. Once again, Mark and I refused to go over there unless the whole band went. The tension escalated and reached the point where we had to sit down with Hal and tell him we could not have the life of the band controlled and directed by the girlfriend of any one of us. So Hal was faced with this awful choice: the band or his girlfriend. He chose his girlfriend, left the island and so was not credited on one of the bestselling albums of all time.

It was a very upsetting moment. Hal was a great guitar player, we loved our time with him and I'm pleased to say we remain good friends to this day. But shit happens, especially in bands — and we were there to work, so there was no moping and we cracked on with the recording. Mark laid down Hal's guitar tracks for the recording and the search began for a guitarist to come on tour with us. There was some urgency to that because the opening show was in Split in late April 1985, and we were going to head out to Yugoslavia a few weeks early to rehearse. We had a few candidates in mind, but now that we had become quite successful, there would be plenty of top players out there happy to join the line-up.

I remember one afternoon when we were recording 'Money for Nothing'. The 'I want my MTV' line at the end was inspired by Mark seeing The Police talking on an advert for MTV and simply saying, 'I want my MTV.' He'd mated that with a few notes from Sting's composition 'Don't Stand So Close to Me'. In the studio, Mark happened to remark, 'I wish Sting was here to sing this part.' And someone said, 'Well, he is. He's here on holiday!' The Police had recorded on Montserrat for a couple of years and it turned out Sting loved to come to the island to windsurf. He'd been spotted out jogging, pounding the dirt lanes in the mornings. We had played quite a few gigs with The Police, mainly in Germany, and got to know them quite well, so – a phone call later – Sting came and joined us for supper one evening. We played some of the tracks from the album and he loved 'Money for Nothing' so Mark popped the question: 'Why not come and sing on it?'

So the next morning, warming up, Sting started singing, 'I want my MTV,' over and over. And that was it. His work was done. It's what you hear on the song. It was a small contribution, but it really added something – and it meant that Sting was credited as co-writer. The song was released in June 1985 and it became our most commercially successful single, topping the US Billboard 100 for three weeks and reaching number four in Britain – a success we were all delighted with.

We were staying out of the country for most of the year to avoid the punitive tax back home, so we went straight from Montserrat to New York to mix and put the final touches to the album at the Power Station. We had moved quickly to replace Hal on guitar, bringing Jack Sonni, a friend of Mark's, over to Montserrat from New York. It was a speculative move that paid off handsomely for all concerned. Jack worked in Rudy's guitar store, our favourite haunt, a few blocks away from the Power Station in Lower Manhattan, where Mark had met him. He could certainly play, and we all got along, so it was decided that Jack was going to join us to play on one of the biggest-selling tours in rock history. I remember Mark saying, 'Sometimes it's nice to play Father Christmas.'

We brought in a number of other top session musicians to the Power Station, including bassists Tony Levin, who played on 'Why Worry', and Neil Jason, who helped out on the song 'One World'. This needed a funk bass sound, which I don't do but Neil does very well. Tony played a bass instrument called a Chapman Stick that looks like a large version of a guitar fretboard and is held almost vertically. He was highly experienced and had played with a host of top acts such as King Crimson and Peter Gabriel. He was a bit rusty at first after six months away from music, but soon found his groove.

We were only in New York for a couple of weeks so there was no point renting an apartment and we stayed in the Mayflower Hotel on Central Park, a well-known rock 'n' roll hotel that you might describe as bohemian if you were in a good mood, or cheap and seedy in a bad one. There was an irritating game you had to play with the hotel reception which involved the guest making several trips up and down in the ancient elevator to complain about their room. Up and down we went, politely requesting one that was not looking out on to a brick wall or the kitchen extraction fan and that boasted a toilet that actually flushed and a shower from which water, preferably hot, came out in something more powerful than a dribble. The hotel was half empty, but between us we made about a dozen trips to the lobby before being given half-decent rooms on the street side, there being little point staying in the Mayflower unless you get that stunning view of Central Park and the Manhattan skyline. It was sad when they bulldozed the hotel a few years back, punching out a tooth in that famous row of buildings, and built 15 Central Park West, one of the fanciest addresses in New York. The apartments in it are occupied by the great and the good and the extremely wealthy.

During this incredible period with the band, it was not going so great with Pauline and we both knew it was going to be very difficult to recover the happy times, that it was all but over. While in New York, I made that area of my life that much more complicated by getting entangled with a Norwegian girl, so when the band members eventually flew home to see our wives, girlfriends and kids, it was probably just as well it was only for a couple of weeks. I had barely set foot in the door at home, kissed Pauline and James hello and unpacked my bags . . . when I was packing them again, kissing Pauline and James goodbye, pulling the door behind me and climbing into the car to take me back to Heathrow. I was probably at home for a week or so, but it didn't feel like that. Then we were on the road for a year and a day: 248 concerts in 118 cities in 23 countries. No wonder the wheels on our magic music bus were starting to wobble by the time it was over. A great deal in our lives was about to change.

Chapter 20

Jerusalem Syndrome

I felt I was living my life with the fast-forward button stuck down, coursing with adrenaline at the prospect of an epic tour that would see us play live before two and a half million people. Every gig was sold out and more and more shows were being added to the schedule. It was going to be remorseless and exhausting, but I was excited. There was a sense the band was peaking and, marshalled by Ed and Paul, we had become a very well-organized and powerful machine on the road. We had a great album about to come out and, thanks to Chas Herington's lighting, each show would be as much a spectacle as a music concert.

Pauline had been impressively stoic about my nomadic lifestyle, which kept me out of the country for all but a couple of months of the year. Even when I was back in the UK, I was often touring or recording. Home life suffered. It must have been so tough for her bringing up a toddler without his father. We were comfortable for money by then, but that was little consolation. I loved Pauline very much but — lonely, bored, carried away, flattered, whatever — I had strayed a couple of times, the ceaseless temptations proving beyond my endurance. So, I set off again, high on my own excitement, high on myself perhaps, not as sensitive to Pauline's situation as I should have been. Success is a powerful drug. So, too, is playing live and travelling to over a hundred of the world's great cities. Touring and playing live is like an addiction.

We flew to Dubrovnik, now in Croatia but then part of Yugoslavia and brewing up for a brutal war that was soon going to devastate the Balkans. Dubrovnik is a beautiful ancient city on the Adriatic coast, so popular with tourists today the authorities want to start limiting numbers. That's not the city we experienced over the two weeks we were there; it was going through a tough time. It was visibly falling apart, nothing worked, there was very little food in the shops and a great tension and despondency hung in the air. It was even worse in Split, where we spent a second fortnight rehearsing. Again, a very beautiful city, further up the coast, but even more gloomy and destitute. Most days there was no coffee or tea at breakfast, occasionally there was an egg, but mostly we ate the local cheese with some Gulag-quality bread. There were scarcely any staff, apparently because the wages were so low there was little point in working. In the market, there were only ever a couple of stalls selling root vegetables. The experience was brightened somewhat when the journalist and presenter Mariella Frostrup, then working in the Phonogram PR department, flew in for a few days. She was a breath of fresh air with her constant smile, quite possibly the only one on view in the country at the time.

It was just as well that our opening show of the tour, in Split, didn't set the tone for the rest. It was by some distance the roughest audience we had ever played for, making the excitable crowds in Italy look like a kid's birthday party. The audience, in the aptly named Gripe concert hall, was 90 per cent male and it was consumed by a violent energy. There was no joy on stage either, watching the fans brawling among themselves and with the security people. There were bottles flying, flares being thrown – indoors! It was great to get on the plane the next day and head to Jerusalem, a true war zone but an absolute delight by comparison.

I had never been to Israel, had only seen the news reports about the ongoing struggle with the Palestinians and the Arabs. We had the luxury of a few days to explore the city before the concert on the last day of April – and what a remarkable and bizarre few days they turned out to be. Paula Yates, soon to be married to Bob Geldof, arrived with a crew to film a documentary about us for the Channel 4 music programme *The Tube* and they followed us wherever we went. Paula was an absolute delight, so warm and natural, and she transformed what might have been a tiresome experience into a bit of harmless fun.

God knows how the production team managed to clear it with the authorities, but one day we found ourselves sitting on donkeys and loping our way through the narrow, cobbled streets in imitation of Jesus entering the Holy City. The footage shows me looking utterly ridiculous with my long legs on this tiny donkey, my shoes trailing on the ground. We got some very strange looks from the locals.

The concert was staged at the Sultan's Pool, a rare honour for a band, and it was one of the most memorable we ever played, for good reasons and bad. The Sultan's Pool is a water basin dating back to the time of King Herod, situated on the side of Mount Zion, overlooking the city. It was surrounded by very high stone walls, and when we arrived and took a peek from the stage it was rammed with an almost solid, roiling mass of people. There was not a yard of space to move. Alarmingly, there appeared to be no police or security personnel, just half a dozen young soldiers below the stage, next to a section reserved for about a dozen wheelchair users.

When we walked out on stage, there was mayhem. The crowd

surged forward and overwhelmed the wheelchair users' area, causing a crush right below us. It was a horrifying few minutes, and it felt like we were witnessing a disaster unfold just a few yards from where we stood. Paul Cummins says he aged ten years in those minutes; it was the most scared he had ever been for the safety of a crowd. He ran around trying to help sort it out, but there were no police — or if there were, they were lost in the melee. At the same time, there was the arresting sight of half a dozen fans abseiling down the walls. It was like a medieval siege. There was bedlam in the shoving, jostling crowd behind, unaware of the trouble up front. The wheelchair users were lost to view in the jam, but then, miraculously, one by one, they emerged from the throng, their chairs lifted up by the other fans and handed on to the stage. There had been no serious injuries among them, thank God.

It turns out, we learned later, that those few young soldiers we'd hoped might be useful for security had come to the gig instead of reporting for duty. They were subsequently disciplined.

We were pretty shaken up by the time the show finally got going, but we soon found our stride. A month later, thirty-nine people were killed and six hundred injured in a stampede and crush at the Heysel Stadium disaster in Brussels. The sports and entertainment industries had yet to wake up to the dangers of poor crowd management. Two gigs into the tour, we had experienced one riot and one potentially catastrophic stampede.

We headed south to a more ordered world in the modern commercial city of Tel Aviv, where we played two shows in City Park. Looking out from our hotel, we could see four gunboats and heavily armed soldiers on every street corner. Israel is not a place to recuperate if you are suffering from nervous exhaustion. The shows passed off happily, though, and the only alarming incident came after the second, when we went out to a bar and fell in with some airline pilots from El Al, the state airline.

All El Al pilots doubled as fighter pilots with the Israeli Defence Force and it was sobering to hear them explain that if they got the call, they'd be scrambling into their cockpits in half an hour on the wrong end of God knows how many beers and cocktails. We hung out with them until about four o'clock in the morning and, as we said goodbye, all of us pretty smashed, we asked them when they were next on duty. Tomorrow, they said, crewing the 11 a.m. flight to Athens. That was our flight! We were a little nervous, hungover ourselves, as we boarded the 747 just seven hours later, but the pilots were as fresh as daisies when they greeted us. They even invited us into the cockpit for the landing ... which went very smoothly, in spite of the pilots almost certainly being over the limit.

From Greece, we moved on in our massive caravan of tour buses and lorries to the Montreux Festival in Switzerland, where we were reunited with Sting and his new band, which included Omar Hakim on drums. I am not sure he and Terry chatted for too long, but it was great to see him and thank him for his excellent work. A few gigs earlier, Sting told us, just before going on stage, the band had approached him and the management, saying they weren't going to play unless they were given more money. Sting said, 'Fine, no matter, I'll play by myself.' And he did, just him and his guitar in front of ten thousand people. The band were back on stage the next night.

Unfortunately, it was back to Yugoslavia after that for two shows in Belgrade and one in Zagreb, all nightmares. As in Split, the crowds were virtually all male, tens of thousands of hooligans fighting and vandalizing, hurling flares and any projectile they could grab or rip out. It was the only time in ten years of touring that I saw squadrons of mounted police charging rioters outside our arena. On our sixth and final tour six years later, there was a war going on, so we were spared the ordeal of playing there. It had been a dubious privilege at our shows in the Balkans to witness close up the intensity of the ethnic tensions that were to explode into full armed conflict.

The show in Ljubljana, the capital of Slovenia, then also part of Yugoslavia, was a calmer experience, but not without its problems. Not long before we went on, Paul took a call from an official saying the gig could not go ahead without blacking out half Ljubljana. The electrical grid did not have sufficient power for both. Our concerts were now placing strain on the power supply of every local system where we played. Our convoy was made up of twelve huge artics rammed with all manner of musical and electrical equipment. We were ourselves a small town on the move.

The Ljubljana mayor got involved in the discussions and, with impeccable logic, he pointed out that as half of the city was going to be at the show, it didn't matter if the other half spent the evening in darkness. Even with half the city's power at our disposal, it was still not enough, and the crew reported that if all the lights and sound came on together, they both dipped, as did the lights in the city. The sound did keep falling away when we played, but no one seemed to notice or care. Slovenians were a gentler breed of Slav, it seemed, and it was reassuring to see our regular 50 per cent quota of women out there, mellowing the testosterone of the male of the species.

This was turning out to be quite an eventful tour, and we found ourselves crossing the border into the Eastern Bloc for three shows in Budapest. It was certainly an eye-opener seeing a Communist city at close quarters, one half of it old and beautiful, where the regime bigwigs lived and worked, the other half a forest of grim tower blocks and factories, propaganda posters and statues of Lenin. Not that we cared, being former council-flat dwellers on a sink estate, but our hotel was pretty dreary, even though it was the most luxurious in the city. Within four years, the transition to a liberal democracy was complete and I'm guessing no one except the party apparatchiks was sad to see the retreat of it.

We were given a lovely young interpreter, probably because the authorities wanted to show off the beauty and intelligence of their Communist womenfolk. She accompanied us to a fancy dinner given in our honour in a grand building on top of the hill on the posh side of town overlooking the Danube. It was all very upmarket, with white linen tablecloths and liveried staff, and all the other tables were occupied by glum, self-important party officials. We were seeing the hypocrisy of Communism at its most hideous, but the killer revelation came when the interpreter was going through the menu and pointed out with a nervous laugh that the cost of the soup was more than she earned in a week. We left Budapest in our cushy, high-tech tour buses, feeling a little uncomfortable about the good fortune that had come our way, that whatever problems Britain might be suffering, thank God it wasn't Communist.

It was while we were in Budapest that we put together the video for 'Money for Nothing', to be released as our second single from the album about six weeks later. The video, partly animated with computer graphics, was groundbreaking. It ended up being the first track ever played on MTV Europe when it launched a couple of years later in 1987 and it is said to have had a huge impact on the way that music videos developed thereafter. It was produced by British film director Steve Barron, a pioneer of computer animation, and his enthusiasm and skills soon got us all excited about this new video phenomenon. Historians of popular culture will tell you that video was something of a landmark moment in the way we enjoy music. Video became almost as important a part of the musical experience as the audio.

We left Budapest on 21 May, a week after the global release of the album. We were too busy to pay much attention to its critical reception, but as news trickled in we were surprised to learn that some of the early reviews back in the UK were quite negative. The one in the *NME* was particularly harsh, but no one was surprised by that. The *NME* was harsh to everyone. We genuinely didn't give a monkey's, and Mark actually roared with laughter at the review. We knew in our waters we had made something worthwhile. It sounded and felt good to us, and the crowds were loving it.

If the intention of the critics had been to deter music-lovers from buying the album, the ploy failed spectacularly. It went straight to number one in every country where sales are recorded. In Britain, it topped the charts for fourteen weeks in total, ten of them consecutive, and became the bestselling album of 1985. In the States, it spent nine weeks at number one on the Billboard 200 and, in Australia, a staggering thirty-four weeks at the top of the charts. It also became the first CD to sell a million copies. The manufacturer in the States complained that such was the demand that they were unable to print any other albums, and unable even to keep pace with demand for *Brothers in Arms*.

The reception elsewhere in Britain and across the States was far more favourable and, once we had passed the 30 million certified sales mark, most critics had come to the view that maybe it wasn't such a shoddy piece of work after all.

On we marched, like a mini-Napoleonic army across Europe, the eighty-strong crew broken down into constituent units with their own officers, with Paul Cummins the general officer commanding the campaign. We really should have bought him a cane and a peaked visor cap. Every day was an epic logistical challenge, demanding speed of action and very hard labour. We, the band, had it easy. We just had to play the music. The only time the crew weren't working was when they climbed on to the tour bus, grabbed a couple of beers and hit their bunks. After playing live to a large audience, the second greatest joy of touring is the thrill of being part of a small travelling community, each day its own mission with its unique set of challenges at each venue. But the objective was the same every time: make sure the band are walking out on stage at eight-thirty. Our crew didn't fail that challenge once in 248 attempts.

Had Ed been able to book all the shows in one go, no doubt our itinerary would have followed a more logical path, but as demand grew, more venues were inserted into the schedule and we ended up zigzagging north and south, east and west. If you were to draw lines between each of the cities we played in Europe, the graphic you'd produce would resemble a young child's drawing rather than a military operational plan. From Hungary, we crossed western Europe to the Low Countries, then went down to France, on into Spain, back to France, across to Switzerland, to France again, then to Luxembourg, up to Belgium and finished up with three shows in Paris.

In spite of the distances, it was all running very smoothly, the band were playing well and getting on well, the venues were heaving, and our new members, Guy Fletcher and Jack Sonni, proved to be superb in live performance. Jack, in particular, relished his unexpected and sudden transformation into a global rock 'n' roll star (on stage as well as off!). Once we reached the venue, the ritual was the same every time, day after day. On arrival in the morning, the crew jumped to, unloading the trucks and building the stage, the light rigging, the sound system and setting up all the musical equipment on stage. The catering tent, the hub of the operation, was erected and set up at once, 'Quiche' Lorraine dishing out refreshments and snacks and preparing meals for eighty.

We would arrive around mid-afternoon because there's not much the musicians can do on site before it's up and running. By then, the crew would have already run a soundcheck to ensure that all the instruments and amps were in good working order. We would then conduct our own, using the monitors, not earpieces. We wanted to hear it out there, get the levels just right for a large arena. Mark had his own guitar-tech roadie, who also looked after Jack; the keyboard twins had their specialist; and Terry and I had ours for the rhythm section, a Dutch guy called Joop, himself a drummer. Every day was Groundhog Day, and it became a very slick operation. If there was a problem at the venue, it was never caused by our crew.

The final ritual was for the whole team to gather in the catering tent for the evening meal. There was no hierarchy, no top table; we all just grabbed a plate and a seat. I loved this ritual, the companionship of it, the solidarity of belonging to the same team and working together for the same cause. For a number of reasons, we rarely used support acts. This was partly because it was extra hassle for the crew, partly because it made the show too long, but mainly because crowds don't really like warm-up acts. They buy their tickets for the main act and get frustrated by the support band, often someone they have never heard of.

We would wait backstage, listening to the growing hum as the crowd streamed in from the streets, the excitement mounting, the adrenaline filtering into the blood. I never got nervous, just excited. In spite of the pressures of his role, I never saw Mark get flustered. He'd be phlegmatic if you dropped him into a pit of snakes. Then, the great moment, the main reason you do it: you make your way up from the back, guitar over your shoulder, the crowd noise getting louder and louder — and you walk on stage, bulldozed by the solid roar that greets you.

It's hard to describe the emotional and physical reaction to the wave of ecstatic delight that rolls off the crowd and crashes on to the stage. Today, we get a small dopamine hit when someone 'likes' one of our social-media posts. Multiply that by about ten thousand and you'll have some understanding of the extraordinary sensation of entering an arena with eighty thousand people in it. It's not an ego thrill, but closer, I believe, to what an extreme sportsman, a BASE jumper or bobsledder, will experience. In these huge venues, you are no more than a toy soldier up on stage, surveying a vast, swelling sea of happy humanity. You may be exhausted, feeling unwell, have had a bad call from home, but all negative feelings are washed away on this riptide of goodwill. And then the second wave comes when the first note is played or the first beat struck. Before you know it, two hours of your life have passed and you're backstage, drenched in sweat, beer in hand. There would be no drug addicts if this experience were available to all. But then again, maybe that is why so many rock stars get involved with drink and drugs; they're trying to re-create the sensation.

Caen was a memorable show on this leg of the tour because my parents dropped by, having driven over in their Volvo estate, en route to their glorified mobile home on the camping site where — my father now retired — they spent three months every summer, among friends they had made down there over the years. (Dad was a solid Volvo man and, like many of his generation who had fought in the war, he would never buy a German or Japanese car.) They had been to a couple of other shows, and Adrian, one of the roadies, always gave them a warm greeting in his sing-song Welsh accent and kept them well supplied with tea and biscuits. All the crew were lovely to them. On the night, they put their collapsible camping chairs at the side of the stage, and it was a heartening moment for me, seeing their smiling faces, knowing that life had worked out okay for their wayward son in the end. I felt a little pride that I had stuck to my instincts and made it work, that I hadn't let them down after all, hadn't wasted all that hard-earned investment in me.

We'd been on the road for eight years, but we had never played in Spain. Our popularity, modest at first, had grown exponentially and we had become as big there as we were anywhere in the world. So we had built in one show in Madrid, two in Barcelona and one in a massive bullring in Bilbao. There was, on the whole, very little difference between audiences wherever we played, the universality of music transcending all other differences. Oddly, the otherwise reserved Scandinavians and Swiss were among the wildest crowds, possibly because a concert was a kind of Bacchanalian experience in which they could let go and lose themselves in the heady atmosphere before returning to their usual manner of cool, polite detachment. But I get a fuzzy glow when I recall our Spanish experience, the hot nights under the stars, the gentle warmth of the vast crowds. Those shows were as good as it got playing live.

Thanks to Chas Herington's incredible lightshow, our concerts had become as dazzling on the eye as, I hope, they were rousing and moving on the ear. They had to be, because we had to fill each enormous arena with as much drama as we could. Music alone was no longer enough. Most live acts up till then offered little else other than the music, maybe a few fireworks chucked in on the last chord. Chas, who now runs Zenith, a very successful lighting company in the States, was among the pioneers to raise the live experience to a new level. The scale now demanded more. So we gave our audiences the whole toyshop: super-powerful lights, lasers and pyrotechnics. We had worked on the interplay between sound and sight while we were rehearsing in Yugoslavia, the lights matching and enhancing the mood of the song. A clear structure was put in place there so that when we hit the road there was not much more than some tweaking and fine-tuning to work on.

There was no better example of this visual feast than at the Stade Louis II in Monaco, where we headed after Spain via a couple of nights in Toulouse. In Monaco, because there was full cloud cover for once, Chas had the opportunity finally to try out his state-of-the-art laser equipment, beaming images of flying swans over our heads and drawing gasps of astonishment from the crowd.

A little name-dropping, if you'll excuse me, purely in the interests of historical record, of course, but after the show we were visited backstage by Prince Albert of Monaco and Princesses Stephanie and Caroline. Royalty had found their way into our sweaty dressing room to pay their compliments and I am happy to report that they were charming — though not so charming that Mark would hand over his shirt, which was an unexpected request. The first figure of any note to visit us after a show had been a staggering Keith Moon, royalty of sorts himself, of course, but backstage at that stadium was one of those moments when, too busy otherwise to reflect, the full import of your journey through life strikes you between the eyes.

Chapter 21

Live Aid Union

We returned to Britain at the end of June, a few days after the release of 'Money for Nothing'. It was great to get home briefly to see James, but things were a little chilly with Pauline, and there was no time to enjoy family life and break some ice. A couple of days later we were off to Birmingham to play four nights at the NEC, two at the Brighton Centre, then thirteen consecutively at Wembley Arena: three venues, 235,000 people, pretty much the equivalent of the population of Belfast back then. I stayed at home when we played Wembley, but I was using it as little more than a place to sleep, coming back in the small hours, sleeping late then heading back up to north London – not a great way to warm the atmosphere and thaw the frost. I was trapped between a failing marriage and my part in a successful band. This is the stuff of personal tragedies. What was I to do? I couldn't, and didn't want to, trade in one for the other. It could only continue as it was, and I would have to pray it worked out somehow. What would be would have to be. There was no way out.

It was heartening to see 'Money for Nothing' climb up the charts.

This is a fact, not a boast, but it was now being said, though never by us, that we had become the biggest band in the world, and it was for this reason that we were faced with a very awkward moral dilemma. Bob Geldof was manically organizing Live Aid, the now famous benefit concert, to raise money for the victims of a dreadful famine in Ethiopia. It was scheduled to take place at Wembley Stadium, a short walk from the Arena, on 13 July, but he was struggling to persuade many of the big acts and artists to take part, pulling his hair out and banging phones. Bob was very keen — 'I absolutely focking insist' — that the Straits headlined the concert, arguing that if he got us on board, all the others would follow.

It was an honour to be asked to top the bill when there were so many other huge names on the British music scene at the time. The problem was that we were contracted to play the Arena the same night and all the 12,500 tickets had been sold months before. Did we let down our loyal fans, or did we fail to meet an arguably more powerful moral imperative and decline to add our voices to a global appeal aimed at alleviating widespread suffering? As with my marriage, there seemed to be no answer.

Geldof was on our case like a Rottweiler in a cattery, first with Ed, then with Mark, and I ended up in the final discussions too. Bob Geldof is an extremely hard man to say no to. His tenacity and passion for the cause was demonic and angelic all at once. Live Aid was an astonishing feat of organization, the music industry's equivalent of planning for D-Day, the main elements of it being carried out in just a few weeks, and most of it by one very insistent Irishman.

The talks went back and forth and, eventually, Bob had to concede that it was impossible for us to headline, so we agreed to perform in the late afternoon. We understood what was at stake, and it was good to hear that other big acts joined the line-up once we were confirmed on the bill. It was a major breakthrough for Bob, and it's pleasing to know that we played our part in the success of the enterprise. If we

Live Aid with Jack Sonni. What a remarkable day for all concerned.
Well done, Bob Geldof, for pulling off the impossible.

helped save some lives and raise some awareness, then that is an achievement as gratifying as any in the success we enjoyed as a band. It was an extraordinary day, of course, vividly remembered by all who took part and watched it. There was a wonderful informal amateurishness to the proceedings, like a massive school concert, most of the egos of the great names of music deflated for the day.

After our soundcheck at the Arena, we walked across the car park to Wembley Stadium and went on in between U2 and Queen, playing 'Money for Nothing' with Sting and then 'Sultans of Swing'. We may not have been headlining, but we played the longest of all the acts, about twenty minutes in all, in an atmosphere as electrifying as any we had ever played in and in the knowledge that there were close to a billion people watching on television. A billion! That was about a fifth of the Earth's population. Of course we were nervous walking out on that stage, not least because no one got a soundcheck. We just walked on, plugged in, and I had barely pulled the strap of my guitar over my shoulder when Sting started singing 'I want my MTV . . .' Every band had different settings and the crew that day did an extraordinary job in pulling it off. On top of everything else, Live Aid was a logistical feat of the highest order. Our performance didn't let us down but, in retrospect, I'm just very glad we came on before rather than after Queen. Their performance stole the show.

Aware that we had just taken part in a great historical event, it was an odd sensation when, half an hour later, we were out the rear and crossing the car park back to the Arena, with the security guy there hassling us for our passes. That was our tenth show at the Arena and the band was on top form, buoyed up by having just played at the biggest show on Earth. Jack was loving every moment of his new life in the limelight and we also had Chris White, a great saxophone player and an excellent addition to the line-up.

The tour was a five-legger, and a few days after Wembley we found ourselves 30,000 feet above the Atlantic, looking down on Greenland en route for Montreal for the start of a 57-show tour of North America. This time we'd be heading clockwise, down the east coast from Canada, across the south, up the Pacific Seaboard before heading back into Canada over in the west, then around to the Eastern Seaboard again. The plan had been to finish off at Madison Square Garden, New York, one of the great venues, but demand being what it was, a postscript show was tacked on for East Rutherford, New Jersey. Such were the vast distances involved and the tightness of the schedule, with only a couple of days off, that we had two crews on the road, leapfrogging each other all the way around the circuit.

The shows were a mixed bag of medium-sized and huge venues, many of the latter being added when *Brothers in Arms* went stratospheric over there. Ed Bicknell was a very busy man in this period, barely off the phone. It was a gruelling schedule, with dozens of press and PR functions to attend in between the travel, the playing and the occasional full night's sleep. This was not a tour designed for a leisurely bus ride and we often had to take a flight to the next stop. The administrative challenge behind the scenes was every bit as demanding as the logistical one on the ground at the venues. There was a powerful sense of mission throughout, but we were nothing if not a professional team now and every member of the band was a strong character. No one cracked.

A rich diversity of venues and the yo-yoing scale of the audiences ensured there was no danger of us sliding into numbing routine. We began with a string of seven huge shows at sports arenas in Canada before crossing the border, playing a mix of cavernous theatres and vast amphitheatre venues in the north-east, the most memorable, probably owing to its name, being the ski resort of Pine Knob. Two days later we were on stage in Pittsburgh at the Syria Mosque. We were a little surprised when we saw that on our schedule. Had our appeal become so great that the Muslims of western Pennsylvania had granted us special dispensation to strut our stuff in their holy place of worship? As it turned out, the venue, played by dozens of the great music acts from Louis Armstrong and Duke Ellington to Springsteen, Marley and Bowie, was a Masonic temple belonging to the Ancient Arabic Order of the Nobles of the Mystic Shrine. Sensibly, they had abbreviated their name to the Shriners. There are 350,000 members today, in a community dedicated to 'fun and fraternity'. And we did have fun. It was a great venue.

The most spectacular venue we played, right up there with the Roman amphitheatre in Orange and the Sultan's Pool in Jerusalem, was the Red Rocks amphitheatre in Morrison, Colorado, a twenty-minute ride from Denver. It had won the accolade of best small outdoor venue so many times that *Pollstar* magazine changed the name to the Red Rocks Award. Carved out of the solid rock hillside, its views as remarkable as the acoustics, it was a breathtaking setting, with the stage at the foot looking up at what appeared, in the night, to be steepling and never-ending semicircles of stone seating. It is described as a small venue, but we played two nights there before full houses of ten thousand. These were our first gigs after a two-week break. A part of me felt I should fly home and see James and Pauline, but in my heart I knew that my marriage was beyond recovery at this stage. The prospect of ten days of tension at home persuaded me to stay in the States, so I flew to New York and hung out with friends.

The tour resumed in Tempe, an inner suburb of Phoenix, Arizona, a city that receives only three centimetres of rain a year and where the temperature averages 38 degrees Celsius in September. It was there that I made the mistake of smoking some local grass that was so strong I couldn't leave my room for six hours. Thankfully, we had the night off! From there to the West Coast for thirteen shows including four at the Greek Theatre in LA, another stunning amphitheatre with row upon row of horseshoe seating rising up from the stage into the wooded hillside and on into the night sky.

Like Red Rocks, the acoustics, the setting and the warm night air generated a wonderful atmosphere, spoiled only a little by some of the VIPs in the front rows, a mixture of celebrities and music-industry executives. Why do they always put them in front? It is a very American phenomenon for the great and the good to be seen at major public events like boxing matches and rock concerts, a little like British royalty taking the box in a West End theatre. Most of them were there for the music but a few just for the social and photo opportunity, and it was irritating to watch them getting in and out of their seats throughout the shows, many of them apparently suffering from weak bladders and in constant need of having to powder their noses.

We played a couple of nights at the Concord Pavilion in San Francisco, yet another spectacular outdoor amphitheatre facing up over a few rows of seats and beyond a grassy hill, the 'lawn', as they call it. It's similar to Henman Hill at Wimbledon, where the fans are free to sit or wander about. While there, we got word that J. J. Cale was playing a small late gig on the night of our second show. We had listened to his music incessantly back in Deptford and it was partly through a common love of his music that my friendship with Mark was forged.

Paul got hold of J.J.'s people at short notice, tickets were laid on for us and, like excited schoolboys, we finished our show and hurried over the Golden Gate Bridge to a tiny venue in Sausalito. It was rammed to the rafters, three hundred people in a room designed to hold a hundred and fifty. There were people standing on tables, and we pressed into the throng for a better view of the great man, perched on his high stool. After so many months and years taking the stage, it was a thrill for the roles to be reversed and to be concert-goers again. It was just J.J. with his guitar and a guy on a Hammond organ playing the bass notes with his feet. It's the simplicity of the music, the easy rhythm, the restrained emotion, the deep humility of a true out-and-out music man that, for me, makes him one of the greats. Towards the end, J.J. invited Mark to play a couple of tracks with him, and it was touching to see the frontman of what had been called the biggest band in the world looking so chuffed as he climbed on to the stage. Sadly, there was no room on stage for anyone else. Of all the people in the world I'd have loved to play with, it is J. J. Cale.

We headed north for a string of shows in Portland, then Seattle, and then it was over the border into Canada. The extraordinary success of *Brothers in Arms* had led to the addition of even more gigs now and we found ourselves shuttling back and forth between Edmonton and Calgary. If it had continued much longer, it might well have tipped us over into some form of madness. When on the road, it was very rare for us to get an opportunity to explore the cities and regions we had the privilege of visiting. Round and round the world we went, but we saw very little of it. The inside of a hotel room, the interior of a municipal sports arena and our reflections in the windows of the tour bus as it hammered through the night — this was the reality of life in our hermetically sealed tour capsule.

So, it was a joy when Paul arranged for us to travel by boat from Seattle up the north-west coast to the city of Victoria through the islands in the sound, the North Shore mountains dominating the skyline behind Vancouver. We had played Vancouver once before, on the *Making Movies* tour in 1980, but then we were in and out under the cover of darkness and didn't get to see the spectacular landscape and coastline. The boat trip was an opportunity to kick back and play the tourist, but from Victoria we flew the sixty miles to Vancouver by seaplane, a mildly nerve-wracking but thrilling experience, watching the water rushing up towards us before landing with a great splash.

The fatigue was starting to weigh a little when we flew the length of the continent to finish the three-month leg with two weeks back on the East Coast. I have nothing against Portland, Oregon, but there was a collective groan when Ed told us that, the night after playing our third show at the Wang Theatre in Boston, we were to fly all the way back to the Pacific Northwest for one concert, and the next morning catch a flight back to Boston for another gig there. I am not sure the environmentalists would let you get away with that today, but if anyone had protested at the time, we would have happily played the eco card and fallen into line with them. It had become a crazy itinerary.

Crazier still was our experience in New York, as our crew was forced to work under the tyranny of the Teamsters, the incredibly powerful labour union. They took complete control of setting up the three shows in Radio City Music Hall at the start of October, and our brilliant crew were left as mere bystanders and lackeys. It was so absurd that our lot were forbidden from even touching any of the equipment, let alone plugging anything in — heaven forbid – unless or until they were told to do so. They were all experts in their roles, but they had to follow the Teamsters guys around and wait for orders. It was a corrupt racket and they charged so much money that what should have been three lucrative sold-out gigs ended with us hardly breaking even. There was nothing Ed could do about it because they would just refuse to let us play, but it was still a true joy to play Radio City, a historic venue inside the Rockefeller Center.

It was the same story when we played Madison Square Garden on the penultimate night of the leg, the Teamsters taking most of the cash and bossing everyone around. But we just had to deal with it and, besides, we were playing 'The Garden', one the greatest venues in the world, 'the holy temple of rock 'n' roll', as Billy Joel puts it. Billy is a legend in his native New York and we managed to get him to join us on stage for a few songs, along with the great sax player David Sanborn, and the 20,000-strong crowd erupted as if they had all won the lottery when Mark announced them. Billy is a fabulous piano player and one of the best performers of his time, and David lifted the whole crowd with his playing. Getting tired at the end of a very long three months, for the whole band it was like getting a shot in the arm. Billy was accompanied by his stunning model wife, Christie Brinkley, star of the 'Uptown Girl' video, and so much taller than him she could have popped him in her pocket. Maybe we'd been on the road too long, but we were all so captivated by Christie's beauty that we were a little speechless at first.

We may have been physically tired, but there was no flagging of the spirit. That was just as well, because we went straight from the States to Scandinavia for the start of a month of shows in northern Europe, followed by another month in the UK – an itinerary that allowed our bodies no drop in adrenaline, thanks in no small part to the fervour of the audiences that greeted us at every venue. It helped that the tour was so well run, barely a hiccough along the way, and our energy levels were kept afloat on the rising tide of the public response to the album, expressed in the sheer scale of the gigs.

Every one of the 248 concerts on the tour was sold out, most of them very quickly, and you can only speculate as to how much demand had been unmet. How many more stadiums might we have filled? No one said it, but all of us, I suspect, understood that it was never going to get better than this. How could it, unless Ed managed to book us a gig on the moon? We were keenly alive to the good fortune that had come our way; this was our return for almost a decade of effort, for the broken and breaking relationships, for the dislocation of our lives, the emotional burden of which affected us all in some way.

Walk on stage before tens of thousands of people who have paid you the compliment of shelling out good money to come and see you and you want to give them something to remember. The love cuts both ways; it's symbiotic. We've all been to lacklustre shows where the band is tired and listless, giving the impression they'd rather be in bed or down the pub, probably because they are at the end of a punishing schedule. I don't believe we ever let down a venue — except perhaps the Lafayette in Wolverhampton, where, in front of that audience of two, we may have simply been going through the motions.

We kept the show on the road for so long, going from strength to strength, rather than into a slow decline and collapse, principally because we looked after ourselves. We never went face-down in a heap of coke, never smashed up a bar, never threw a TV from the window, drove a car into a swimming pool or wheelbarrowed a harem of hookers around our hotel rooms. That may not be very rock 'n' roll, but at least it meant we could keep playing it. If we said we'd be on stage at eight o'clock, we'd be there. You don't book a table in a restaurant at eight in the expectation of being served at ten. All the temptations were there, but we always kept it to beer and wine and gave the hookers and groupies at the bar no more than a nod and a smile. Well, most of the groupies.

Scandinavia is a fabulous place to play, and they had really gone for us over there. We played the largest indoor arenas in all four countries, but the highlight for me was the smallest. It being the start of the leg, we had an empty day in the schedule while we waited in Stockholm for our equipment to arrive from Norway, and it was suggested we might play a gig at the famous Café Opera, a beautiful eighteenth-century building that holds no more than about two hundred. To avoid thousands descending on the venue, word was quietly put out to the Dire Straits fan club in the city and, a few hours later, we were on stage. The decor was a little more baroque, but otherwise it was like being back in the Hope and Anchor. After the huge stadiums and the tightly choreographed performances, the informality and amateurishness of it was so refreshing, taking us back to our roots and the happy memories of those simpler times. We just walked in and plugged in our guitars, the audience right at our feet, then stuck around for some beers and a chat with them. It was good to feel somewhat normal again.

Christmas arrived through a blizzard of gigs back in the UK, including four at City Hall in Newcastle, Mark's hometown, a moving experience for him and the audience. The local hero had returned. There were seven consecutive nights at the Hammersmith Odeon, then it was time for a break. But I had other work to attend to. Playing music was one thing, facing it quite another. It was time to go home.

Chapter 22

New Worlds

Christmas down at Telscombe brought few tidings of joy. Pauline and I tried to make it as festive as possible for James, now three and a half, but things were difficult between the two of us. There were long walks over the South Downs in the unseasonably mild and wet weather. It's hard to accept that your marriage is struggling when you have brought a child into the world, James playing with his toys by the tree while his mother and father headed towards their separation. So it was with a heavy heart, mixed with some relief, that I flew up to Edinburgh to team up with the band at the Playhouse for three shows, the last on New Year's Eve. Knowing I had a big Illsley family holiday in Montserrat coming up — booked many months earlier — I flew to Oslo straight after Edinburgh to stay with a friend and escape the tension at home.

My parents, my brother Will and his wife, Chris, and their daughter, Corin, joined James and me in Montserrat, but Pauline didn't come. It was a spoiling holiday. We stayed in George Martin's beautiful plantation house, waited upon by the lovely house staff.

My mother had never been in an aircraft and my father only once, when he was flown back from Italy in the war. He rather enjoyed the free drinks. They were almost as excited as James when we transferred from the 747 jumbo at Antigua to a tiny light aircraft for the short hop to Montserrat, the plane landing on a bumpy grass runway next to the wooden-hut terminal.

From the Caribbean, I made my way to Hobart, Tasmania, for the start of the last leg of the *Brothers in Arms* tour. We knew before we had even landed that the tour was going to smash all records for concert attendance in Australasia over the eleven weeks we were there. In the event, 900,000 tickets were sold, a feat not to be bettered until Ed Sheeran's tour in 2018. Australia's population was 14 million at the time and, if you subtract the very young and the elderly, the amount of people coming to see us represented a sizable proportion of the country's teenagers and adults. There were to be fifty-six shows, twenty of them at the Entertainment Centre in Sydney, four of which were tacked on right at the end to meet a demand that, it was coming to feel, could never be satisfied.

There was no time to mope about my marriage and it was far easier for me to cope than it must have been for Pauline. I had the distraction of touring, the focus of playing music, and I was, physically at least, as far from my personal problems as I could be, enjoying the heat of a late summer in a country I had come to love. For Pauline, back at home in frozen, leafless London, in the grimmest month of the year, it was much harder.

After two massive outdoor shows in Hobart and one in Adelaide, staged in the vast wide-open spaces of the cities' Aussie Rules football stadiums, we headed to Melbourne for thirteen consecutive nights indoors at the Sports and Entertainment Centre. Bob Dylan, still in town after playing a gig with Tom Petty and the Heartbreakers, met up with Mark for lunch and Mark asked if he might like to come and play one night. He joined us for the sixth show, on 19 February, and there was a very loud roar from the crowd when Mark announced him.

Bob Dylan, for me the Picasso of music, has always been prepared to take risks. Never bothered by what others might think, he does what he likes. That means he can be a little frustrating to see live sometimes, when he plays so many obscure versions of his songs. When Mark and I saw him at Brixton Academy, we played a little competition we called 'Spot the Song'. I think we only got one between us. But it was a huge thrill to be sharing a stage with one of the iconic cultural figures of the twentieth century. We played four of his songs, including 'Knocking on Heaven's Door' and a rousing version of 'All Along the Watchtower'.

After Yugoslavia and Italy, the only time I ever feared an outbreak of crowd violence was in New Zealand, where we played two shows in Auckland, one in Wellington and one in Christchurch, both outdoors. Being at the bottom of the world, it's a big deal when successful bands drop by. New Zealand is a homely, friendly place, more village than country, and they head out to big concerts like it's the annual fete. Over 10 per cent of the country's 3 million people came out to see us.

It was in Wellington that it looked as if there was going to be some serious trouble. Rival Maori gangs were a major problem for the New Zealand police force at the time, and about a hundred gang members, no strangers to the tankard that day, had decided to park themselves right under the stage. The Maoris enjoyed special legal rights as an indigenous people and the police were wary about being too heavy-handed with them for fear of infringing their rights and, presumably, for fear of getting into a tussle with them. There were some very big units just below our feet and they certainly hadn't come to the concert in a spirit of peace and goodwill to all men. The crowd behind them was being kept at a distance, and it was disconcerting to play with this huge buffer zone between the stage and the vast ocean of fans fifty yards away, held back by a cordon of police. The Maori crowd pressed forward but never broke through and, in the event, the violence never got worse than some pushing and shoving and the odd fist. It was probably just as well that our brand of music tends to have an upbeat and soothing effect on audiences. The evening might have turned out to be very different had we been a metal or punk band.

Sydney was our next stop and, unusually for touring, it became our home for almost two and a half weeks. Every day we hung out like regular citizens, heading down to the beach, eating lunch in a restaurant, before clocking in for work at the Entertainment Centre down in the Haymarket area an hour or two before we took the stage. We stayed at the Sebel, where Billy Connolly was also a guest. At the peak of his popularity in 1986, he was packing out the Sydney Opera House night after night. We'd be back at the hotel bar after our show when Billy would stride in, still telling hilarious, rambling stories. He was virtually talking to himself – it just so happened that others were also in the room. You had the impression that he probably hadn't stopped declaiming since walking out of the Opera House and that he would probably still be regaling the walls and furnishings up in his room. On a night off, we went to see him at the Opera House and I was laughing so hard I had to leave the auditorium for fifteen minutes to recover. What a lovely and extraordinary man.

But he wasn't the only entertainer among us. My artist friend Brett Whiteley had appointed himself as unofficial tour mascot and, as we had arranged a pass for him, he accompanied us to almost every show in Australia. He loved his music, even more the live experience and the sensory impact of it, the effect that one second of music could have on a crowd of eighty thousand people. 'You hit one bass note, mate, and the equivalent of a whole town goes nuts right there and then. I've been painting twenty-five years, but when I put on an art exhibition, I'm chuffed if three hundred people show up — and none of them jumps up and down and starts screaming with delight.'

Brett was fascinated by the different ways that art and music connect with people. He loved the instant hit of music, quite possibly because he liked the instant hit of almost anything, especially drink and drugs and chicken livers. A hard presence to ignore, he was one of those characters who walked into a room and made things happen, creating some kind of stir either by his antics or by the powerful energy of his character and the frankness of his opinions. His was a restless, busy soul, his mind a hive of curiosity; he was always searching for some higher truth, always engaging with his surroundings to find meaning and fun. He just wanted to connect, and that's probably why he was so mesmerized by music's power to capture and enrapture an audience so easily. And with Brett the connection was instant. I hope he knew that his paintings do have a similar effect on the viewer as music has on the listener, at least on me. They are so arresting they, too, have the power to stop people in their tracks.

Perhaps it was a fear of boredom, but unless Brett was hiding himself away for a few weeks dealing with his addiction issues, his dynamic, twitchy personality never stilled and, playing the court jester for us, he was hugely entertaining on that tour. He was an odd mix: a bit of a lad and a carouser, but blessed with the most exquisite artistic sensibilities, his capacity for crudity and raw fun coming in roughly the same measure as the refinement. The expression 'There is never a dull moment . . .' might have been coined for him, a truth underlined in comic fashion one evening when we were having sushi at the Hyatt Hotel. One of Brett's very few material indulgences was a small white 3-series BMW convertible, and he had parked it out in the street a little along from the hotel. He was enjoying his sushi — about the only other dish he'd eat apart from chicken livers — when the maître d' asked if anyone owned a white BMW.

'I think you'd better come outside,' he said to Brett, when he said it was his.

We were met by the most extraordinary sight. A car was nose down in his. Apparently, a woman in the multistorey car park adjacent had slammed her car in a forward gear instead of reverse, ploughed through the wall and plummeted into Brett's soft-top. Somehow, she escaped with only minor injuries.

It was while we were in Sydney that the end of my marriage was sealed. It was there that I met Louise, who was to become the mother of my second child, Jess. Our paths crossed as I headed on to the tennis court she was vacating. We dated, hit it off straight away and she joined me for much of the rest of the tour, though not in Perth, where Pauline's family were coming to see us play.

In spite of all the troubles back home — or maybe because of them — I loved the whole tour to Australia and New Zealand. The scale of the tour was almost overwhelming. Ordinarily, we'd bounce from one city to the next, night after night, but with most of Australia's population concentrated in just half a dozen cities we got to lay our hats for long periods in the same place. It was rare to be able to unpack and get to the bottom of a suitcase.

Sydney was great, and from there we decamped to Hamilton Island, off the north-east coast, in the heart of the Great Barrier Reef. It's been overdeveloped since, of course, but back then the island was largely unspoilt. The only large building was the newly built luxurious Reef View Hotel, which we used as a base and a jumping-off point, flying by light aircraft over the Outback every night for a show in Queensland or the Northern Territory: Rockhampton, Mackay, Townsville, Cairns and Darwin.

In Darwin, over twice as many people attended the gig as lived in the town. The population of the Northern Territory, covering an area twelve times greater than England, was about 160,000, about a third of whom were there at the Showgrounds to see us, undeterred by the unrelenting torrential rain. That was a tough show for me. I had picked up a pretty savage stomach bug, and after every song I had to go to the side of the stage and puke into a bucket. Incredibly, of the thousand-plus shows we played, none of us ever missed one through illness. In spite of being a smoker then, Mark never suffered a chest cold or a sore throat. There are no understudies in a band, so you have to play. In somewhere as remote as Darwin, as far from a major city or 'civilization' as any town on the planet, the cancellation of a big show would come as a major blow. Sadly, one show that did have to be cancelled was the one planned for Uluru, right in the heart of the Outback. We had all been looking forward to playing at this beautiful, iconic site, but we were warned off it by Peter Garrett, the lead singer of Midnight Oil, who explained that the Aborigines disapproved of their sacred site being desecrated. Fair enough, but it was disappointing not to pay a visit.

After our week in Perth, way out west, we flew the two thousand miles back to Sydney — the same distance as London to Cairo. The Australians weren't done with us yet, and we packed out the Entertainment Centre again for four nights on the trot. It had been an incredible three months, and I was very happy to have had the distraction of touring, with all the diverting sights and experiences that brings. It was fortunate that the tour was so long and intensive because it stopped me from descending too deep into painful soul-searching and self-recrimination. For that reason, I didn't really want the music to stop. When finally it did, the adrenaline ebbed away and I found what I expected to find: that my emotions were an undressed tossed salad of grief, guilt and anxiety — and now that I was an item with Louise — served with a garnish of happiness and hope. When I looked back I felt melancholy; when I looked forward I felt exhilaration. I was a little confused.

I had decided to stay on in Sydney for a while, to be with Louise, clear my head and work through the difficult decisions that needed to be made before heading back to London. I waved off the rest of the band from the Sebel as they headed to the airport for the flight home, so it was a surprise when I went into the bar that evening and found them all having a beer. The jumbo jet had developed engine trouble, apparently, and had had to turn back. Australia 1986 really was the tour that refused to end.

It was hasty, but I'm pleased I did it: I bought an apartment in Sydney within a few weeks of the tour's end. I guess I was trying to be decisive, drawing a heavy line under the past and making a firm statement about my future. It was time to move on. The apartment was in Point Piper, right on the beach, with superb views over the harbour and downtown Sydney. Many happy years were to be spent there.

There will be scars, but time does heal and I am very happy that Pauline and I are still in touch and that our son, James, has turned into a fine man. Our marriage was the victim of my life on the road. I could beat myself up for the couple of times I strayed from my marriage vows, but those transgressions were symptom not cause, flings not affairs, regret them as I might. Pauline never did anything wrong and I am sorry that she had to suffer and sacrifice her happiness for my career.

Chapter 23

What Now?

So what now? That was the question none of us asked but were all thinking when we finally went our own ways after a year and a day on the road — make that a year and two days, after the aborted flight. For the immediate time being, I wanted to do little more than soak up some Australian sun, sleep, get to know Louise better and, I suppose, gather some strength to go home and deal with the practicalities of divorce and building a new home life. When the tour drew to its end, Mark and I were of the mind that the band was over. There had been no talk of the next album, the next tour. After this tour of 248 concerts, and almost ten years on the road, and being in and out of studios, airports, hotels, tour buses, media functions and concert venues, there was no appetite for an immediate continuation of that grinding lifestyle. It was time to take stock and tidy up our somewhat messy private lives. For the next three years, whenever I saw or spoke to Mark or had lunch, the words 'Dire Straits' were rarely uttered.

Mark's creative appetite is insatiable, and it's only recently that I have discovered the full scale of the projects in which he involved himself almost as soon as he returned to the UK. Within a few weeks of the tour he had formed the Notting Hillbillies, whose full line-up would include Steve Phillips and Brendan Croker on guitar, Paul Franklin on pedal steel guitar, Marcus Cliffe on bass, Guy on keyboards and, rather surprisingly, our manager, Ed Bicknell, on drums. (Ed, in fact, is quite an accomplished drummer.) It would take an entire page to list all Mark's projects in the years that followed. He wrote scores for films such as *The Princess Bride* and *Last Exit to Brooklyn*, produced albums for other artists, including Randy Newman's *Land of Dreams*, played on others, appeared live . . . He may have had enough of tour buses, but he couldn't keep away from the music.

I was happy to hang up the bass for a while, play at being a dad to James, having missed so much of his growing-up and, for the time being at least, enjoy a quieter life. But I'm not by nature the type of person to sit around on the sofa for too long. I need a project either on the go, or in the making. I don't like being idle. I was thirty-seven when the tour finished and I still wanted to be active, to get involved, to engage with the world in a new way. It was just a question of how and what. I had travelled the globe, round and round, but in a rather extraordinary, self-contained little bubble. It was time to emerge from the space capsule and start exploring.

While in Sydney, I was introduced to the Reverend Ted Noffs, one of the most remarkable people I have met, and I have met a few. A Methodist minister, Ted came to practise what he had been preaching from the pulpit — and with spectacular results. Dismayed and fed up with picking up and offering passing help to countless homeless people, drunks and addicts, in 1964 he set up the Wayside Chapel in the Kings Cross area of Sydney, turning his active pastoral care into a movement that came to be called Life Education. Soon, there were Life Education centres in almost all Australian schools, aimed at advising the young about the perils of drugs and bad living. When

Prince Charles met Reverend Ted earlier in 1986, he was so impressed by his work and message that he was keen to try and establish the charity in the UK. I met Ted around the same time, sat in on some classes and instantly felt an eagerness to get involved. There was a personal element to this decision. I had seen drink and drugs wreak their havoc close up and had lost a few good friends to addiction.

Back in the UK, the phone rang one morning when I was still in my dressing gown. It was Prince Charles's equerry, and moments later I found myself in conversation with His Royal Highness. Soon after, Ted Noffs came over to lay the foundations for Life Education in the UK. I became a trustee and, under the Dire Straits umbrella, bought their first mobile classroom in Britain. Today there are 120 of them and the movement became so successful that, for funding reasons mainly, in 2009 it amalgamated with Coram, the country's first-ever dedicated children's charity, established in 1739 as the Foundling Hospital in London's Bloomsbury by philanthropist and sea captain Thomas Coram and backed by King George II and ranks of gentry. Two hundred and eighty years on, Coram goes from strength to strength.

It has been a privilege to be involved with the charity for so long and it was satisfying to discover how many successful people there were doing good work behind the scenes but keeping it quiet and not making a song and dance about their efforts.

My involvement with the charity led to a visit in 1987 to Number 10 Downing Street and a meeting with then prime minister Margaret Thatcher. However severely she may have come across in public, she was wonderful with the children who had come along and she gave us a tour of the famous building, pointing out all the portraits of her predecessors that line the stairwell.

We had been so busy for a decade that there had been few gaps in the schedule to back good causes. Other than Live Aid, the most we had managed was to perform a few times with a host of other big-name acts at concerts for the Prince's Trust, Charles's charity to help the young find jobs or get into education and training. Our first appearance was at the Dominion Theatre in London's West End in 1982, memorable mainly for the awkward fun of watching pop idols Duran Duran struggle through their performance. Even though it was a charity gig, their management hadn't wanted to miss the publicity opportunity and they had bussed in a couple of coaches of screeching teenage girls from their fan club to greet them.

It was perhaps some sort of divine retribution that, first on, they went straight out on stage, having come direct from a recording studio. Their sound man slapped on a tape of backing tracks from the recording studio and the plan was to sing and play the rest over the top. To their bewilderment and annoyance, the play speed on the tape machine was set wrong. The confusion it unleashed was soon obvious on the faces of the audience and the members of the band. Realizing they were a semitone or so flat, the band adjusted their instruments, Simon Le Bon his voice, but no sooner had they done so than the sound man, also realizing the problem, had switched the speed to normal. Chaos reigned again. The moral of the story is that if you are going to play before two and a half thousand people, it is probably best to rehearse and prepare for it.

In 1985, the Prince's Trust 'Rock Gala' at Wembley Arena was effectively a Dire Straits concert with guest appearances by Sting and The Who's Pete Townshend. Playing with Pete was a genuine privilege. He was as wild as ever on stage, and the most charismatic and delightful man off it. That show was also memorable for the performance of my son, James, then just three. He was given the honour of presenting Princess Diana with a bouquet of flowers during the line-up on the red carpet. As soon as the royals arrived, James couldn't contain himself and ran straight for Diana, completely out of sync with the tight choreography. She couldn't have been more

*One of many Prince's Trust shows we did. I suspect Princess
Di was more into the music than her husband.*

charming, bending down to take the flowers and talk to him. I found myself sitting next to her at Grosvenor House a couple of years later for a Life Education function — and she really was every bit as gentle and warm-hearted as she has been portrayed. The day after the Wembley show, the front of the *Daily Mirror* carried the picture of James and Diana and, thirty-five years on, it sits proudly in its frame on the wall of his loo.

We were back at Wembley the following year for an all-star performance for the Trust. All the big names were there: Paul McCartney, Elton John, George Michael, Rod Stewart, Mick Jagger, David Bowie, Eric Clapton, Status Quo, Paul Young, Midge Ure and Phil Collins. Phil, Eric and Elton were on stage throughout and the rest came and went over the evening. British music could hardly have produced a more stellar line-up, and it was a strange experience to stand playing bass behind McCartney on his acoustic guitar, singing 'I Saw Her Standing There', a record I used to listen to on my Dansette in my bedroom in Market Harborough.

Tina Turner's rendition of 'Better Be Good to Me' and Eric's 'Tearing Us Apart' were, for me, the highlights of the night, and not even the late arrival of Jagger and Bowie could upstage Tina. There was a clamour in the auditorium when Paul McCartney announced that the two men were coming on. Their double-act performance of 'Dancing in the Street' was a memorable one for everyone . . . with the possible exception of Bowie and Jagger themselves. The duo had been at a wedding all day, and you didn't need a breathalyser to know they'd had a very enjoyable afternoon of it. Consummate pros, they pulled it off and brought a raucous energy to the proceedings — and to the party backstage afterwards.

But I think it was probably Tina who stole the show. We had got to know her when, a couple of years earlier, we played on her recording of 'Private Dancer', the song Mark had given to her. The only one of us who didn't play on the recording was Mark, who was in the States working with Bob Dylan. That was a shame, because Jeff Beck played quite an eccentric solo that drew some very uncomplimentary remarks on the song's release. Amazing guitarist, Jeff, but that probably wasn't his finest moment in the studio. In gratitude for the song, Tina had asked the band to put down the recording with her in a north London studio, and it was a joy to spend the day with her. It's unlikely you'll meet a lovelier woman on the music scene, and her infectious enthusiasm is all the more impressive with all the suffering she has endured in her private life. Her performance in the studio was quite extraordinary — she belted it out as if she was playing to Wembley Stadium. She loves a curry, does Tina, and after we packed up someone called out to the local Indian restaurant and we spent the rest of the evening sitting around in a sea of bhunas, kormas and tikka masalas. She liked 'Private Dancer' so much she gave its name to the title of her album and we were all delighted for her when it was released and quickly went huge around the world, triple platinum in the UK and five times platinum in the States.

I had given the house in Clapham to Pauline as part of our divorce settlement, so Louise and I rented a flat in Chelsea for a few months before we bought a house in South Kensington and a one-bedroom mews house in Holland Park — a perfect space for conversion into an art studio. I still have the house today.

On 11 June 1988 we headlined the Nelson Mandela seventieth-birthday concert at Wembley Stadium. Mandela was still in prison and we wanted to add our voices to the general admiration for the man, as well as to the mounting clamour around the world for his release by the apartheid regime. We were not very popular with the authorities over there after donating all our South African royalties from our first album to Amnesty International. When the government banned our music from being broadcast, they scored an own goal, because sales of the album went even higher.

Our gesture was not forgotten on either side of the political divide, and when the organizers approached us to top the bill we didn't need to go away and think about it. The chief organizer this time was impresario Tony Hollingsworth and, like Bob Geldof with Live Aid, he was eager to get us on board early, not so that other acts might follow our lead this time but so that global broadcasters would sign up. The whole point of a seventieth-birthday tribute to Mandela was to raise worldwide consciousness of his imprisonment and expose the iniquities of the apartheid regime. Our participation is said to have made a major difference. If we, the performers, had any influence over Mandela's release from prison eighteen months later, then so much the better. I don't usually like to mix politics with music, but on this occasion it felt right.

Hollingsworth managed to upset Ed Bicknell by insisting that we rehearsed before the show on the grounds that we hadn't played together for over two years. Winding up Ed should be made a national sport. It's an easy game to play and it's fun to watch. It was heartening that he had our backs covered at all times, but we weren't too bothered by that stipulation to rehearse. We always liked to be well rehearsed before going on tour and we happily reconvened at Brixton Academy to get back into the groove and run through our set list. Even better, we were then booked in for a couple of nights at the Hammersmith Odeon in the build-up to Wembley. Short of a rhythm guitarist after Jack Sonni returned to New York for the birth of his twin girls, we needed a replacement. We were delighted when Mark asked Eric Clapton to join us on guitar for the Odeon and Wembley shows, and it is a source of nagging regret that the Hammersmith shows weren't recorded.

As a music and entertainment festival, the Nelson Mandela 70th Birthday Tribute was a magnificent and moving occasion, over a hundred acts taking the stage throughout the day — comedians and actors as well as musicians. It made a bigger emotional impression on me than Live Aid because we were backstage in the stadium all day, mingling with the other bands and artists, soaking in the atmosphere generated by the 82,000 people out on the pitch and in the stands.

If Freddie Mercury had stolen the show three years earlier, it was the largely unknown American singer Tracey Chapman who did so this time. It catapulted her to worldwide fame before a global audience of 600 million in sixty-seven countries, the largest-ever after Live Aid. (The official viewing figure is said to have been considerably higher because a number of free licences were handed to some of the countries in Africa.) She ended up making two appearances as a result of the big backstage drama on the day. The intransigence of his management team had made it very hard for the organizers to book Stevie Wonder, but they got their man in the end. Stevie wanted to play and, late in the day, called Hollingsworth himself to ask if there was still space in the schedule. He was in luck because the organizers had been unable to persuade Prince and U2's Bono to appear, and the twenty-five-minute slot was all his.

When he arrived at Wembley, it was discovered that the hard disk of his pre-recorded synthesized music had been lost. Stevie was, naturally, very upset and apparently left the stadium in tears, refusing to play. No one in the audience knew about this because his appearance had been intended as a surprise. With no notice, Tracey Chapman stepped in to fill the gap and produced another very moving performance, doing her international profile no harm in the process. Before Wembley, her eponymous album had sold 250,000 copies. In the two weeks following, she sold 2 million.

There was a happy postscript to the drama. Stevie Wonder returned to Wembley, the lights dropped, and he slipped on to the stage, triggering a thunderous roar around the stadium when the first notes of 'I Just Called to Say I Love You' rang out. We came on about twenty minutes later to close the show, straight after Billy Connolly, who carried on where he had left off in Sydney, giving the impression that he prepares nothing, that he's talking to 600 million people just as he would if he were propped on a bar stool regaling a stranger. We played 'Walk of Life', 'Sultans of Swing', 'Romeo & Juliet', 'Money for Nothing', 'Brothers in Arms', 'Solid Rock' and Eric's 'Wonderful Tonight'.

Three decades on, a number of our shows come back to me vividly from time to time, deeply buried memories erupting out of the blue, but if I was forced to choose the concert that left the biggest impression on me, it was this one. It was that day when I saw so clearly the importance of music beyond its primary function as entertainment. I saw and heard its capacity to unify, to create a solidarity greater than the ephemeral two-hour experience of a crowd enjoying a night out. Whether or not the concert made any difference to Mandela's release from captivity can never be known, though the strength of feeling most certainly would not have gone unnoticed by the South African authorities. In a way, it didn't matter. The concert succeeded in bringing together one-tenth of the world's population for a day, and you could only rejoice and be moved by the power of music to achieve that. Few other shared human activities can do that.

These were great times for me personally. Louise and I were getting on really well. She was fun to be with: fresh, natural, down-to-earth and streetwise, like so many Australians I had met. The remote, rural retreat in Telscombe became our main home, and it was down there at the beginning of 1988 that she announced she was pregnant. In September, she gave birth to our daughter, Jess.

But . . . let no one ever persuade you that absence makes the heart grow fonder. It is one of the great myths. Absence, as I had already discovered with Pauline, is a killer. I was soon to be reminded of that hard reality when Louise's father fell seriously ill back in Australia. A good daughter, Louise flew back for long periods to be at his bedside and help out her mum, taking Jess with her each time. I am not good at being alone. I never saw the absence of a wife or girlfriend as an opportunity to play the field, but it always created a kind of emotional vacuum in me, a lust not for sex but for intimacy and company. I never overlapped girlfriends, but there was never a long gap between them either, and back then I was always equally drawn to female company as to men's. I didn't notice it at first, but the upshot of Louise's absence from my life was that it triggered the start of a slow decline in our intimacy.

The phenomenal success of *Brothers in Arms* continued for years after the tour, and we received a host of awards from the music industry. In 1986 and 1987 we were given about thirty major accolades, most of them from the Grammys, the Brits and MTV, and we were sent so many framed gold and platinum discs from around the world that we asked to stop receiving them. There was one, however, that made me feel genuinely honoured — the Ivor Novello Award for Outstanding Contribution to British Music, given to me and Mark jointly in 1988. You won't find many trophies in my house today, but that little bronze statue sits very proudly.

It wasn't long before the pull of music drew me back to my guitar and, there being no band, in April 1988 I started work on my second solo album, *Glass*, which I recorded in George Martin's AIR Studios near Oxford Circus and co-produced with Dutchman Albert Boekholt. Mark, Alan and Guy all dropped in to make contributions to tracks I had started writing while on tour, but over a dozen musicians were involved in all, including the brilliant country guitar player Jerry Donahue.

After its release, again with Brett Whiteley's artwork on the cover, the song 'I Want to See the Moon', about my relationship with my son, James, was played extensively on local radio up and down the country and in Europe. I even heard it myself a few times driving back and forth between London and Sussex. It was, as they say in music circles, 'on heavy rotation'. Chuffed, I asked Ed how the distribution and sales of the single were going. He contacted Phonogram only to discover, to his horror and then mine, that the record label hadn't got the record in the shops. There was no single for anyone to buy! I was upset and, in truth, insulted by that, I have to confess. However, it wasn't hard to get that disappointment in perspective following the news that our sound guy, lovely Pete Granger, had been killed in a hit-and-run accident walking down the street with his child in his native South Wales. That was a terrible blow to all of us and kicked all our petty worries into the long grass.

After the Mandela gig, the band regrouped twice more in the late eighties, first in a hotel in Mark's native Newcastle to honour a young girl called Joanne Gillespie after she won North East Personality of the Year for her book, *Braveheart*, about her battle with cancer. It was a moving occasion and there were a lot of tears from the seven hundred guests – tears of admiration and happiness for Joanne and tears of laughter when comedian Frank 'It's the way I tell 'em' Carson took to the stage. (I'd have hated to have been stuck in a lift with him and Billy Connolly.)

A year later, the band played at the Knebworth Festival before a hundred thousand people to help raise money for Nordoff Robbins Music Therapy, rock music's favourite charity. We were joined by Phil Collins on drums, Elton John on piano and Eric Clapton on guitar, all of us buffeted by very strong winds. I took James along because, warned that the roads around Knebworth Park would be gridlocked, we were flown up in an Augusta 109 from Battersea heliport in south London. This delighted James, who was obsessed by helicopters at the time. In spite of all the excitement of the day, one memory that has stayed with me most clearly is the kindness that Elton and Phil showed him, fussing over him and keeping him supplied with snacks and drinks backstage throughout the day.

Lifting away from Knebworth to return to London that evening, looking down at the stage and the hordes of music fans, I felt a heavy wave of nostalgic sadness wash over me. It had been good to be playing again and I thought that was probably the last time I'd experience that exhilarating sensation. Then, a few weeks later, Mark called and asked if I fancied meeting for lunch, and a couple of hours in, with no more excitement in his voice than he had expressed in ordering his soup, he wondered whether I might fancy putting the band back together. He had a few 'Dire Straits' songs that might make a decent album, he added laconically. In a couple of months we were back in the studio, me thinking, *Jesus, here we go again* . . .

Chapter 24

Here We Go Again

I'll say it again: it is a drug, playing live, a natural drug, but a drug nonetheless. I say it again because it's a drug that plays havoc with musicians' private lives, and it was to wreak havoc once again with mine. Playing live is the reason why Elton John is on his 254th 'farewell' tour and why bands like The Stones and The Who, whose heyday came in the age of black-and-white three-channel television, still crane themselves out of their ergonomic reclining armchairs, put their teeth back in and shamble on to the tour bus. I am an addict myself and, today, still fit and healthy, I am still playing gigs and probably will continue to do so until arthritis and amnesia get the better of me. The key thing for me is that I no longer tour, playing only from time to time, because my home life, the third version, has become sacrosanct.

I was genuinely surprised by Mark's reunion suggestion, but only for a few minutes. What was I thinking? Of course we were going to have another crack, one more lap of the world, but there was trepidation in my bones. I had lost — sacrificed, perhaps — one partner to the irresistible lure and demands of my passion for music, and by retreating to the studio for a few months, then hitting the road for fifteen months, I was playing Russian roulette with another. There's nothing like a good long tour to wreck a relationship. Fifteen months away from home! That's how long it was going to be this time. Ed knew this was probably going to be our last album and tour and he was eager to get in as many dates as he thought we could handle.

The band gathered at Mark's mews house in west London in early autumn 1990 – and off we went again. It would be two years and two months before it was all over. While we worked through Mark's latest set of songs, Ed started booking the biggest stadiums he could find. Paul put the crew on alert and began prepping the mammoth logistical operation and, as the shows were confirmed, started mapping out the itinerary, booking hotels, flights and tour buses.

As with *Brothers in Arms*, it was the four of us who came together for the pre-recording session – Mark, Guy, Alan and myself – and, as last time, there was the same anticipation to hear the new material for the first time. The lyrics were complete, but some of the songs were in an embryonic state and ready to be worked on, with us all contributing. The early days working on new material were always magical.

I have often wondered how Dire Straits' music might have turned out had Mark played with a completely different set of musicians. It may well have sounded exactly the same, or very close to what's out there today, but I doubt it.

The most striking example of this creative process was 'Telegraph Road' on *Love Over Gold*, a song that was gradually pieced together over dozens of sessions. But every song needed work and received input, sometimes just a little, sometimes a lot more. Mark was only interested in producing the best result. If something wasn't working, he was the first to say it.

Once again, there were to be new faces in the line-up. Phil Palmer, a fine all-round guitarist who had played on my solo albums, took over from Jack Sonni. Anyone who has played with Eric Clapton for so many years had to be halfway decent. (It is also Phil's very distinctive acoustic guitar you hear on George Michael's track 'Faith'.) Paul Franklin, a master of the pedal steel guitar and a delightful man, also joined us, both for the recording and the tour.

Terry Williams left the band after the Mandela concert following six years' sterling service and great company. Such a nice man and a great drummer — we were going to miss him. In our search for a replacement, we were fortunate to discover that Jeff Porcaro of the American band Toto was available. He had been working with Mark on a film soundtrack and it was fabulous that he was free because Jeff is regarded as one of the all-time greats. His services were constantly in demand — you will have heard his drumming on a multitude of tracks.

There was an amusing episode when he turned up for his first session at AIR Studios at Oxford Circus, when Jeff casually announced he was off for a quick spliff before we got underway and I was a little alarmed that the session might go pear-shaped. But when we settled down to the songs, far from Jeff's playing being a problem, he was brilliant — or 'seriously in the pocket', I think was the expression used afterwards. There was no post-session talk with Jeff. If he played like that, he was welcome to smoke a farm's worth of the stuff before picking up his sticks. He was with us for no more than a week before he went on his way, having nailed every track to perfection. It was a huge shock when, two years later, while we were in Scandinavia, we received the news that he had died of a heart attack at his home in California, aged thirty-eight.

Jeff's work was completed early on in the recording before others added their contributions: Chris White on sax, Manu Katché and Danny Cummings on percussion, Paul Franklin on pedal steel guitar, Vince Gill on guitar (and backing vocals on 'The Bug'). George

Martin himself got involved, too, when we brought in an almost full orchestra for 'Ticket to Heaven'. He put together the string arrangements and conducted the orchestra. It was a very impressive team, which made putting *On Every Street* together a genuine pleasure. We also had a brilliant sound engineer in Chuck Ainlay, Neil Dorfsman worked his magic again in the mixing process, and Bob Clearmountain, who had mastered most of our albums, completed the production process.

The big difference with this recording was that there was no time pressure at all and we were in there for six months, the longest time we'd ever spent in a studio. For that we have to offer some thanks to Iraqi dictator Saddam Hussein, President George Bush Snr and PMs Maggie Thatcher and John Major. The original plan was for us to start the tour in the spring of 1991, four or five months before the release of the album, but when the Gulf War kicked off in January, we were forced to rip up the schedule and start over. With security and border checks heightened the world over, but mainly in Europe, the tour would likely have descended into a logistical and bureaucratic nightmare. With the schedule being so tight, a gig almost every night, there was a very strong possibility that our immense convoy of trucks would be held up and shows would be cancelled. So Ed and Paul binned Plan A and went to work on Plan B, and the band — comprising nine musicians — set off in August, first stop the Point, Dublin, after two months of rehearsals at Bray Studios with the band and the crew to coordinate sound and lights. This was quite an involved process now that all the equipment had been digitalized, and we had an infinity of options to play with.

A staggering statistic was to emerge from the tour. By the time it was over and the headcount was complete, over 7 million people had come out to see us play at 229 shows, an average of 31,000 per concert. That's almost three times more people than the 2.5 million who attended concerts on the *Brothers in Arm* tour — a tour we thought could never be trumped for magnitude. In terms of numbers through the door, I believe *On Every Street* remains one of the biggest tours in history.

Other new faces in the touring line-up included Chris Whitten on drums, Danny Cummings on percussion, with Chris White on saxophone returning for his second tour. Chris Whitten was an excellent session drummer who we had met at AIR Studios, where he had been working with Paul McCartney on the *Flowers in the Dirt* album in the adjacent studio, and he had also drawn praise for his playing on the Waterboys' *This is the Sea*, notably on its best-known song, 'The Whole of the Moon'.

I guess *On Every Street* was never going to scale the heights of *Brothers in Arms*, but I am very fond of the album. There are some great songs on it and an interesting mix of feel and styles. Reviews were mixed, but they always were and that never bothered us. A band cannot be all things to all critics. The proof was in the public reaction, and the response was very positive. The album went to number one in every country apart from the States, where, once again, without a single for the thousands of radio stations there to play, it never got the exposure it needed for runaway success. All told, it sold getting on for 15 million copies and, if that's failure, we felt we could cope with that.

Ed Bicknell was living out his 'Why let the truth get in the way of a good story?' life dictum, I believe, when he was recorded as saying, 'The last tour was utter misery. Whatever the zeitgeist we had been part of had passed.' As always with Ed, the truth was a little less dramatic and more prosaic. If the passing of a 'zeitgeist' results in over 7 million people attending 229 rapidly sold-out concerts, I'd like to see what success looks like. But, again, as always with Ed, there was a core of truth buried within the theatrical proclamation.

Inevitably, a tour of such length across every continent bar Antarctica and South America will grind a band down. It demands physical, mental and emotional stamina — another reason why so many musicians turn to drink and drugs to buoy themselves up and sustain them from one show to the next: the next midnight bus ride, the next hotel and the next call home to a partner growing increasingly vexed by your absence. I remember at one breakfast having to ask the waitress what country we were in and, towards the end, Chris White asked me, 'Is it just me or are our hotel rooms getting smaller?' They weren't, but I knew what he meant. We existed in a parallel dimension, cloistered like monks from the world beyond, but perhaps not adhering quite so assiduously to our holy vows.

That all said, this was a great band and my memories of the tour are largely happy ones. But as the itinerary ground on and the fatigue started to bite, as on all previous tours, it was the camaraderie of the crew, our surrogate family, that made each day bearable and often joyful. The sense of being on a mission or a journey of exploration, of having to hack and drag ourselves to the next milestone or watering hole day after day, invigorated all 150 of us every morning. We were all weary after a time, tensions arose, the odd row broke out or an issue back home flared up, and there were a few occasions when hearts were opened or stern words issued. Paul Cummins was a brilliant man-manager and took care of the 'pastoral' needs of the crew, so thankfully these incidents were few and far between. Today, I look back in awe that, bar the odd dust-up or emotional collapse, everyone held it together in the main, a year and a quarter of our lives away from our homes and families.

From time to time, our partners and families would fly out to see us for a couple of days if there happened to be a day's break in the schedule, allowing us to spend time together. I got to see James and Jess when they flew out to Oslo for a weekend with a nanny, but Louise and I were not getting along and I knew that when I returned home I was going to be a single man once again.

Fifteen months was way too long to be away from home — even

soldiers get leave, merchant sailors long spells on land – and by the time we staggered through Customs at Heathrow, two autumns on, there wouldn't be many wives and girlfriends there to greet us in the Arrivals terminal. Mine wasn't the only relationship to crash and burn; many of our relationships ended up in the departure lounge, scheduled for flights to destinations unknown.

As with Pauline, it was fortunate that I didn't have the time or headspace to grieve over the break-up too hard. I parked those feelings and would deal with them down the line, and it would take some rigorous counselling to set me straight. It was as hard for Louise as it had been for Pauline, stuck at home with no husband to help care for her child. To her, I was just gallivanting around the world from one exotic city to the next, having a riot, banging cocktails and playing to oceans of adoring fans. The reality was quite different, of course, the only true happiness being found on stage for a couple of hours each day, but I can see how she or anyone else might come to believe I was leading a life of impossible glamour.

It didn't help our relationship that, not long before the tour, I had bought a wreck of a house down on the south coast, a house I intended to make my home for ever and which I still live in today. The building needed an immense amount of work to make it habitable and it probably did not improve Louise's view of me that she was left to oversee the renovations. Only about two rooms were okay to live in and, with little Jess in tow, only just walking, Louise camped down there in the middle of nowhere for long periods to deal with the team of builders, electricians and plumbers. Here's a relationship tip for you: don't go skipping around the globe playing music and drinking beer for a year or so and leave your girlfriend and young child in a damp, crumbling house ten miles from the nearest cappuccino. Trust me – she won't cover you in kisses for that privilege.

The epic scale of this tour struck me in Rotterdam, early in the first European leg, when Paul and I were making our way over to one of the three tour buses for the journey to Brussels after three consecutive nights at the Ahoy arena before a total of 180,000 people.

'Jesus!' I said. 'Look at all those lorries. Rotterdam certainly shifts a lot of freight.' Or words to that effect, anyhow.

Paul burst out laughing. 'Every one of those lorries is ours. All forty-seven of them.'

The organization of that was all his work — an astonishing feat. Again, we never missed a show, never came on late and there were no disasters or mishaps of our own making. And so it was that we rolled on for another year, the convoy hammering through 120 towns and cities in 19 countries — Helsinki and Halifax, Sacramento and Sydney, San Sebastian and Nuremburg, Gateshead and Grenoble — the names flicking before our eyes like an electronic departures board on constant reset. There was less travelling for the band members on this tour because, for most of the legs — two in Britain and Ireland, two in Europe, one in North America and one in Australia and New Zealand — it had been arranged that, wherever the itinerary allowed, we would set up base in a hotel as central to the region as possible so that we could fly back and forth to shows. This had the twin virtues of saving a bit of money and ensuring we got a decent amount of sleep.

Flying in small aircraft wasn't without its anxieties. The logic behind the original schedule, before Saddam and Bush messed it up, was that we would not to have to travel in very cold climates in the dead of winter. This wasn't about the comfort of the band; it was to make the work of the crew a little easier and avoid any problems caused by adverse weather. The itinerary rejigged, we found ourselves in Canada in March 1992, and I have never felt cold like it. There were snowdrifts so high that at one hotel they had to dig a tunnel through to the entrance so that the guests could come and go. Driving from one gig back to the airport, we had the heating on full tilt the whole way, but it made virtually no difference and the condensation on the inside of the windows turned to ice. On the runway, it was unsettling to see the ground crew spraying de-icer on to the two propellers, which had locked fast. All but a couple of the eighteen shows we played in Canada were staged in arenas ordinarily used for ice hockey, spaces only marginally warmer than outdoors. The ice of the playing area was covered in some sort of carpeting, but it was still so cold that our performance enjoyed the percussive accompaniment of several thousand people stamping circulation into their feet, while on stage we had banks of heaters blowing down on us to stop our fingers freezing.

Mercifully, over the fifteen months on the road, there were no serious accidents or illnesses. The worst incident, of course, involved me. We were in Madrid closing the show, as we always did, with 'Local Hero' and 'Going Home', the songs acting as signals to the stage crew that they could start the task of packing up in order to hit the road as early as possible. One of the roadies had opened up a flight case behind me and, taking a step back, I tripped and threw out a hand to stop myself, making an ignominious fall to the stage floor.

I must have had a great deal of adrenaline coursing through me because I was completely unaware of the injury I had suffered. I carried on playing, jiving and smiling away at the crowd, and then I noticed people near the front staring at me in horror, eyes agog and hands over their mouths. I turned to the stage wing and there was Paul, gesticulating frantically at me to make my way towards him. I shrugged and screwed up my face in bewilderment but made my way over, grinning — until he pointed at my trousers. The whole of my right leg was sodden with blood and a great chunk of flesh was hanging off my hand. I hadn't felt a thing. Fortunately, the last song was almost done, and afterwards Paul wrapped up my hand and whisked me to hospital, where my wound received sixteen catgut stitches. A week later, a doctor turned up at the venue to take out the stitches before the show. I was appalled to see that he was drunk. The scissors in his hands were shaking so much I decided to remove the stitches myself with my six-blade knife ('*A six-blade knife can do anything for you . . .* '). Fortunately, this was right at the end of the tour and I was able to play through the last few shows without too much pain or difficulty.

So, at Zaragoza's La Romareda stadium on 9 October 1992, the last note ever played by Dire Straits faded into a starry Spanish night and we returned home to face up to the hard truth that there was a great deal more than a tour that had come to an end.

The hand was just a flesh wound that would heal. Deeper, truer pain was waiting for me at home. The tour was over, and Dire Straits were over. The dissolution of the band was never formally announced — a meaningless gesture to my mind and, of course, you never say never — but in our weary bones Mark and I knew that we had reached the end of a very long road. Even if it wasn't the end, it would be a very long time before we undertook an enterprise as grand and grinding as a tour on that scale, by which time we would be getting on for fifty and enjoying, so we hoped, a quieter life.

The live album *On the Night*, which was recorded at the Roman amphitheatre in Nimes, sold very well. Over fifteen years we had produced six studio albums, all backed up by world tours, plus two live ones. That felt like quite enough, thank you very much. You could tell by a couple of the songs on *On Every Street* that Mark's mind was maybe beginning to wander away from Dire Straits towards fresh creative pastures. I wanted fresh challenges, too, but quite what form they might take I had no clear idea, just a vague notion about maybe taking up painting.

Before I could sort my life out though, I needed to sort my head out. It was something of a messy artist's palette.

Chapter 25

When the Music Stops

Remember that feeling as a kid when you jump off the moving merry-go-round at the fairground and you lurch about for a bit, your head swimming, trying to right yourself? You're looking around for your family or friends because you've just leapt off at random and don't know where you are or where they are in the crowd. There's a lot of noise and a lot of bustle. That's how I felt on my return to the UK when the members of the band went their own ways after Zaragoza and how I was to feel over the weeks and months that ensued — a year, or more even. That ride had been spinning for fifteen years, and now I was on my own two feet, reeling a little, wondering where to go, how I might connect with my family and find my friends.

I had had a wonderful time and I had the security of some money in the bank. Great, but so what? What now? It's always about *what next?*, isn't it? It's the way we are wired. I had two failed relationships behind me, and two kids who knew the nanny better than they knew me. I had nowhere to live with a family, just the one-room mews house with its galley kitchen and poky bathroom, plus an empty house in the country. I had no job, no purpose, no mission, no reason to get up in the morning, no wife or girlfriend, no plans, no idea. I'm not the kind of person to cover my walls with gold and platinum discs from around the world, then sit on the sofa admiring them and congratulating myself.

I was only forty-three, fit as a springer spaniel and, unlike many of my peers in the music industry, I had no substance problems or health issues. That much was good. My body was fine. It was just my head that needed some maintenance work, my soul some nourishment. It wasn't only that I was disorientated and directionless. There's no avoiding it: the life of a musician in a successful band is a selfish one. Or rather, it's difficult to avoid becoming self-centred when you have become the centre of attention. The band had come first in my life, all else trailing in its wake, my family so often taking second place. It was time to put that right and find my next purpose.

My first priority was the children. It seemed incredible that James was now in his eleventh year, his fourth at proper school, a couple of years from his voice breaking and becoming a teenager. Had it really flashed by that fast? Jess was four, a walking, talking little girl. Four years old! Surely it was only a couple of months ago that she was born? My sense of time was completely out of sync with the rhythms of everyday life.

What I can now recognize as 'normal' life felt utterly abnormal. *Wash my own clothes! Drive my own car! Book my own tickets! Shop for my own food! Cook my own meals! Take the Underground! Really?* Inevitably, I had become rather spoilt. I almost had to go right back to the beginning and start adulthood all over again. It was James and Jess that helped me to start that process. Children see life for what it is, no filters, and they live and love it in the moment. I needed a bit of that. On Friday evenings, I would load up the car with food and goodies and drive around London, picking them up from their respective mothers, and motor down to the house on the coast for the weekend. It was a relief, and therapy of sorts, to discover that the only people more self-centred and demanding than rock musicians are young kids, and they have the unarguable excuse of knowing no other way. It's entirely natural, especially for very young kids, to insist on attention, activity and love. I began to relish those weekends, messing around on the beach and in the woods, scoffing pizzas on the sofa in front of a video, doing something for someone — my own flesh and blood — rather than just for myself.

James and Jess helped me to take the first steps back towards good mental health, but I was still fumbling in the dark and I couldn't find the light to guide me out. Mark was dealing with his transition to civvy street by the simple expedient of not going there. He continued to immerse himself in music and cracked on, playing with other artists and turning his mind to a solo career. I hung up my bass for the foreseeable future. I wanted and needed to do something different to deal with the transition.

I saw a good deal of Paul Cummins around this time. He had become a very close friend and he remains one to this day, one of a handful of people I can talk to about anything. It was his suggestion that I got in touch with Chuck Schwartz, an American friend of his, a potter and Jungian dream analyst. It was for his therapy, not his crockery, that finally, after a few weeks, I picked up the phone and called him. It turned out that Jungian dream analysts were in high demand in London at this time. Chuck's schedule was full, but he said he could fit me in during his lunch break on Wednesdays if I didn't mind him eating a sandwich during the session. So, every Wednesday for the next year or so I drove down to see Chuck in Wandsworth. Any scepticism I might have harboured about the process was soon banished.

In a café in the south of France with Paul Cummins.
A great mate to spend time with.

Part of that wariness arose from the fact that I never had dreams, so what would Chuck have to work on?

'Don't worry, you will, you will,' Chuck assured me at our first meeting. There was a blockage in my mind, he explained, but just by committing to the treatment I had already started to loosen it. 'Put a pen and some paper at your bedside and scrawl down what you dreamed as soon as you wake up and we'll have plenty to discuss next week.'

Sure enough, that very night the dreams came at me like I had been dropped into a crazy, action-packed animated movie, all of it in vivid colours. As my subconscious stirred up and bubbled, at first I was more disturbed than relieved by the flood of mental activity. All those repressed feelings had been well and truly uncorked. A great deal of my issues, Chuck contended, were related to my self-centred, occasionally thoughtless treatment of Pauline, Louise – and a few other women along the way. Since problems had arisen in my relationship with Louise, there had been a number of fleeting encounters and relationships, including one I was pretty serious about. It all became even messier, but I could no longer hide from my commitments by disappearing around the world. I had to address this.

Jung understood dreaming as a process through which the mind probes and communicates with the subconscious and believed that there are symbols with hidden, coded meanings that throw light on our feelings and behaviour. Slowly, Chuck helped unpack my mind, allowing me to re-pack it in a more orderly way. It was painful at times to face up to some hard truths, but the process came to change my view of myself and of my world. It gave me a self-understanding I had never previously sought. My big problem, so it was confirmed, was a fear of commitment, not wanting to be tied down. 'You have to realize that you and only you are responsible for how you think, feel and behave,' Chuck kept saying. 'No one else. Just you. Only you can make yourself better. Think about how you'd like to change and do it. That's it.'

You can laugh about the notion of Jungian dream interpretation, but it genuinely worked for me. Part of that might have been down just to talking to someone, to going deep and subjecting myself to fierce self-examination. Whatever – I came out the other side of it a happier, humbler, healthier person and I will always be grateful to Chuck for that. I was stuck. Chuck unstuck me. He liberated me.

I had been thinking a great deal about taking up painting again ever since I met Brett. He had fired my imagination. Chuck was delighted about this longing of mine and encouraged me to paint as often and as furiously as I could. It was art as therapy. In the same way I was releasing my subconscious through dreams, painting allowed me to express those inner, deeply buried feelings and thoughts on to canvas. I took him at his word and spent day after day in the garage space at my mews house, painting and drawing. I painted hundreds of pictures, many of them pretty poor, but that wasn't the point. It was helping. I was distracted. The more I painted and the more I saw Chuck, the less I felt the need to head out and mess around in fleeting relationships that brought little joy to either party. It gave me a new purpose and, as the quality of my work improved, a sense of progress and direction and a more meaningful sense of fulfilment.

My painting started to get markedly better when, following up a suggestion from Ed's secretary, I went down one evening to Heatherleys, a famous old art school on Lots Road in Chelsea, to meet Binny Mathews. She was in the middle of a class when I arrived, but she came out and I introduced myself and told her I was after some lessons. The first question Binny asked was, 'Do you have any champagne with you?'

I confessed I hadn't.

'Well, go and get some and we'll talk.'

That was the start of a very long friendship. Binny is a brilliant artist and tutor, and over the coming months she taught me so much. I didn't tell her I had been in a band, didn't play the rock-star card, and she wasn't that keen on the idea of private lessons, which is what I'd had in mind. 'You'll have to come along to the classes, like everyone else,' she said. But, over the champagne, it was revealed that she had taught art with my sister-in-law, Chris, Will's wife, at Oakham School up in Rutland. I got my private lessons.

I have been painting ever since and now have a studio down at my house on the south coast. I spend a great deal of my time there; it has become my sanctuary. It still works as therapy, but I have become decent enough to be taken on by a couple of well-regarded galleries over the years and have staged a number of solo exhibitions in

London and overseas. The only exhibition that didn't go down so well took place in Sydney in 2004. I had twenty-five paintings shipped over at great expense, all of them big canvases. I was excited, not least because on the opening night at the Christie's gallery in the eastern suburbs, I was to be sharing the space with an earlier sculpture exhibition that was yet to be removed. I was co-exhibiting with Rodin! Helped by a full-page article about my exhibition in the *Sydney Morning Herald*, the glamorous Sydney society crowd arrived in numbers and I was feeling pleased that we had attracted so many people through the door. So, I was a little taken aback when a local artist sauntered over and said, 'Jeez, mate, you've got a bloody nerve, haven't you?'

'What do you mean?' I stammered.

'You've got your work cut out here, that's for sure — unless you're David Hockney or Rodin. Aussies like to buy Aussie art. Good luck to you is all I'll say.'

'Cheers, thanks for the encouragement.'

But he was right. It was true: Aussies prefer to buy home-produced talent. Oh, well, it was good to be back in Sydney, at any rate.

I am still painting today, still playing music — and so far have seven solo albums to my credit — still trying to connect and communicate, still trying to express myself. I have never properly understood where that impulse comes from, this urgency to connect with people, but it's always been there and shows no sign of going away. From my school days, musicians and artists have been tribes to which I have always wanted to belong, but I think the drive to play and paint goes deeper than that and, through Chuck Schwartz, I discovered that it is indivisible from who I am. There's nothing I can do about it.

For me, music has the edge on visual art if you measure it through 'connection'. There's nothing like playing live to feel that connection. It's not just an awareness but a physical sensation. Today, when I am pottering around the kitchen, or driving, and a Straits song comes on the radio, I feel that bond with my past and all the other people listening. That is a thrill that has grown over the years as technology revolutionizes how we listen to music. I get letters and emails from all over the world, from Chinese people and Finns, Mexicans and Filipinos. It's remarkable to think that our music keeps speaking to people, and God knows where — a hut, an igloo, a shack, a mansion, up a mountain, down in the swamps. No other form of art can do that so immediately — provoke instant and strong emotion in people everywhere and anywhere.

So I painted and I talked and I saw my kids and I messed around on my acoustic and I planned to put down another solo album, and still my life didn't feel complete. I needed to find someone I wanted to spend the rest of my life with. I understood now the difference between fleeting happiness and deep fulfilment. And I knew the moment I met her that I had found it.

I met Steph in the summer of 1993 at a fundraiser for Life Education. I had put a rough band together — including Phil Palmer — and I was put on the hosts' table, next to Steph. I knew before I had finished our first course that I was looking into the face of my future — and a beautiful future it was too. By happy coincidence, she lived down the road and walked past my mews house every day on the way to her office. Everything moved quickly. It's strange how you just know. Soon we were going out.

It is not to dishonour the good times I had with Pauline and Louise to say that my marriage to Steph has been the best thing to happen to me, not least in its production of two more delightful children, Harry in 1996 and Dee Dee in 1998, both of whom, funnily enough, are very musical. James and Jess are both very happily married, to Beth and Moses respectively, and have two children each. So, a lovely wife, four children and four grandchildren.

Mark met Kitty, now his wife, around the same time as I met

The plaque on the council flat where the band was born was unveiled in 2009. We knocked on the door, but the woman who lived there refused to answer!

Steph, and she is the same for Mark as Steph is for me — so now two close friends have become four. It's always fun when we meet up for a long lunch or dinner together, and we leave looking forward to the next time. It's wonderful to have maintained such a friendship after our long and eventful journey. To have led such an extraordinary, creative and fulfilling life with a lovely family and friends makes me feel truly blessed.

Acknowledgements

Writing an autobiography felt like a Herculean task, but those involved have made it a joyful experience . . .

Annabel Merullo, my literary agent at Peters Fraser + Dunlop, thank you for getting the ball rolling. Your persuasive powers did the trick!

I am truly grateful for the enormous commitment of my editor Andrea Henry at Transworld, skilfully assisted by copy-editor Sarah Day and also Danai Denga. Thanks also to Michelle Signore for spotting the opportunity.

Niall Edworthy, huge thanks for all your forensic research. You've been remarkably patient and professional, but, most importantly, enormous fun to work with. You made a marathon feel like an effortless sprint.

My thanks must also go to the many musicians who have contributed so much to the band — David Knopfler, Pick Withers, Alan Clark, Hal Lindes, Terry Williams, Mel Collins, Tommy Mandel, Guy Fletcher, Danny Cummins, Phil Palmer, Chris White, Paul Franklin, Jack Sonni and Chris Whitten. Cheers to all the crew, caterers, truck drivers and promoters who worked so hard with the band with such good humour over the years. Some now sadly gone, but not forgotten.

Thank you to James Harman, our lawyer, for keeping us in the safe zone all these years. And to the inimitable Ronnie Harris, now a good friend, and his team of able accountants, for taking such good care of the finances for over forty years.

Where would the band have been without Ed Bicknell and Paul Cummins, our brilliant, creative and consistent management team? Ably assisted by those at the Damage Management office. And thanks also to Robyn Becker, PA to MK. And to my own PA, Janine Penney, for your loyalty through the years.

The Dire Straits phenomenon began after a chance meeting with Mark Knopfler in a council flat in south London. A remarkably gifted songwriter and musician, and one of my oldest friends, he continues to be a constant inspiration and an exciting person to know.

Finally, love and thanks to my family — all of you.

Picture Acknowledgements

The publisher would like to thank the following for kind permission to reproduce images. While every effort has been made to trace the owners of copyright material reproduced herein, the publishers would like to apologize for any omissions and will be pleased to incorporate missing acknowledgments at the earliest opportunity.

Integrated Photographs

Pages 7, 10, 40, 85, 99, 110, 139, 154, 157, 173 and 303 courtesy of John Illsley; pages 81 and 84 © Colin Bodiam; pages 92 and 97 © Andra Nelki; pages 143 and 184 © Adrian Boot/Urban Image Music Photographic Archive; pages 129 and 163 © Barry Schultz; page 196 © Getty; page 232 © Rob Verhorst/Redferns/Getty; page 260 © Duncan Raban/Popperfoto/Getty; page 281 © Clive Limpkin/Alamy Stock Photo; page 308 © Will Strange Photography.

Plate Sections

Section One

Page 1 both courtesy of John Illsley; page 2 © Glenda Bogdanovs; page 3 © Colin Bodiam; page 4 © Heritage Auctions, HA.com; page 5

Index

Page numbers in *italics* refer to illustrations